CIVIC SERVICE

CIVIC SERVICE

Service-Learning with State and Local Government Partners

David P. Redlawsk

Tom Rice

and Associates

Foreword by Kay W. Barnes

JOSSEY-BASS
A Wiley Imprint
www.josseybass.com

Library of Congress Cataloging-in-Publication Data
Civic service: service-learning with state and local government partners/
[edited by] David P. Redlawsk, Tom Rice and associates.
       p.   cm.
   Includes bibliographical references and index.
   ISBN 978-0-470-37374-3 (cloth)
   1.   Service learning—United States. 2.   Education, Higher—United States.
   3.   State government—United States. 4.   Local government—United States.
   5.   Political planning—United States. I. Redlawsk, David P. II. Rice, Tom W., 1959-
   LC221.C54   2009
   378.1'03—dc22   2009013921

Printed in the United States of America

FIRST EDITION
HB Printing 10 9 8 7 6 5 4 3 2 1

The Jossey-Bass
Higher and Adult Education Series

CONTENTS

FOREWORD

In reflecting on the teachings of Peter Drucker and the future of leadership, one writer concludes: "The most effective way to seize opportunities to manage 'the future that has already happened' is to be proactive, take advantage of emerging trends, embrace change, and become a change leader" (Maciariello, 2006, p. 25). What an apt description of the potential of service-learning.

As the mayor of a major city for eight years, with a graduate degree in public administration, I have developed a comprehensive perspective on the value of service-learning with government partners. As the authors of this book note, such partnerships are indeed win-win for everyone.

Government has an impact on our daily lives in a variety of ways, ranging from the provision of basic services to creating a vision for the overall community. The variety of service-learning experiences possible in the governmental sector is far-reaching. Through my experiences in local government, I have witnessed people engaged in service-learning activities ranging from researching and preparing a needs assessment in a declining neighborhood to leading the planning and implementation of an official visit of a foreign dignitary to city hall.

An important component of those service-learning experiences is the integration of the hands-on activity with the academic rigor necessary to maximize the learning process. For example, a needs assessment of a declining neighborhood will include focused conversations with residents and a visual exploration of the neighborhood's assets and liabilities. Academic resources can be tapped regarding scholarly interview techniques and tested fieldwork methods for collecting visual impressions when planning those activities. In addition, after completion of the assessment, determination can be made about the insights students gained regarding not only the assessment content but also the impact on them and the cognitive and psychological changes in students as a result.

The preparation for the visit of a foreign dignitary is more than ordering the punch and cookies for the reception. Involved in the process is the protocol expected by the participants, language challenges, and allaying the possible discomfort of those not used to multicultural gatherings. Certainly the academic portion of the experience lends itself to researching the country represented by the dignitary, interviewing and integrating local residents into the experience, and reflecting on one's own reaction to the event.

Service-learning with state and local government partners can have a crucial impact on our country's future. If we are to successfully navigate the unscripted future we all face, we must raise the bar in confronting the multiple challenges in our society. Just as the problems facing us are real, so are the opportunities for vision, for renewal, and for tapping into fresh, creative approaches to addressing these problems.

The ultimate question each of us faces today is, "How can I make my own unique and best contribution to enable our society to be one in which each of us can live out our lives in dignity and have the opportunity to reach our individual potential?" Service-learning in government settings goes a long way in helping us address that question.

■ ■ ■

KAY W. BARNES
DISTINGUISHED PROFESSOR OF PUBLIC LEADERSHIP,
PARK UNIVERSITY
FORMER MAYOR, KANSAS CITY, MISSOURI

References

Maciariello, J. A. (2006). Peter F. Drucker on executive leadership and effectiveness. In F. Hesselbein & M. Goldsmith (Eds.), *The leader of the future 2: New visions, strategies, and practices for the next era* (pp. 3–29). San Francisco: Jossey-Bass.

ACKNOWLEDGMENTS

We would like to acknowledge the support of the Benjamin F. Shambaugh Memorial Fund, which allowed us to hold a conference at the University of Iowa bringing our contributors together. The result, we think, is a stronger set of chapters, benefiting from discussions and debate over the many ways to conceive of service-learning projects. We also thank Jean Florman of the University of Iowa's Center for Teaching whose efforts to inculcate the pedagogy of engagement and service-leaning at Iowa has inspired us both. With support of the Iowa provost's office, Jean organized a series of service-learning summer institutes that brought together fifteen faculty members each time to learn how to "do this work." Both of us participated in the first of these, which greatly impacted our own teaching and thinking about engagement. At that institute we met Edward Zlotkowski for the first time. Thanks to Edward for suggesting this project and encouraging us along the way, as well as for making connections that led to some interesting chapters for this book. Finally, we must thank the staff of the political science department at the University of Iowa—Wendy Durant, Carole Eldeen, and Karen Stewart—for their work in handling the logistics for our Shambaugh Conference. It's not easy to manage the logistics for more than a dozen academics for several days, but they did the job with competence and good humor.

■ ■ ■

DAVID P. REDLAWSK
TOM RICE
IOWA CITY, IOWA

THE EDITORS

David P. Redlawsk is professor of political science at Rutgers University. During the writing of this book, he was associate professor of political science at the University of Iowa. He holds a B.A. from Duke University, an M.B.A. from Vanderbilt University, and a Ph.D. from Rutgers University. Redlawsk was director of the University of Iowa Hawkeye Poll, which routinely involves students in the process of developing and carrying our survey research. His research interests include voter information processing and the role of emotions in decision making, as well as the role Iowa plays in the presidential nominating system. He is coauthor of *How Voters Decide: Information Processing During Election Campaigns* (Cambridge University Press, 2006) with Richard R. Lau and editor of *Feeling Politics: Emotion in Political Information Processing* (Palgrave Macmillan, 2006).

■ ■ ■

Tom Rice is chair of the Department of Political Science at the University of Iowa. He has also been on faculty at the University of Vermont, Iowa State University, and the University of Northern Iowa. His research interests include voting behavior, community politics, and social capital. He has been active in several non-profit organizations and government agencies.

THE CONTRIBUTORS

Jeffrey L. Bernstein is associate professor of political science at Eastern Michigan University. He was a 2005–2006 Carnegie Scholar with the Carnegie Foundation for the Advancement of Teaching. His research interests include public opinion and political socialization and the scholarship of teaching and learning.

■ ■ ■

Terry Christensen is professor and chair emeritus of the Department of Political Science at San José State University and executive director emeritus of CommUniverCity San José. Among his nine books are *California Politics and Government* (Wadsworth, 2007) with Larry N. Gerston, and *Local Politics: A Practical Guide to Governing at the Grassroots* (M. E. Sharpe, 2006) with Tom Hogen-Esch.

■ ■ ■

Joseph A. Gardella Jr. is professor of chemistry and director of the University of Buffalo/Buffalo Public Schools Interdisciplinary Science and Engineering Partnership at the University at Buffalo, State University of New York. He has published widely in the areas of surface and analytical chemistry and in service-learning, with a focus on environmental science, public policy, and K–12 education. He received the 2003 Lynton Award for his service-learning work and a 2005 Presidential Award for Excellence in Science, Mathematics and Engineering Mentorships for his work mentoring women and minority students and faculty.

■ ■ ■

Anthony Gierzynski is associate professor of political science at the University of Vermont. His research focuses on elections, parties, campaign finance, and the media. He is author of *Money Rules: Financing Elections in America* (Westview, 2000) and *Legislative Party Campaign Committees in the American States* (Kentucky, 1991), and he is currently working on a book on electoral reform.

■ ■ ■

Johnny Goldfinger is assistant professor of political science at Indiana University–Purdue University Indianapolis. His research focuses on liberal democratic theory, political deliberation, and social choice. He is currently working on a book that examines the deliberative theories of Jürgen Habermas and John Rawls.

■ ■ ■

Charles Hadlock is the Trustee Professor of Technology, Policy, and Decision Making at Bentley College in Waltham, Massachusetts, as well as professor of mathematical sciences. He is the author or editor of several books published by the Mathematical Association of America—one of them on service-learning opportunities in the mathematical sciences. He is also a member of the American Political Science Association and collaborates with political scientists on agent-based models for voting behavior and for other social phenomena. In an earlier consulting career with Arthur D. Little, he worked with many public and private sector clients in the United States and abroad, emphasizing energy, environment, and health issues.

■ ■ ■

Mara B. Huber directs the Center for Educational Collaboration at the University at Buffalo, State University of New York, which leads, promotes, and facilitates collaboration between University at Buffalo faculty and staff and regional K–12 schools, with a focus on the University at Buffalo/Buffalo Public Schools Partnership. She earned a Ph.D. in psychology from the University at Buffalo.

■ ■ ■

Jennifer Infurna, MPH, worked on Pandemic Flu Planning Support for the Commonwealth of Massachusetts as the day-to-day client representative when she was a research analyst for the Joint Legislative Committee on Public Health of the Commonwealth of Massachusetts. She is currently director of management systems and analysis for the Partners Healthcare System.

■ ■ ■

Melinda Jackson is assistant professor of political science at San José State University. Her research focuses on public opinion, voting, social capital, and civic engagement. She has coauthored a chapter in *Polls and Politics* (SUNY Albany Press, 2004) with Lawrence Jacobs, and several articles on the role of social capital in community electronic networks in *Political Behavior, Journal of Social Issues, American Behavioral Scientist,* and other journals.

■ ■ ■

Steven G. Jones is associate provost for civic engagement and academic mission at the University of Scranton. He edited the second edition of Campus Compact's *Introduction to Service-Learning Toolkit* and is coauthor of two other Campus Compact monographs: *The Community's College: Indicators of Engagement at Two-Year Institutions* and *The Promise of Partnerships: Tapping into the Campus as a Community Asset.* He is also coeditor, with Jim Perry, of *Quick Hits for Educating Citizens.*

■ ■ ■

Kendra A. King is associate professor of politics at Oglethorpe University in Atlanta, Georgia. She serves as the director of the Rich Foundation Urban Leadership Program, a four-course certificate degree program of the university. She earned her Ph.D. in political science from The Ohio State University.

■ ■ ■

Timothy M. Koponen is a Trustee Lecturer in the School of Public and Environmental Affairs at Indiana University–Purdue University Indianapolis. He teaches the introductory and capstone classes in the undergraduate public affairs fields and places students into hands-on internships. His interests are varied but focus on the economic impact of nonmonetary values. In addition to several articles, he is a chapter author in *Making Nature, Shaping Culture* (University of Nebraska Press, 1995) and has written on the social construction of economics with a chapter in *Industrial Ecology and the Social Sciences* (Edward Elgar Publishers, 2008).

■ ■ ■

Peter Koutoujian, J.D., M.P.A., has been a member of the Massachusetts House of Representatives for eleven years and is currently chair of the House Committee on Public Health. He has led many major public health initiatives in the commonwealth, and occasionally teaches courses at the Boston University School of Public Health and other universities.

■ ■ ■

Heather M. Maciejewski is a seventh- and eighth-grade science teacher at School 19, the Native American Magnet School, one of the Buffalo, New York, Public Schools involved in the Interdisciplinary Science and Engineering Partnership (ISEP). She also serves as an educational specialist in the chemistry department at the University at Buffalo, State University of New York. She was the founding collaborator of ISEP and has been recognized locally and nationally for her innovative classroom work and development in middle school science. She earned degrees in psychology from the University at Buffalo and a master's degree in education from D'Youville College in Buffalo.

■ ■ ■

David C. Manns is a doctoral candidate at Cornell University, having completed honors bachelor's degree studies in chemistry at the University at Buffalo. He has also worked in the environmental testing industry.

■ ■ ■

Tammy M. Milillo is a doctoral candidate in chemistry at the University at Buffalo, State University of New York, having worked in the fields of geographic information analysis and environmental chemistry starting as an undergraduate. Her doctoral research focuses on the geographic information analysis of environmental pollutants in urban neighborhoods.

■ ■ ■

Rosa Ramos Morgan has been the administrator of the Community Neighborhood Renaissance Partnership since its inception in 2001. She has served on the board of directors of both the Florida Association for Microenterprise and the Asset Building Coalition. As the founder and CEO of Community Assets, a consulting firm, Morgan has engaged in neighborhood revitalization, economic development, and civic engagement for the past ten years. She is a graduate of the University of South Florida.

■ ■ ■

William Oakes is associate professor of engineering education at Purdue University, where he directs EPICS, Engineering Projects in Community Service. His research interests include service-learning in engineering education, the impact of cognitive and noncognitive variables on student persistence, and design in engineering education.

■ ■ ■

Gunwha Oh is a doctoral candidate in geography at the University at Buffalo, State University of New York, specializing in geographic information systems and map design.

■ ■ ■

Joseph Ohren is professor of political science and director of the master of public administration program at Eastern Michigan University. His primary teaching and research interests are public management, public budgeting and financial management, and local government politics and administration. He is a frequent consultant for local governments in southeastern Michigan.

■ ■ ■

Christine Pappas is associate professor of political science at East Central University in Ada, Oklahoma. She received both her doctorate and J.D. from the University of Nebraska and has published articles in *PS: Political Science* and the *Journal of Political Science Education*. She was named 2005 Oklahoma Political Science Teacher of the Year.

■ ■ ■

Jennifer Ricci is a graduate of Bentley College. She was a leading member of student government during her college career and graduated with honors in managerial economics with a minor in health sciences and industry. She is currently a securities analyst with Lewtan Technologies.

■ ■ ■

Charlotte Ridge is a graduate student at the University of Iowa. Her research interests include women and American politics, feminist theory, and media issues.

■ ■ ■

Gaurav Sinha is assistant professor of geography at Ohio University in Athens, Ohio. He completed a Ph.D. in geography at the University at Buffalo, specializing in geographic information systems.

■ ■ ■

Marsha K. Turner was the first director of Service Learning Programs at Florida State University from 2001 until she retired in 2007. Her research focuses on the assessment and evaluation of service-learning as it relates to students' outcomes and impacts and was recognized in 2007 as exemplary by the International Association for Research in Service-Leaning and Community Engagement. She holds a B.S. in English and education from the University of Alabama and an M.S. in library and information science and Ph.D. in information studies, both from Florida State University. She has thirty years of experience working in education in a variety of teaching and administrative capacities with the

Florida Department of Education, University of South Carolina, and Texas Women's University. In her retirement, she continues to work in and with communities.

■ ■ ■

Fredric A. Waldstein holds the Irving R. Burling Chair in Leadership and is professor of political science at Wartburg College, where he is also director of the Institute for Leadership Education. He was appointed by Iowa governor Terry Branstad to serve as a founding member of the Iowa Commission on Volunteer Service, and subsequently was elected its chair. He is a founding member of the American Association of State Service Commissions and has served as board chair. Waldstein is a graduate of Wartburg College and holds a Ph.D. in political science from Washington University in St. Louis. He teaches courses in leadership education and political science. His current research interests pertain to the development of new educational paradigms to foster skills of critical inquiry, civil discourse, and service-learning as tools necessary to encourage civic engagement as a means to sustain democratic society.

■ ■ ■

Nora Wilson is a graduate of the University of Iowa and is studying law at the University of Wisconsin Law School.

Civic Service

CHAPTER ONE

WHY CIVIC SERVICE

Tom Rice, David P. Redlawsk

One of the most exciting developments in higher education in recent decades is the rapid expansion in service-learning. Broadly defined, service-learning is an educational method that combines out-of-classroom service experiences with reflective in-class instruction to enhance student learning and build stronger communities (Eyler & Giles, 1999; Furco, 1996). It is precisely this productive reciprocal relationship between the service and classroom experiences that distinguishes service-learning from traditional on-campus courses and off-campus internships. On-campus courses often fail to make academic material pertinent to students, and off-campus internships often fail to augment on-the-job experiences with germane academic material. Service-learning bridges these gaps by connecting service experiences with classroom exercises rooted in traditional academic material (Marullo & Edwards, 2000; O'Byrne, 2001).

The growth of service-learning has spawned a plethora of literature on the subject. While we encourage our readers to explore this work and provide a very brief overview at the end of this chapter, this book is principally about how to do successful service-learning. More particularly, our goal is to encourage our readers to undertake service-learning courses by sharing with them several diverse and successful efforts across multiple disciplines. These examples come in the form of many inspiring courses, each described in the chapters that follow. What ties this together is a common focus on service-learning with government partners such as city councils, school districts, and public agencies. Even so, much of the material is easily transferable to service-learning courses with businesses and nonprofit organizations. What sets this book apart from many others that summarize successful courses is that its perspective reaches beyond teachers and students. Instead we take a comprehensive look at all of the constituencies served by service-learning, including, of course, teachers and students, but also government agencies as community partners, higher educa-tion administrators, and community citizens. It is our hope that the book can motivate our readers, regardless of their constituency, to take the lead in getting their own service-learning courses started. The world will be a better place if they do.

WHY GOVERNMENT PARTNERS?

One answer as to why this book focuses on service-learning with government partners is that both of us as editors are political scien-tists. There is, however, more to it than that. Traditionally, service-learning partners have tended to be service organizations such as soup kitchens, halfway houses, animal shelters, senior centers, and the like (Speck & Hoppe, 2004; Stanton, Giles, & Cruz, 1999) These nonprofit organizations epitomize what is meant by service, and they draw heavily on volunteers such as students. Most govern-ment agencies are not such obvious targets for productive service-learning relationships. There are, to be sure, some agencies that fit the traditional view of human service providers, such as public health clinics, but many agencies, such as transportation depart-ments, planning and zoning commissions, and municipal utilities, may not seem to be obvious service-learning partners. Fortunately, this has begun to change in recent years as more political scien-tists have engaged in service-learning and as more professors from other disciplines have come to realize that government agencies are good partners for their service-learning classes (Battistoni & Hudson, 1997). Nevertheless, there remains significant potential in this area. By focusing on government partners, we hope to spot-light this potential.

We also focus on government partners because of the wide-spread concern that young people are disconnected from the public sphere. Putnam (2000) and others lament the decline in social capital and the dense civic involvement it engenders. There is good evidence that young people are volunteering in large numbers, but there is equally strong evidence that this is not translating into further involvement in civic affairs. Young people might be volunteering to staff homeless shelters, but they are not working with others in their communities to help solve the homeless problem (Keeter, Zukin, Andolina, & Jenkins, 2002). Thus, a deeper level of engagement is missing. Without actually entering this debate or even commenting on its merits, we suggest that whether social capital matters and whether it is (or was) declining, civic engagement is, as Martha Stewart might put it, "a good thing." It seems particularly appropriate and timely to be concerned with helping students develop the necessary skills, knowledge, and understandings to become productively engaged in the civic life of their communities.

This is precisely what service-learning aims to do, and evidence is growing that this is indeed what it does. A study of alumni from a Catholic liberal arts college showed that students who participated in either community service or service-learning as undergraduates were much more likely to be involved in their community after graduation than those who did not (Fenzel & Peyrot, 2005). In another study, a survey sent to students during their first year of college, four years after, and finally nine years after they started college, was used to track the effects of undergraduate volunteerism. The results showed that doing volunteer work during the last year of college nearly doubles a student's chances of volunteering after college (Astin, Sax, & Avalos, 1999). And in a particularly relevant study, participation in service-learning was found to have a stronger effect on future commitment to activism than did simple community service activities not tied to course work (Astin, Vogelgesang, Ikeda, & Yee, 2000). It may be that, as Birney (2005) suggests in a different context, service-learning activities help increase political efficacy. Finally, Longo, Drury, and Battistoni (2005) find that students in engaged courses learn that they are not in it alone, that others are similarly situated, and that the work they do has an impact on the community. The bottom line is that service-learning offers hope for reversing the troubling downward trend in civic engagement.

DEFINING GOVERNMENT PARTNERS

In this book, we define government partners quite broadly. The specific service-learning courses highlighted in the chapters that follow include partnerships with a wide variety of government units, from quasi-governmental neighborhood groups to state legislatures. Several of the chapters discuss extensive service-learning initiatives between campuses and communities that involve many different academic courses and government agencies. Examples include Indiana University-Purdue University Indianapolis (Chapter Two) and CommUniverCity San José (Chapter Three) in particular. If there is a dominant theme to the type of government partners featured in the coming chapters, it is that most of them are local governments. The predominance of local government examples reflects the reality of available government partners. There are more than eighty thousand local governments across the nation, ranging from cities and counties and all of their agencies and divisions, to school boards, emergency service areas, water districts, environmental zones, and many more (Christensen & Hogan-Esch, 2006). Not only is there a huge array of local government units, every campus is located near several of them, making it easy for students to travel to and from these partners.

While local government partnerships are featured in most of the examples in this book, we urge our readers to explore partnerships with state and federal government agencies as well. Campuses close to state capitols or in large urban centers are likely locations for partnerships with these units of government. It is even possible to partner with state and federal agencies from a distance. For example, Gierzenski and Rice, in Chapter Ten, on partnering with the Iowa and Vermont state legislatures, explain how they were able to do this even though their students seldom met with the lawmakers and almost never went to the statehouse. Projects such as these show that with a little creativity it is possible to build successful service-learning partnerships even when students and their government partners are miles apart.

So far, our definition of government partners includes all local, state, and federal government agencies. To this broad range, we added political campaigns. At first blush, this might seem puzzling because campaigns are, technically, not government entities; they are independent short-term nonprofit organizations. Moreover, one of the primary goals of service-learning is to build better communities, and a case could be made that this is not a primary concern of campaigns, especially in this era of heightened negative campaigning. We take a different view, perhaps because we are political scientists. Campaigns may be private organizations, but their central purpose is to elect people to public office in anticipation that they will help make society better. Campaigns are about ideas for improving society, and campaign discourse is often about which ideas are better and why. Students who work in campaigns are part of this process to try to make society better, and they often learn, we contend, positive civic skills that they can employ the rest of their lives. Political campaigns, then, are deeply intertwined with the process of governing, and they foster the development of desirable civic skills. For these reasons, we see campaigns as opportunities for meaningful and productive service-learning partnerships. In Chapter Eleven, Redlawsk and Wilson show some of the challenges and benefits of involving students in campaigns as part of a service-learning class.

PENTAGON OF CONSTITUENTS, CIVIC ASSETS, AND TANGIBLE IMPACTS

Service-learning courses with government partners have the potential to engage five constituencies: students in the service-learning classes; professors teaching the classes; officials with government agencies; other individuals and groups on the campuses (especially administrators, but also students and faculty not directly involved with the classes); and the citizens served by the government agencies. In Figure 1.1 we arrange these constituencies in a pentagon and connect each constituency with every other by way of a double-headed arrow. Three of the constituencies and the paths between them are central to the service-learning experience. Every service-learning project with a government partner must engage students, professors, and government agencies, and every project activates the paths joining the three constituencies. Quite simply, it is not service-learning if these three constituencies are not engaged and in contact with each other.

FIGURE 1.1 PENTAGON OF CONSTITUENTS, CIVIC ASSETS, AND TANGIBLE IMPACTS

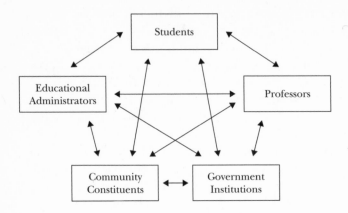

The other two constituencies, higher education administrators and community citizens, are engaged and have the paths to other constituents activated in some project but not others.

Figure 1.1 is a useful model for understanding service-learning with government partners and its many potentials. Consider, for example, the origins of the service-learning courses presented in this book. The majority of service-learning courses, including those in this book, start with professors motivated to engage their students in meaningful real-world activities. But successful courses can be, and often are, initiated by one of the other constituencies in the model. One of the two legislative policy research courses reviewed in Chapter Eleven got its start when a state legislator and a student approached a professor about using students to help the legislature. Chapter Nine reports on an activist university president who galvanized his faculty and local public educators to serve low-income and disadvantaged school children in the local area. Chapter Eight tells of a single student who approached her professor about helping to fix up her neighborhood.

These examples underscore that any of the constituencies in Figure 1.1 can initiate service-learning courses. This is one of the most important messages in this book. With an idea and a little energy, almost anyone can be the catalyst for a service-learning project. Government officials who need assistance should not hesitate to contact professors and higher education administrators about their needs. Higher education administrators can often motivate faculty to offer service-learning classes simply by asking or by providing a few resources. Students should certainly not be shy about approaching individual faculty members, department chairs, and even administrators about starting service-learning classes. Even citizens, individually or in groups, can bring universities and government agencies together to offer these courses. We will have more to say about how to get service-learning courses started later in this chapter.

Another way that Figure 1.1 is useful is that the double-arrowed paths between constituents draw attention to the vast array of civic assets that can result from the connections made possible in service-learning courses. Service-learning itself builds the civic connections between individuals that are so critical to the formation and perpetuation of social capital. And it is not just the students who develop civic assets from service-learning courses. Successful courses also help the other participating constituents become better civic citizens. This is a point often lost in the rush to extol the virtues to students of service-learning, and it is a point that makes the case for service-learning even more compelling.

In addition to signifying the potential to build positive civic skills and commitments, the double-arrowed paths represent the positive tangible impacts that constituents have on each other. For example, when students in an urban planning class help build a neighborhood playground, they have a direct tangible impact on the citizens in the area: they provide the citizens with a playground. Thus, quite apart from the civic skills citizens might pick up from being a part of the project, they also gain a playground. And when administrators at a college provide resources for professors to offer service-learning classes with government partners, they have a tangible impact on the professors: the professors have the resources to teach new classes. In turn, the professors, when they offer their courses, have a tangible impact on their students: they teach their students material and skills quite apart from any civic skills the students pick up.

The paths, then, represent two important processes that result from the interactions between constituents: the building of civic assets and the production of tangible impacts. These dual processes are another one of the central messages of this book. Service-learning has always been touted as a method for allowing students to make a tangible impact in the real world. It has also long been recognized for its potential in building civic-minded students. What Figure 1.1 makes plain is that these two processes reach well beyond the students. The recipients of the civic assets and tangible benefits of service-learning can be any or all of the other constituents. Indeed, in almost every service-learning project, the three core constituents—students, professors, and government officials—develop civic assets and receive tangible benefits as a result of participating in the project. Many courses provide the same assets and benefits to the other two constituents: higher education administrators and community citizens.

ADDING CONSTITUENTS' VOICES

Each service-learning project summarized in the chapters that follow provides readers with both a full understanding of that particular project and generalizable information and lessons to help readers start their own courses. Indeed, this book is not meant as an academic treatment of service-learning with government partners, but rather as a how-to blueprint for those interested in practicing service-learning. There are many other books with the central purpose of providing hands-on advice for doing service-learning. Almost all, however, are professor focused; that is, they are written by professors for professors, taking a professor-centered view of service-learning. There is, of course, nothing wrong with this focus, but it often fails to speak to the questions and concerns of other constituents who might be interested in learning about and starting service-learning courses.

We have made a concerted effort to speak to all five of the service-learning constituents in this book. Our chapter authors, most of whom are professors, have endeavored to include perspectives and viewpoints from the other constituents. While some have included partners as authors, each chapter is followed by at least one short piece written by a constituent in that particular service-learning project other than a professor. We call these pieces "Voices," and each provides valuable insights and advice about service-learning from the perspective of that constituent.

The primary purpose of these pieces is to help constituents other than professors understand service-learning and get the most out of it. It is our hope that these pieces will encourage nonprofessor constituents to enter into service-learning projects when given the opportunity and to consider initiating projects on their own. These pieces also offer professors a unique and valuable look at how other constituents may view their projects. We suspect that even seasoned service-learning professors will pick up a thing or two from these voices that will help them improve their courses.

HOW TO GET STARTED: APPROACHING OTHER CONSTITUENTS

Our observations and experience suggest that the biggest challenge in service-learning is getting started. Once the constituents are in contact with each other, project ideas seem to flow freely, and course opportunities seem to take form. This is not to suggest that planning and executing successful service-learning courses is easy, but it is to say that a certain positive momentum often takes hold once various constituents in the process are brought together. The reason for this is very straightforward: service-learning is usually a win-win for participants. If done well, it benefits all of the constituents, and many of the potential benefits are usually very obvious, even in the early planning stages. Thus, once constituents start talking about the possibilities, successful service-learning courses are often the result. The hard part is frequently bringing the constituents together in the first place.

GETTING STARTED: PROFESSORS

Getting started is so critical to the development of successful service-learning courses that we want to provide some simple and generalizable advice on how to do it. Thus, the next few pages act as a quick primer on how to approach other constituents, beginning with the professors who will teach these courses. The most obvious constituent group for professors to target is government officials in agencies that might be able to offer projects relevant to their academic courses. We encourage professors to think broadly when making a list of possible agencies—good partners are not always easy to spot. It makes sense, for example, that an American history professor might find partners in historical societies and museums. He or she may also find a good partner, however, in a university press that publishes books in American history and could use a student to help in this process. Or perhaps a state-owned promotional magazine would welcome a student who could work on a history feature. Still further, maybe community and neighborhood organizations would be interested in working with students to chronicle their histories. The key for professors is to think creatively about partners; there are often more possibilities than initially come to mind. For example, one of our Iowa English department colleagues, associate professor Teresa Mangum, has worked with the city-run animal shelter as part of a course on the representation of animals in Victorian literature, and in doing so has connected the in-class discussions of this literary genre to the real world of caring for cast-off animals. Her course description for Literature and Society reads in part:

> This class is a service-learning course, which means that in addition to the usual requirement to attend class and discuss readings, students are required to commit 16 hours to a community project that involves service and research. . . . Community partners include the Iowa City/Coralville Animal Care and Adoption Center, the Friends of the Animal Center, and other local organizations focused on animals and human-animal interaction. . . . Our goal in these research projects will be to move from theoretical perspectives on the roles animals play, as literary and imaginative subjects, to investigating how metaphors, representations, and associations with animals affect the practical environments in which we interact with animals, shape policies governing animals, and even "speak for" animals.

Once target constituents are identified, professors need to contact them. The easiest way to do this, and often the most successful, is to simply call and talk to whoever answers the telephone. Explain who you are and that you are interested in having some of your students involved with the group as part of a class project. This person will often put you in touch with someone who could use student help. At this point, you should once again explain who you are and that you are interested in having some of your students assist the group. Very few government officials will know anything about service-learning, so they will likely think of this as an internship opportunity for students. That is fine; you can always explain the unique nature of your service-learning class in a later meeting. In this first conversation, the key is to convey to the official your seriousness and to explore possible projects for the students. If the official is interested, schedule an in-person meeting to go into detail about the project and your course. If the official is not interested, ask if there is someone else in the agency who might be able to use student help.

GETTING STARTED: STUDENTS

Students can play a major role in getting service-learning courses started, but they do so primarily by motivating other constituents— usually professors, government officials, higher education administrators—to contact each other about initiating courses. When approaching professors, students should choose those who offer classes in areas in which they would like to do service-learning projects. Students interested in law, for example, would probably do better approaching professors in political science or criminal justice than in English or art. If a target professor has offered service-learning classes in the past, the students will not need to explain service-learning. They can move instead to immediately talking with the professor about the type of service-learning classes they would enjoy. If the professor is not familiar with service-learning, the students may need to do a little education, which might start by recommending this book to the professor!

Another target for students is government agencies that work in areas in which they would like to do service-learning projects. If students can convince agency officials that they want to work in the agency, they can often enlist the officials to help them approach professors. In approaching agency officials, students must be knowledgeable about the responsibilities of the agency and ready to make the case about how they can be of value to the agency. It is not necessarily important to explain service-learning, but it is important to explain that students receive course credit for their work. Many officials initially think that the students are offering to do traditional internships. There will be plenty of time later for the officials to be educated about the unique requirements of service-learning. If students elicit interest from the agency officials, then they, perhaps along with the officials, can approach professors whose areas of expertise intersect the agency's responsibilities. Having an agency already interested should greatly improve the chances that faculty members will be interested.

A third point of entry for students can be their institution's administration. This certainly means department chairs, but it might also include deans or provosts. Success with the latter two groups is likely only if a well-organized group of students clearly articulates a case for service-learning. Since administrators generally do little teaching, the purpose of seeing them is to lobby for their influence and resources. If administrators are convinced of the value of service-learning, they can do a great deal to encourage professors to offer service-learning classes. There are many examples of administrators playing a key role in promoting service-learning on campuses, so students might be effective if they make a strong case.

Regardless of whether students approach their professors, government officials, or higher education administrators, they are more likely to be successful if they come as a group and present a clear, articulate case. A single student is not as likely as a group to motivate other constituent groups to embrace service-learning. After all, service-learning is a classroom-based exercise. A single student wanting the opportunity to make a difference outside the classroom is a better candidate for a traditional internship, but a group of students, especially if they are all in the same academic major, can make a strong case of significant demand for service-learning classes. Likewise, students with a clear, coherent message are more likely to succeed than those who are unprepared. Students need to respect the time of professors, public officials, and higher education administrators, and make their case succinctly and powerfully, and to do this, they must be prepared. Finally, it is worth noting that students should not underestimate their ability to get service-learning classes started. Generally, people are supportive of students who express educational needs, and they are often inclined to help.

GETTING STARTED: GOVERNMENT OFFICIALS

Government officials can also take the lead getting service-learning courses started. Officials will probably have the most success by approaching professors and department chairs, although large agencies that could partner with several professors across several academic disciplines may want to approach deans and provosts or, in some cases, even presidents.

Navigating a college or university to find partners may seem a bit daunting at first. A good tactic is to first identify the academic departments that seem to have the most in common with the responsibilities of your agency. For some agencies, the likely target departments will include political science, public administration, and public policy. In many institutions, public administration and public policy are part of the political science department. For other agencies, the target departments will be more directly related to their service area. Human service agencies might look at the departments of social work and sociology, in addition to political science. Transportation agencies might consider looking at urban planning departments (which sometimes go by a different name). Another helpful tactic is to see if the college or university has a central unit that helps arrange and administer internships. If so, this office should be able to provide advice about which departments to approach, and the office may even make contacts for you. If the college or university happens to have a unit dedicated to arranging and supporting service-learning (the number of such units is increasing), this is the most logical first stop.

Once a likely academic department has been identified, the next step is to contact individual faculty members about the possibility of offering a service-learning course with your agency as the government partner. If you cannot determine which faculty members are the best to approach, ask the department chair for assistance. Be clear to faculty members about your needs, and ask if they would work with you to arrange academic credit for students who help you. Many professors are unfamiliar with service-learning and will be thinking in terms of traditional internships. If a professor is interested, you can express your desire to form a service-learning partnership at a later meeting. The key during the initial contact is to spark the professor's interest. Most professors will be impressed that you are interested in working with their students, but some will be reluctant to take on what they might see as extra duties.

GETTING STARTED: HIGHER EDUCATION ADMINISTRATORS

Service-learning can be part of the fabric of a college or university if administrators establish it as a clear goal and provide resources to make it happen. Four of the best examples in this book are the extensive service-learning programs at Indiana University–Purdue University Indianapolis (Chapter Two), San José State University (Chapter Four), University at Buffalo, State University of New York (Chapters Five and Nine), and Wartburg College (Chapter Twelve). The chapters that cover these programs focus as much on individual government partner projects as on the campuswide service-learning initiatives, but they do give a sense of what is possible with an ambitious and visionary administration. They also bring to light the very different approaches administrators can take in emphasizing service-learning.

GETTING STARTED: COMMUNITY CITIZENS

Individual citizens or groups of citizens certainly can help facilitate service-learning projects between higher education institutions and government agencies, but our guess is that this happens only rarely. We do not have an example of a citizen-initiated project in this book, but it is easy to imagine one. For instance, citizens in a small town could work to put local government officials in touch with a professor at a university in a nearby city who can use his or her students, as part of a service-learning project, to work with local officials to test groundwater quality in the area. Generally government agencies in need of the kind of help that a service-leaning relationship could provide probably contact higher education institutions directly, but occasionally citizens might initiate the contact, as in this example. We mention this possibility so that citizens realize that they can make service-learning work for them too.

We have noted that various constituencies might see initial approaches as attempts to simply set up traditional internships. It is probably obvious then that service-learning is different in some important ways. Two of these are abundantly illustrated throughout the chapters of this book: reflection and the connection of the service activity to in-class work. The idea of reflection is that students will not just "do" service but will also give serious thought to what they learn in their service projects and make connections between their on-site learning and their in-classroom learning. Guided reflection is used to help bring this about: students are given assignments that include writing prompts designed to develop critical thinking skills and connections. Redlawsk and Wilson (Chapter Eleven) provide examples of the reflection prompts used in a local politics class. These prompts ask student to consider not only what they have learned but how that contributes to their understanding of the nexus between the theory of the classroom and the practice of the service-learning activity.

SERVICE-LEARNING RESOURCES

Our hope is that this book will excite people to start service-learning courses with government partners. For us, the emphasis is as much on starting courses as it is on service-learning. Put another way, we are less concerned with whether new courses meet some commonly agreed-on criteria of service-learning right away than we are about getting courses started. When professors team with government officials to offer courses where students work in government and share their experiences in the classroom, good things happen, even if the core tenets of service-learning are not always practiced. That is why the authors of the successful service-learning projects described in the following chapters spend less time on how the projects met service-learning criteria and more time on how the projects engaged the constituents in Figure 1.1 to contribute to student learning and build better communities.

This book is more about action than theory. That said, we are firm believers in service-learning theory and guidelines. Every new course that brings professors and government officials together to educate students and improve communities will be made better if the general principles and goals of service-learning are understood and applied by everyone involved. In Appendix B we provide a brief overview of the some of the best work on service-learning. This is a good introduction to the vast service-learning literature, but it is just an introduction. We urge our readers to go well beyond our very limited summary and explore the expanding literature on service-learning and civic engagement.

The Rest of the Book: Key Lessons

This is the place where the editors traditionally summarize each of the coming chapters to perhaps whet the reader's appetite. While we certainly hope our readers will go through each chapter in detail, we also know there are some key lessons to be learned in each. Here we provide a short sense of what those lessons might be.

The story presented in Chapter Two of the projects undertaken at Indiana University–Purdue University Indianapolis (IUPUI) is fascinating for a whole host of reasons, including the wide range of possibilities for an urban university in the state capital. But we are particularly struck by the reminder that students at all levels of achievement can benefit and contribute to service-learning projects. Some of the students who did the best at IUPUI were not necessarily those who would rank among the best academic achievers. Furthermore, and maybe even more interesting, the IUPUI project detailed here was particularly student driven. Although the professor structured the course itself, students structured much of their experience, organizing their own working teams, sorting themselves out according to their interests, and driving much of the process. For many faculty, the idea of giving up the authority to structure a course and manage the classroom is rather daunting. From IUPUI we learn just how well it can work.

CommUniverCity San José (Chapter Three) is an institution-wide effort to engage a university located in the middle of a city with the neighborhoods that surround it and the city government. The partnership in many ways is not all that unique; a number of universities have engaged in their communities. But what is unique, and of particular interest, is that the service-learning experiences at CommUniverCity are driven not by faculty or the city government but by the neighborhoods themselves, which determine their priorities, needs, and goals, to which the university and the city respond. This is engagement at the grassroots: the residents of the neighborhoods decide what they need, and the experts (and their students) implement those decisions.

Chapter Four takes us to Eastern Michigan University, where two professors collaborated on one service-learning project supporting a local government effort to pass a tax referendum to rebuild and maintain local streets. The chapter points out that not all service-learning has to be transformative in the way that perhaps working at a soup kitchen might open a student's eyes to inequity. Working directly with local government can help students break down barriers to understanding what goes on in their backyards and challenge their stereotypes of politicians. This is transformative in its own way and should provide students with a better appreciation for the role of local government officials and agencies in the everyday life of the community.

One clear lesson in this book is that service-learning with government partners need not be limited to political scientists. Indeed, government is, of course, involved in so many facets of modern life that nearly any discipline can find ways to connect to it in service-learning courses. Our Iowa English department colleague noted earlier is one example. Chapter Five represents another, where chemistry students become immersed in the issues of environmental policy through providing technical services to communities and agencies dealing with the cleanup of heavily polluted areas. Students not only learn about the chemistry and analysis involved, but they also develop a keen awareness of the challenges of dealing with governmental agencies that are attempting to serve many masters. It is also worth noting that even here, in a course where those of us who are social scientists would expect there to be few papers and other writings, students use written reflections to help connect the experiences in the community to the classroom.

In Chapter Six, we learn about an ambitious project that had students in a capstone course at Bentley College, a well-ranked independent business school, develop a comprehensive pandemic flu planning document for the Commonwealth of Massachusetts. The sheer scope of the project comes through clearly in this chapter; the resulting document was more than 150 pages, detailing existing emergency preparedness measures as well as identifying gaps that need to be addressed. Many of us would shudder at the idea of developing such a project in a single semester, even for a capstone course such as the one described here. But it becomes clear through the details presented that a team-oriented approach, managed jointly by the professor and a student project manager, can accomplish valuable work on behalf of government partners while providing students with the real-world skills that they need on graduation.

Like many other universities, Oglethorpe has been engaging students in community service for decades. Chapter Seven tells the story of how this commitment to student outreach evolved over the years and how the institution has come to embrace the service-learning model. For Oglethorpe, service-learning is just the most recent iteration of student engagement activities to take hold at the institution. And Oglethorpe has something important to add to the basic service-learning model. Long before it instituted service-learning, the institution held issue forums that brought together community leaders to discuss local problems. More recently, some of these forums have been held at the end of service-learning courses, thus bringing students together with a wide range of community leaders. This has proved valuable to the students and the leaders.

The story of a service-learning project in Oklahoma starts with an unusual question: What happens when you do local service-learning without government partners and instead of working *with* the local government you are working *against* it? The neighborhood of Hammond Heights in Ada, Oklahoma, was all but neglected by the city until a student and her professor tried to make a difference. As Chapter Eight describes, they set up a table and offered to "work for you" in addressing problems the community faced. The project snowballed, and the city was forced to take notice. We will not give away the whole outcome here, but suffice it to say that sometimes working against government results in bringing government to the table.

What happens when a university president challenges his institution to address a community problem? The result, as described in Chapter Nine, is inspiring. In 2004 the new president at the University of Buffalo asked his institution to help him improve the public schools in Buffalo. Working closely with Buffalo public school administrators and teachers, the university responded in many ways, including several service-learning initiatives across many disciplines. This chapter tells how the unique partnership between the university and the public school system operates and how it has also involved the State of New York and even the federal government. It relates a particularly successful service-learning venture that has been a key part of this broader effort, the Interdisciplinary Science and Engineering Partnership. In this effort, faculty and students from the university have worked in a service-learning setting to enhance the professional development of public school teachers, start and staff after-school programs, foster learning relationships between parents and public school students, and bring learning units into public school classrooms.

Chapter Ten describes two service-learning courses, one in Iowa and one in Vermont, where students conduct policy research for state legislators. The courses differ somewhat in format, but the students in both prepare high-quality nonpartisan reports that are available to all legislators. One interesting feature of these courses is that the students rarely meet with their partners, the legislators. In fact, the students are located in communities many miles from the state capitols. Most of the contact between the students and lawmakers is by e-mail, which works well. Another interesting feature is that every student works on an extremely wide variety of policy issues every semester, often including topics in agriculture, civil rights, education, the environment, health care, human services, public safety, taxes, and transportation.

Except for Chapter Eleven, partners in this book are generally existing agencies of local government, state government, and school districts. In Chapter Eleven we turn directly to politics. Students in a local politics course at the University of Iowa do their service-learning in the context of local political campaigns. Although the organizations with which they work are more ephemeral than ongoing governmental agencies, the authors argue that the work is just as important. Political campaigns are about informing voters and encouraging them to participate in the process of electing those who govern us. While the organizations are not the typical ones of service-learning, the course engages students in theory in classroom work, practice in political campaigns, and reflection through detailed exercises, which the authors have detailed here.

Campuswide service-learning is possible even in a small, rural community. At Wartburg College in Waverly, Iowa, service-learning was introduced in a few classes years ago, and now dozens of courses are offered by several disciplines and they receive assistance from the newly created Center for Community Engagement. Chapter Twelve describes how service-learning reaches partners throughout the small community and how it extends to its larger neighbor, Waterloo, Iowa. The chapter also details one particularly successful service-learning course, State and Local Government. The triangulated learning approach in the course introduces current events to the service-learning model. In addition to working with their partner and their traditional course work, students analyze current news stories to see how the stories relate to the text material and their experiences on the job with their partners. This serves to further illustrate the link between course material and the real world.

Not all our authors come from political science. Chapter Thirteen introduces us to a multidisciplinary approach undertaken at Purdue University that engages students in the engineering and computer sciences, as well as those in many other majors, in projects that result in practical deliverables to the partners with which they work. This chapter tells of large-scale, multisemester projects, focused on building important engineering skills of design and development for students as they work in teams to identify community needs and ways to fulfill them. Perhaps most exciting in this chapter is the partnership that has developed between the university and the Indiana Department of Corrections vocational program. Students design the projects, and participants in the vocation program build them to professional standards.

Chapter Fourteen tells the inspiring story of how a comprehensive group of community leaders and citizens came together to assist a declining neighborhood in Tallahassee, Florida. This effort, which is ongoing, has benefited from service-learning projects through Florida State University. What started as a few faculty members engaging their students in service-learning projects has blossomed into dozens of long-term service-learning partnerships. This illustrates an important benefit of linking service-learning to large-scale community initiatives: the interconnectedness of communitywide initiatives makes it easy for civic leaders and university personnel to see additional service-learning opportunities. Service-learning becomes, in a sense, contagious, with existing projects spawning ideas for further projects.

Appendix A presents brief summaries of several other successful service-learning courses with government partners. The courses come from an extremely wide range of disciplines, underscoring that service-learning with government partners is possible in almost any academic discipline. Some of the disciplines represented by the course summaries are physical education, music, psychology, French, math, and horticulture. A contact person has been included with each summary so that readers interested in learning more about a particular course will be able to do so.

References

Astin, A. W., Sax, L. J., & Avalos, J. (1999). Long-term effects of volunteerism during the undergraduate years. *Review of Higher Education, 22*(2), 187–202.

Astin, A. W., Vogelgesang, L. J., Ikeda, E. K., & Yee, J. A. (2000). *How service learning affects students.* Los Angeles: University of California, Higher Education Research Institute.

Battistoni, R. M., & Hudson, W. E. (Eds.). (1997). *Experiencing citizenship: Concepts and models for service-learning in political science.* Washington, DC: American Association for Higher Education.

Birney, M. (2005, September). *Does civic participation contribute to political engagement? Using fixed effects panel analyses to investigate correlations and causation.* Paper presented at the annual meeting of the American Political Science Association, Washington, DC.

Christensen, T., & Hogan-Esch, T. (2006). *Local politics: A practical guide to governing at the grassroots.* Armonk, NY: M. E. Sharpe.

Eyler, J., & Giles, D. E., Jr. (1999). *Where's the learning in service-learning?* San Francisco: Jossey-Bass.

Fenzel, L. M., & Peyrot, M. F. (2005). Comparing college community participation and future service behaviors and attitude. *Michigan Journal of Community Service Learning, 12*(1), 23–31.

Furco, A. (1996). Service-learning: A balanced approach to experiential education. In B. Taylor (Ed.), *Expanding boundaries: Serving and learning* (pp. 2–6). Washington, DC: Corporation for National Service.

Keeter, S., Zukin, C., Andolina, M., & Jenkins, K. (2002). *The civic and political health of the nation: A generational portrait.* College Park, MD: Center for Information and Research on Civic Learning and Engagement.

Longo, N. V., Drury, C., & Battistoni, R. M. (2005, September). *Democracy's practice grounds: Classrooms and campuses as platforms for democratic civic education.* Paper presented at the annual meeting of the American Political Science Association, Washington, DC.

Marullo, S., & Edwards, B. (2000). From charity to justice: The potential of university-community collaboration for social change. *American Behavioral Scientist, 43*(5), 895–912.

O'Byrne, K. (2001). How professors can promote service-learning in a teaching institution. In M. Canada & B. W. Speck (Eds.), *Developing and implementing service-learning programs* (pp. 79–88). San Francisco: Jossey-Bass.

Putnam, R. D. (2000). *Bowling alone: The collapse and revival of American community.* New York: Simon & Schuster.

Speck, B. W., & Hoppe, S. L. (2004). *Service-learning: History, theory, and issues.* Westport, CT: Praeger.

Stanton, T., Giles, G., & Cruz, N. I. (1999). *Service-learning: A movement's pioneers reflect on its origins, practice, and future.* San Francisco: Jossey-Bass.

CHAPTER TWO

PARTNERSHIPS THAT WORK

Developing and Sustaining Service-Learning Partnerships with Government Agencies

Steven G. Jones, Johnny Goldfinger, Timothy M. Koponen

The pedagogic value of service-learning in political science courses is well documented (see in particular the special section, "Service-Learning in Political Science," in the September 2000 issue of *PS: Political Science and Politics*). It can complement what is taught in the classroom, help develop political skills, and foster an interest in civic engagement. However, to take full advantage of these benefits, service-learning experiences must be effectively designed (see Ball, 2005; Delli Carpini & Keeter, 2000; Dicklitch, 2003; Hepburn, Niemi, & Chapman, 2000; Kahne & Westheimer, 2006.). Eyler and Giles (1999), in their seminal work *Where's the Learning in Service-Learning?* highlighted five basic characteristics of effective service-learning programs: placement quality, application, reflection, diversity, and community voice.

In this chapter, we examine two of those characteristics, placement quality and community voice, and show how they can be advanced through service-learning partnerships involving government agencies. We begin by discussing how service-learning partnerships at Indiana University–Purdue University Indianapolis (IUPUI) complement the mission of the campus. Next, we define our understanding of service-learning partnerships. Finally, we present a case study of a service-learning partnership with a government agency that produces reciprocal benefits for students, faculty, and the agency partner.

About IUPUI

Indiana University–Purdue University Indianapolis is a comprehensive urban campus located in a metropolitan area with a population of 1.6 million people. It is composed of twenty-two schools and academic units, which grant degrees in over two hundred programs. IUPUI was created in 1969 as a partnership between Indiana and Purdue universities, with IU acting as the campus administrator. It is the second-largest campus in the Indiana University system, serving over twenty-nine thousand students. It is particularly notable for its graduate and professional programs in medicine, law, dentistry, nursing, health and rehabilitation science, and social work.

IUPUI is geographically well situated to implement service-learning partnerships with government organizations. The campus is located in downtown Indianapolis, the state capital of Indiana. It is less than a mile from several large complexes of state, county, and city government offices, along with several major public attractions. Consequently there is the potential for many types of partnerships that can complement a variety of academic needs. This flexibility is useful for IUPUI because of its large student population and diverse number of academic programs. The close physical proximity of students, faculty, and government officials is also particularly advantageous in that it facilitates the creation, ongoing maintenance, and mutual success of service-learning partnerships.

Another factor that contributes to the success of service-learning partnerships at IUPUI is the institution's civic engagement mission and the administrative support given to that mission. The stated mission of the university is

> to advance the State of Indiana and the intellectual growth of its citizens to the highest levels nationally and internationally through research and creative activity, teaching and learning, and civic

engagement. . . . IUPUI promotes the educational, cultural, and economic development of central Indiana and beyond through innovative collaborations, external partnerships, and a strong commitment to diversity [Indiana University, 2005].

In 2002, IUPUI completed a self-study on civic engagement as part of the institutional reaccreditation through the North Central Association. In preparation for this institutional review, a campus task force defined civic engagement as "active collaboration that builds on the resources, skills, expertise, and knowledge of the campus and community to improve the quality of life in communities in a manner that is consistent with the campus mission" (Hatcher & Bringle, 2004) as it was explicitly identified as a fundamental mission for IUPUI.

Civic engagement has no geographical boundaries and includes university work in all sectors of society (nonprofit, government, and business), as well as the local, regional, national, and international settings where this work happens to be situated. However, as a public, metropolitan university, IUPUI assumes a special responsibility for being accountable for the impact of its civic engagement activities within central Indiana. This aim is reflected in a recent statement of IUPUI's institutional values:

> In developing and implementing new and revised programs, IUPUI will do so with a sense of RESPONSIBILITY to build on its distinctive history, urban location, and academic and research strengths. IUPUI will provide leadership in the education, research, and civic engagement necessary to sustain a world class community by meeting its responsibilities to . . . prepare graduates to become engaged citizens and civic minded professionals with documented competencies required to meet the region's economic, social, governmental, and cultural needs [Indiana University, 2005].

Consistent with these values, civic engagement has become integral to IUPUI's institutional identity, fundamental to student learning, and a basis for scholarly research by faculty.

The IUPUI Center for Service and Learning (CSL) has primary responsibility for advancing civic engagement at the campus level; however, civic engagement is also the responsibility of each academic unit. CSL fulfills its responsibility through faculty grants, faculty and staff development related to service-learning, the organization of campuswide community service activities, collaboration on campuswide assessment of civic engagement, oversight of community-based Federal Work Study, and serving as a catalyst for campus-community partnership programs.

Recently IUPUI has focused its attention on the political dimensions of civic engagement. IUPUI is one of 219 campuses participating in the American Democracy Project, a national undertaking of the American Association of State Colleges and Universities (AASCU) that supports efforts to "produce graduates who understand and are committed to engaging in meaningful actions as citizens in a democracy" (AASCU, n.d.). IUPUI was also selected in 2006 as one of eight campuses to participate in the Political Engagement Project, an initiative sponsored by the Carnegie Foundation for the Advancement of Teaching, AASCU, and the *New York Times*. Given IUPUI's new emphasis on political engagement, service-learning partnerships have advanced this goal of political engagement by giving students hands-on experience in the operations of the government.

DEFINING SERVICE-LEARNING PARTNERSHIPS

We define service-learning partnerships as mutually beneficial projects and programs between university faculty and local community organizations in which service-learning is used as the primary strategy for achieving identified student learning objectives while contributing to the accomplishment of short- or long-term agency needs and priorities. It is important to keep in mind that this definition assumes very specific meanings for the terms *service-learning* and *partnerships*. First, we are speaking of *service-learning* partnerships, as distinct from internship programs, practical experiences, work-study placements, and other types of experiential learning activities that might occur in a community setting. Second, we are referring to *partnerships* rather than projects tied to a specific course. By focusing on partnerships, we emphasize the ongoing nature of the relationship between faculty and agency partners over time and how developing and sustaining such relationships can contribute to the overall effectiveness of service-learning. Effectiveness, in this case, refers to both the service rendered to agencies and the learning experiences of students.

Although our definition of service-learning partnerships is broad enough to include partnerships with nonprofit as well as governmental organizations, we focus on partnerships with government agencies. We believe service-learning partnerships with government agencies offer additional benefits from service-learning to political science students that may not occur in nonprofit settings. For example, when political science students are placed in government agencies as part of their service-learning assignments, the result will be a greater realization of "application," a term coined by Eyler and Giles (1999) and defined as "the degree to which students can link what they are doing in the classroom to what they are experiencing in the community and vice versa" (p. 170). Depending on the learning objectives, students are more likely to see the role of government in addressing important societal issues when their service experience takes place in a government setting.

Exposure to the actual workings of the government is an important consideration for service-learning in political science courses. Service-learning that occurs in the private or nonprofit sector is usually lacking in governmental experiences. Students may gain an appreciation of a particular issue or set of issues, as well as a deeper appreciation of actors in civil society. However, they will not necessarily learn what government does to address those issues. Indeed, this is one of the critiques of service-learning in political science: students become engaged but do not necessarily learn anything about politics. Walker (2000) refers to this situation as the "service-politics split" in which students perceive service and politics "as very different types of activities with different values structures," and in which service is seen as morally superior to and more satisfying than politics. We believe that service-learning partnerships with government agencies can contribute to bridging the service-politics divide. When service-learning occurs in a governmental context, students will be able to see government in concrete rather than abstract terms and have the opportunity to reevaluate their personal definitions and beliefs about politics. In addition, students gain applied work experience in the public sector and the opportunity to explore service career options.

It is important to keep in mind that all forms of service do not necessarily meet the requirements of service-learning partnerships as we define the term. A key factor is a sustained working relationship between the faculty member and the organization over time. Sporadic or short-term relationships do not produce the quality of interactions and benefits envisioned by service-learning partnerships. Consequently, relatively transitory forms of service-learning, such as working on political campaigns or coordinating independent events, may not offer opportunities for sustained collaborations between faculty and organizations. Even ongoing service-learning relationships, such as positions with political officials or agencies, do not secure the benefits of partnership if the principals do not cooperate to develop complementary objectives over time. In both cases, placement quality suffers and community voice is stifled.

EXAMPLES OF SERVICE-LEARNING PARTNERSHIPS AT IUPUI

Because of IUPUI's commitment to community engagement, faculty have been encouraged to develop a number of what we are calling service-learning partnerships, which emphasize long-term, coordinated relationships. For example, one of us, Steven Jones, has developed a partnership with La Plaza, a coalition of community agencies that serve the local Hispanic population. Not only has the partnership yielded several successful service-learning projects, but Jones and his partner at La Plaza have collaborated on grant proposals and have shared information and resources on other non-service-learning projects.

Other examples of ongoing service-learning partnerships between IUPUI faculty and government agencies include the Fit for Life program, a partnership between faculty in the Department of Physical Education and four public schools that focuses on the reduction of childhood obesity. The Cultural Trails project is a city-county project to connect several historic neighborhoods through bicycle trails and public art and culture displays supported by faculty in anthropology, geography, history, and public affairs. The Child Welfare Program in the School of Social Work integrates service-learning into first- and second-year social work courses partnering with city, county, and state child welfare agencies.

Another successful service-learning partnership at IUPUI includes collaborations with a variety of governmental agencies. The development of these relationships required extensive networking and coordination. Because of its ambitious nature, this service-learning partnership is worth examining in detail.

A Case Study of Service-Learning Partnerships

The School of Public and Environmental Affairs (SPEA) at IUPUI trains students to address and solve problems facing society. Its curriculum includes preparation for public service. To advance this aim, service-learning partnerships have been instituted in a capstone class for public affairs majors. This course, Management, Leadership, and Policy, seeks to integrate learning across the SPEA curriculum through experiential learning. Two sections of this class were recently reworked to incorporate service-learning partnerships that gave students the opportunity to experience the pressures and workloads of public sector employment. These sections have thirty-five students, divided into eight teams of four to six members, depending on the needs of the government partners and the preferences of the teams themselves.

Government partners include the State of Indiana Office of Management and Budget (OMB), the Department of Environmental Management (IDEM), the Department of Family and Social Services Administration's (FSSA) First Steps program, and two divisions of the Secretary of State's Office, the Division of Elections and the Division of Securities (respectively, SoS-E, and SoS-S). The participating students are seniors in public affairs within SPEA, and their studies focus on one of three major subfields: public management, civic leadership, or public policy.

The primary purpose of the service-learning component is to give students a group experience driven by the needs of the government body for which they are working and an experience that they can apply to their job search before and after graduation. Secondarily, the capstone is meant to evaluate the program itself in terms of student satisfaction and the fit of the course work to a variety of entry-level tasks students will experience in public service occupations.

One of us, Timothy Koponen, negotiated placements with the four agencies in this pilot project over the summer of 2006. Contacts were available through other engagement work with the state, including a statewide program to recruit college students as poll workers. Contact with IDEM was made through an adjunct lecturer in SPEA. Koponen provided a set of criteria for the projects he could use in the class and met with the division leaders of the specific offices to negotiate which projects would be presented to students in January 2007. Projects had to include certain features to fit well into the class, including a requirement that each project present some sort of data analysis or collection. Projects also needed to reflect a broad appeal to and potential impact on various stakeholders who had organized groups or advocates within the policy process in Indiana. Each project also should have a direct research and policy component, where students could apply their accumulated knowledge to the tasks before them and derive policy recommendations based on their accumulated course work.

On the Indiana state government's side, each project had to be of a relatively low priority yet still important enough to get students excited about the effect of their work. This is because as a pilot project and with undergraduate students, we did not want to risk vital reports or time-dependent results on untested undergraduates. Koponen suggested as a rule that projects be outside the top ten priorities for each office, but that they be in the "low teens." This, both parties agreed, was the level at which any work done by undergraduates would be beneficial, yet no risk was being taken with students being given too much responsibility from the state government office.

The projects themselves concerned various aspects of state government functions that needed to be evaluated within the next year, or projects concerning questions that state administrators wanted answers to, but did not have the resources to commit. This gave the students projects that were important, yet not crucial, to the state (see Table 2.1).

TABLE 2.1 STATE PROJECTS FOR CAPSTONE CLASS

Agency	Office	Group	Number of Students
FSSA	First Steps	Average cost of child in First Steps	4
FSSA	First Steps	Recruitment and "child find" for First Steps	4
IDEM	Office of Pollution Prevention and Technical Assistance	Comparing subchronic exposure level in various states	4
OMB	Government Efficiency and Strategic Planning	Compliance with One Indiana purchasing program	4
OMB	Government Efficiency and Strategic Planning	Governor's span of control and sunset laws on commissions	4
OMB	Government Efficiency and Strategic Planning	Use of pooled purchasing by school corporations	5
SoS	Elections Division	Precinct worker training and recruitment for Help America Vote Act compliance	6
SoS	Securities Division	Survey of college student financial knowledge for securities division	4

Some offices offered more ideas along these lines than were usable given the resources of the class. The OMB had a potential of about a hundred projects in a report given to the governor and state assembly in 2006, each of which could have qualified. In general, we found that there is, as one might expect, an overabundant number of these projects across the state's agencies. As this is written, negotiations are in progress with the Department of Workforce Development, the Indiana Department of Agriculture, more areas of FSSA, and the Department of Natural Resources to develop future service-learning projects. Each of these departments has projects that fit our criteria, and they have shown interest in having students do polling and analysis (Department of Natural Resources and FSSA), statistical analyses of collected data (Department of Workforce Development), and comparative policy analyses of state agricultural policies.

With the projects designed with the partners beforehand, the class could begin. Student reflection on these projects was integrated into the course in various ways. A series of reports, some individual and some by group, was required to get a sense of how students were keeping active on the projects and also to evaluate how their experiences were becoming integrated in their educational goals.

All students were required to start the course with an initial self-evaluation. Looking back into their classes and their experiences outside class, students gave a summary of their strengths and weaknesses that was then used as the information needed to evaluate their interests in the projects. These assessments were meant to create inventories of skill sets that students could use as reflective tools later in the course and also to identify skills and interests when choosing their respective project groups. Over the first two weeks of the course, students explained to each other what kind of projects they would be interested in and what skills and talents they would bring to the team. State agencies presented during this initial period as well, with most offices submitting three or four projects for students to choose as teams developed. Koponen asked the students to create teams with a variety of skills appropriate for each project they desired, and the classes as a whole selected teams and projects with little input from the professor. This self-organization and team building was the first lesson in independent activity in the class.

Project meetings with the government partners were then arranged by students with some input through the professor or his service-learning assistant. (Service-learning assistants are students who receive scholarships, awarded through the IUPUI Center for Service and Learning, to provide administrative support to service-learning faculty.) As teams met with their project partner, enthusiasm for the projects was high, and students began to get a sense that they were doing work that could have an impact on people's lives. Team members then began the tougher parts of the group work: dividing the labor for each project and counting on one another to do their respective tasks. Team reports kept students focused and fostered dialogue among the teams, individuals, the professor, state partners, and the classes as a whole. Discussion items ranged from personnel problems and how to motivate individuals who had "dropped off the map" in projects, to technical or organizational issues with the projects themselves or with the state as an organization.

In one instance, the group was focusing on calculating the average cost of child development programs for the First Steps program. Reports of delays in obtaining needed data got students to refocus on comparisons with other states and allowed productive work to proceed while our state partner obtained the data from those who held it elsewhere. This was discussed in the class as an example of problem solving and an explanation of how sunshine and privacy requirements within the state bureaucracy can create data fiefs within the organization as well.

Group reports were turned in biweekly. They covered the subjects around which class discussions and lectures were organized: data, stakeholders, and policy. These reports offered students opportunities to reflect on their accumulated skills as they applied to their own projects, and class time was taken to let students share their projects with other groups in the class. These reports also offered the opportunity to identify group members who were falling behind in their work commitments and to give some feedback to both the professor and the partners within the state government. Free riders in various groups were then remotivated to increase their participation to acceptable levels.

Feedback was also obtained from students in another class assignment that required them to put together a job marketing plan and a résumé. With the assistance of IUPUI's Career Center, students were given class time to see various models of résumés and encouraged to make appointments with the Career Center to individually write and review their résumés. One résumé builder that most students had was their contribution to and participation in the group project with their state partner. Some students included the partner project supervisor as a reference for future employment in the public sector.

As the final reports of each project became due, students worked cooperatively to reflect on the knowledge gained, skills used (including interpersonal skills), and the effect their work had on the effectiveness of the state of Indiana with regard to their specific project. The groups' presentations to fellow class members allowed each group to share lessons learned to familiarize others with the work they had done. Students also wrote a final reflective paper on the changes they perceived in their competencies and knowledge of how the public sector works through the insights they gained with their project. At the end of the class, a networking party was held with people from various public sector, political, and nonprofit agencies to allow students to discuss the projects and their interests with those who would be most able to help them in placement in the future.

One of the primary lessons we learned is the payoff in getting the right kinds of projects and willing partners to cooperate with academics in providing meaningful yet low-risk projects for students. One myth that was dispelled was that only the best students should take advantage of these kinds of opportunities. Our partners could easily see which groups were diligent and able and could distinguish those students who were not up to par for the overall project. This is a management skill they use often, as the pool of state employees is on average about the same as our students. Making sure that partners knew the variability among students in advance of project assignment and the team building that developed over the course of the project ensured mutual understanding among the partners and resulted in valuable insight from the partners for student evaluation and the future of the program.

Another valuable lesson was that the best students do not always make the best team leaders, and the most diligent team workers are not necessarily the hardest-working students. The real world requires a variety of qualities and interests from students, and often group leadership and highly productive and dedicated work emerges from academically less-than-stellar students. This finding should encourage a greater focus on average students, offering them opportunity and counseling to prepare them to shine when their time comes.

A by-product of the program was an increase in paid and unpaid student internships from the government partners. Some projects were too big for a one-semester course. This led the state agencies to cherry-pick students with whom they had working relationships and offer them work related to their projects (some were offered more complicated roles) within the state agency. This of course strengthens the relationship between the SPEA and the state agencies in a way that bodes well for both partners as well as for the individuals involved.

The Benefits of Service-Learning Partnerships

Given the resource limitations that exist everywhere at the state level, the increasing expansion of public demands on the state, and the reluctance of taxpayers (or their representative) to fund these expansions, the creation of government-academic partnerships is a valuable tool for state managers. One main benefit is that back-burner issues, projects that are good for the functioning of the agency but demand more resources than are available, can provide mutually beneficial opportunities for cooperative arrangements. The secretary of state of Indiana has a vested interest in providing sufficient numbers of trained and qualified poll workers to count the votes of its citizens. The FSSA has an interest in understanding the best practices for recruiting children into preschool programs for the developmentally disabled. IDEM should have time to compare its environmental protections with those of similar states. These become of secondary importance, however, in the face of too few resources. The IUPUI public affairs capstone program and the other projects developed as a result have allowed students to gain experience doing important work for the government and, as important, has let state managers receive low-cost or free reports to prepare these secondary issues for follow-up by their professional staffs.

At the same time, hiring from the pool of students involved in these projects furthers the mission of the SPEA. The students who participate in our course are better trained and have practical knowledge in organizing work, dealing with interpersonal issues within work groups, and applying organizational skills that are otherwise hard to develop in the typical classroom setting.

Already, state partner managers have commented on how much more attractive these students will be on the job market and how much more able in their first job in public service because of their experience.

Through the use of students and the cooperation of schools like SPEA at IUPUI, the government has direct access to resources that used to be hidden behind the veil of the university. When government partners have access to faculty in setting up and solving problems or access to students applying their honed research skills in university-based databases to agency-identified projects, there are clear mutual advantages to faculty, government partners, and students. Faculty learn much about the practical working of the government that can be incorporated into the classroom. State managers develop faculty relationships that they can use to address a variety of problems outside the purview of specific projects themselves. Students are able to apply their disciplinary skills to the types of projects they will encounter as future professionals. These types of programs tear down that wall between the largest funders of state university education— the government—and those who benefit from that support the most—the faculties and students.

Finally, perhaps the most valuable outcome of these programs is the building of professional networks for the students, managers, and faculty. Students develop connections to public service within Indiana, which advances the goal of stopping the state's brain drain of qualified college graduates to other states. Managers become personally acquainted with the future pool of labor and can assist in tweaking the political science and public affairs curricula to better educate the next generation of public servants. Professors have contacts with whom they can collaborate in projects and work together to solve outstanding problems within the state.

CONCLUSION

In the introduction to this chapter, we defined service-learning partnerships and identified several criteria by which to evaluate the effectiveness of such partnerships, particularly placement quality and community voice. We also noted that service-learning partnerships with government agencies play a distinctive role for political science and public administration educators in that they provide students with opportunities for application that may not be available in partnerships with nonprofit organizations.

Our case study has demonstrated how these criteria are met through a capstone course in which teams of students complete research-based projects for government agencies. These projects had been planned and organized prior to the course by Koponen and his government partners. In addition, the government partners provide ongoing information and feedback throughout the projects, important characteristics of establishing and maintaining community voice.

Furthermore, the case illustrates how placement quality requires give-and-take among the faculty, the partners, and the students themselves. Koponen ensures placement quality by asking the government partners to identify relatively low-priority yet necessary projects that require the application of important data collection and analysis skills. Thus, both the partners' and the faculty member's needs are met. In addition, students themselves contribute to placement quality by having the opportunity to match their particular strengths to the requirements of the projects available to them. Consequently they are able to apply prior knowledge and skill sets to real public sector projects, as well as network with public service professionals. Thus, they not only use what they learn in the classroom, but become familiar with the types of knowledge and skills they will need to become successful professionals after graduation. Such experiences are consistent with Eyler and Giles's (1999) concept of application.

The professional benefits of service-learning partnerships are readily apparent for students and organizations. The former gain experience and insights, while the latter receive labor power and support. The professional benefits for faculty, however, are not so obvious. Developing and maintaining service-learning partnerships can be time-consuming tasks. Consequently, it is worth pointing out the potential benefits they can provide to faculty members.

In general, faculty are expected to make contributions in teaching, research, and service. Service-learning partnerships are an important pedagogical tool that can enhance the student's learning experience and teaching effectiveness. Like many other service-oriented assignments, they tie theory to practice, thus allowing students to move from abstract thought to concrete application. The ongoing nature of these partnerships makes them particularly useful. Course design can benefit, for example, because the structure of the service can be adjusted in successive courses to fine-tune the learning outcomes. There are also unique opportunities for the scholarship of teaching and learning. The pedagogical and administrative lessons learned through the repetition of collaborations with the same partners can be theoretically and practically valuable.

Faculty can also benefit from service-learning partnerships in terms of other types of research. On many campuses, there is an increasing emphasis on applied research that can benefit the surrounding community. Because service-learning partnerships emphasize community voice, they give faculty members an opportunity to learn firsthand the needs of their partnering organizations. The close working relationships can also facilitate research collaborations that are applied or even more traditional.

Service-learning partnerships, in addition, offer new opportunities for faculty service in the community. Because these partnerships require faculty members to be more actively involved and interested in public organizations off campus, they are exposed to new professional networks. Thus, they have a chance to expand their understanding of the needs and problems of different groups in the community. With this knowledge, faculty members can more effectively target organizations that can use their expertise and services. Service-learning partnerships therefore allow faculty to develop their own service to the community.

When service-learning in political science incorporates the principles of partnership that we have identified in this chapter, a variety of mutually reinforcing benefits accrue. Students apply disciplinary skills while also developing skills identified as necessary by the partners. Government partners gain access to low-cost yet valuable resources needed to fulfill their public missions. Faculty have increased opportunities for teaching, research, and service, thereby improving their own professional development.

Voices: Social Service Agencies as Government Partner

Mary E. Chalmers

Timothy Koponen approached me about having some of his students in his senior capstone classes participate in a project at the statewide government program where I work. We agreed, and my colleagues and I identified four projects. From those possibilities, he put together two suitable projects. The director of our program spoke to the capstone classes to give the students an overview of the program and some background about working in state government.

THE STUDENT GROUPS

Two groups of four or five students chose to work with us. We asked for a single contact person for each group, and the projects began. A colleague and I met with the students at the government building to discuss the program and the project, and we provided resources and suggestions. The students initiated a couple more meetings once they had done the background work and asked some insightful questions.

THE PROJECTS

Both projects involved analyzing data to address questions that our program wanted to know but did not have the time to pursue. Once we had the data, we met with the students again to discuss the data and provide guidance for their research. This was critical: the students did not have sufficient understanding of the program or of how to engage the data on their own. Students then analyzed the data and wrote a report that described the program, the project assigned, their analysis, and their findings.

SOME LESSONS LEARNED

As a first-time experiment, the projects went well, and I am interested in working with other groups of students. The students seemed excited and proud of the work they had done, and they clearly had learned a lot. Several of the students on graduation even landed jobs in other government agencies because of their work with our program.

Suggestions to make these types of projects even more valuable include:

- Conversations with government agencies about what projects would work need to take place and be finalized before the school term begins. Students lost several weeks because our data were not available.
- Guidance from the state biweekly would increase student contact with and understanding of the government program, though time constraints might make this difficult.
- Alternatively, these interim meetings could be between the professor and the students. These projects may be the most independent exercise the students have engaged in as undergraduates; checking in with the professor would provide an important sounding board and guidance.
- Providing specific suggestions about how to analyze the data is essential. While the data we provided were not extremely complicated, they were probably more data than most students had been asked to understand and analyze in their undergraduate courses.
- Ideally, the students ought to present their findings to the state before they write their final reports. This would provide an opportunity for the state to ask questions and for the students to practice defending their work before a potential employer.

Overall, students did a great job taking the initiative, asking questions, seeking out resources, and providing a timely report;

they needed more guidance in analyzing and reporting on the data, issues that can be addressed through the suggestions I have made. The insight and experience that the students gain takes them beyond their undergraduate experiences. This hands-on experience inside the government helps prepare them for what comes next in ways that are invaluable.

■ ■ ■

Mary E. Chalmers is First Steps program consultant in the Family and Social Services Administration in Indiana State government.

References

American Association of State Colleges and Universities. (n.d.). *American Democracy Project.* Retrieved January 8, 2009, from www.aascu.org/programs/adp/.

Ball, W. J. (2005). From community engagement to political engagement. *PS: Political Science and Politics, 38*(3), 287–291.

Battistoni, R. M. (2000). Service learning in political science: An introduction. *PS: Political Science and Politics, 33*(3), 615–649.

Delli Carpini, M. X., & Keeter, S. (2000). What should be learned through service learning? *PS: Political Science and Politics, 33*(3), 635–637.

Dicklitch, S. (2003). Real service = real learning: Making political science relevant through service-learning. *PS: Political Science and Politics, 36*(3), 773–776.

Eyler, J., & Giles, D. E., Jr. (1999). *Where's the learning in service-learning?* San Francisco: Jossey-Bass.

Hatcher, J. A., & Bringle, R. G. (2004). The civic engagement inventory. *National Clearinghouse for Leadership Programs, 12*(1), 5–7.

Hepburn, M. A., Niemi, R. G., & Chapman, C. (2000). Service-learning in college political science: Queries and commentary. *PS: Political Science and Politics, 33*(3), 617–622.

Indiana University. (2005). *Eight campus identities, one shared destiny: Mission differentiation at Indiana University.* Retrieved January 12, 2009, from www.iun.edu/~aaupnw/Archive/mdpreport%20combined%20%2004%2005%2005.pdf.

Kahne, J., & Westheimer, J. (2006). The limits of political efficacy: Educating citizens for democratic society. *PS: Political Science and Politics, 39*(2), 289–296.

Walker, T. (2000). The service/politics split: Rethinking service to teach political engagement. *PS: Political Science and Politics, 33*(3), 646–649.

CHAPTER THREE

CommUniverCity San José

Building a Partnership for Service and Learning

Terry Christensen, Melinda Jackson

CommUniverCity San José is a partnership for service, learning, and empowerment between a *community* of neighborhoods, San José State *University*, and the *City* of San José, hence the name CommUniverCity. In its first two years of existence, CommUniverCity San José has concentrated 21,281 hours of student and community service in these neighborhoods, all based on priorities set by the residents, not those of the university or the city. This is a story of collaboration—how it was achieved and the challenges we have faced.

COMMUNITY, UNIVERSITY, CITY

The uniqueness of CommUniverCity San José is based on three crucial and equal partners. The community is an underserved neighborhood near the university campus. The university is San José State University, where service-learning and civic engagement

---

Debra David, director of the San José State University Center for Service-Learning, contributed to the "Community, University, City: How CommUniverCity Came Together" section of the chapter. CommUniverCity VISTA volunteer Becky Herhold contributed to portions of the case studies section.

are high priorities. The city is the City of San José, which is committed to improving selected neighborhoods through its Strong Neighborhoods Initiative.

COMMUNITY

The Five Wounds/Brookwood Terrace (FWBT) area is made up of half a dozen neighborhoods with their own identities. The first half of the area's name comes from the Church of the Five Wounds, whose two towers next to a major freeway make it the most visible and monumental building in the area. Five Wounds is the Portuguese national church and the center of an old Portuguese community still characterized by shops and restaurants catering to San José's now dispersed Portuguese population. But Portuguese culture still remains strong in the Five Wounds area, with band halls and a community center in addition to the shops and the church. The second half of the FWBT name comes from a relatively new in-fill development of modern tract homes, Brookwood Terrace. Between these two are older neighborhoods with homes dating back to the early twentieth century. Apartments are scattered through FWBT with a concentration of low-rent four-plexes at the southern end, abutting another freeway. A creek borders FWBT on the west, separating it from a pricier, gentrified neighborhood that lies between FWBT and the San José State University campus.

The demographics of FWBT tell their own story (Table 3.1). This is a low-income community where the majority population is Latino, a majority of residents were born in another country, and a majority of households speak a language other than English at home. Income is low relative to the rest of the city, where the cost of living is among the highest in the nation. In a city of home owners, renters are the majority in FWBT. Voter registration and participation are low. In short, the demographics tell a tale of need as well as foreshadowing the challenges of serving—and engaging—such a community.

But demographics do not tell the whole story. Despite its disadvantages, FWBT has never been a neighborhood without hope. A solid core of loyal home owners forms the basis of half a dozen neighborhood associations, two of them strong and stable, with a long history of fighting to protect their communities.

TABLE 3.1 DEMOGRAPHICS OF FIVE WOUNDS/BROOKWOOD TERRACE AND
THE CITY OF SAN JOSÉ

	FWBT	San José
Total population (2000 Census)	18,284	893,899
Percentage Latino	66.3	30.2
Percentage white	16.2	36.0
Percentage Asian	12.1	26.2
Percentage "other"	2.1	7.2
Percentage foreign born	52.4	36.9
Percentage only English spoken at home	22.5	48.8
Median household income	$43,207	$70,243
Percentage households below poverty level	13.3	7.2
Percentage households renting	62.7	38.2
Percentage high school education or higher	48.4	78.3
Percentage B.A. or higher	8.1	31.6

The Portuguese community remains cohesive, thanks to the church and a vibrant community center. The schools, while facing many challenges, remain important community institutions. Public facilities include a branch library—a Carnegie library dating from 1910—and two small parks. A commercial strip on a major city street includes the merchants of "Little Portugal" as well as Latino shops and restaurants and a growing number of Vietnamese shops and restaurants. But abandoned stores also dot the streetscape along with large plots of land left vacant by a steel mill and a lumberyard. Five Wounds/Brookwood Terrace is a diverse neighborhood with apparent challenges as well as less obvious strengths.

UNIVERSITY

San José State University (SJSU) is one of twenty-three California State University campuses—the oldest, in fact, with celebrations for its 150th anniversary underway in 2007. SJSU is in the heart of downtown San José, a small, dense urban campus in a sprawling suburb-like city. Its thirty thousand students mostly live in San José and the surrounding suburbs and commute. With relatively low tuition, SJSU is affordable for most residents of the area. Many students are the first in their families to attend college, and English is a second language for many. Asians and whites are the largest racial groups; Hispanics are underrepresented relative to their population in San José and the region.

While the tradition of service-learning at SJSU dates back to its founding as a teachers' college, the relatively recent establishment of the Center for Service-Learning in 2000 has encouraged and supported more faculty to integrate service-learning into their courses. That said, university financial support for service-learning is minimal, and with a heavier-than-average workload, many faculty members are unwilling or unable to find the time it takes to develop effective service-learning projects for their students. Student time is also a challenge. Besides commuting, most SJSU students work full time or part time, and many have families. These obligations make it hard for them to participate in activities outside the classroom, and some resist such assignments. Nevertheless, many faculty members believe in the power of service-learning and make time for their projects, and students, once engaged in service, soon see the benefits and enjoy participating in an alternative to traditional classroom teaching.

City

Founded in 1777, San José is the oldest civilian settlement in California. An agricultural market town for two hundred years, San José boomed beginning in the 1950s, growing from a population of ninety-five thousand to nearly 1 million today. The tenth largest city in the United States, San José claimed the title "Capital of Silicon Valley" as high-tech industries came to dominate what once was a valley of orchards. Highly diverse and relatively affluent, San José is a classic Sunbelt sprawling city, with a small downtown surrounded by old neighborhoods like FWBT, and then miles and miles of suburban-style housing—now some of the most expensive in the country.

San José's Web site (www.sanjoseca.gov) describes its form of government as council-manager, but it is better understood as a mayor-council-manager or "adapted" city (Frederickson, Johnson, & Wood, 2004), with both mayor and council playing a more active and authoritative role than is typical in council-manager systems. A confluence of factors prepared the city for partnership in CommUniverCity. One important element was the city's Strong Neighborhoods Initiative (SNI), launched in 2002 by a new mayor and council members in conjunction with some farsighted city administrators. SNI identified nineteen underserved neighborhoods throughout the city and targeted city resources and staff to work with neighborhood leaders on improvement projects identified and prioritized by the residents themselves. To fund the projects at a time when the city's general fund faced annual deficits, the designated neighborhoods were made part of San José's redevelopment area, providing access to funding from a separate and relatively fat pot of money.

But SNI is not only about money. More subversively, the SNI process forces civil servants to listen to the public that employs them and follow their orders. And it forces departmental staff members out of their parochial perspectives and into the community, where they must work with other city staff across departmental lines—traffic planners with police and code enforcement officers—and even with agencies like schools that are not part of city government. Once an SNI such as FWBT is defined, a Neighborhood Advisory Committee (NAC) of residents—usually neighborhood leaders—is formed. The NAC, working with city staff, puts together a plan that sets priorities for the area. Initially these were primarily capital projects: park development and improvements, street lighting, traffic calming, and the like. City staff are then mandated to carry out these priorities—even if the professionals disagree. For example, a stoplight might be installed at an intersection that the residents deem most in need of one rather than one that the traffic planners' data rank higher. With real money to spend and genuine responsiveness from the city, many residents have become—and stayed—engaged.

COMMUNITY, UNIVERSITY, CITY: HOW COMMUNIVERCITY CAME TOGETHER

These components formed the base for CommUniverCity San José: a community with significant issues but a reservoir of strength and a history of activism; a university with a growing interest in service-learning and working with the community; and a city engaged in becoming more responsive to its residents. Exhibit 3.1 details the time line of CommUniverCity San José. In 1997, the California State University system began a strategic planning process for service-learning, encouraging every campus

EXHIBIT 3.1 COMMUNIVERCITY SAN JOSÉ DEVELOPMENT TIME LINE

January 2000
• San José State University (SJSU) Center for Service-Learning established

2003
• Joint University/City Martin Luther King Jr. Library completed
• SJSU and City of San José form Beyond MLK partnership to continue successful collaboration
• SJSU College of Education dean Susan Meyers proposes service-learning town-gown initiative, approved by SJSU Deans' Council
• Five Wounds/Brookwood Terrace (FWBT) SNI area chosen as community partner for town-gown initiative

2004
• City, campus, and community leaders meet to discuss town-gown initiative
• Several service-learning classes begin working with FWBT in Fall 2004

2005
• CommUniverCity San José name, mission, and guiding principles approved; city, campus, and community leaders form steering committee
• First five CommUniverCity service-learning projects begin in fall

2006
• First CommUniverCity day of service in April involves 511 students and residents in FWBT
• Social capital baseline survey conducted in FWBT and comparison SNI area

2007
• Second SJSU/CommUniverCity day of service in April expanded to be an all-university day of service with 830 participants

2005–2007
• CommUniverCity San José service-learning projects involved 1,459 SJSU students and 2,871 community residents in 20,817 hours of service supported by $433,451 in donations, grants, university expenditures, and city contracts

to engage in its own parallel process. Many of the people now involved with CommUniverCity participated in shaping the SJSU strategic plan, which eventually resulted in funding for the SJSU Center for Service-Learning with a part-time director in January 2000. Seeds were also planted by an earlier grant from the Department of Housing and Urban Development for a Community Outreach Partnership Center that involved faculty from education, health science, urban and regional planning, and other departments.

In 2003, Susan Meyers, dean of the College of Education, proposed a campuswide service-learning partnership between a San José neighborhood and SJSU to the Council of Deans, calling it a town-gown initiative. The deans approved but committed no resources. Undeterred, Dean Meyers and Debra David, director of the SJSU Center for Service-Learning, met with the principal of the high school nearest to campus, who suggested working with the City of San José's SNI.

When the leaders of the Center for Service-Learning met with SNI community coordinators, the city team leader for one SNI area near the SJSU campus was immediately enthusiastic about partnering with SJSU. David and a team of AmeriCorps VISTA members undertook an investigation of prospective SNI neighborhoods, focusing on school statistics, health-related needs, proximity to campus, socioeconomic characteristics, and racial and ethnic diversity. The Five Wounds/Brookwood Terrace SNI, whose city team leader had responded with enthusiasm to the idea of a partnership, was selected based on the research and its location near the SJSU campus.

In spring 2004, Meyers convened a meeting of city representatives, campus leaders, and community representatives to discuss the town-gown partnership. Response to that meeting was positive, and in fall 2004, several service-learning classes began working with the Five Wounds/Brookwood Terrace neighborhood, focusing on health, education, urban planning, anthropology, and management information systems. Over time, the city, campus, and community representatives evolved into a steering committee, which in spring 2005 met to discuss project selection, assessment, funding, and other organizational matters. The mission, name, and guiding principles of CommUniverCity San José were approved.

Momentum continued to build, with more courses and faculty coming on board.

Concurrently the top executives of the university and the city were searching for ways to continue and expand their successful collaboration on the completion of the joint city-university Martin Luther King Jr. Library. Because neither the city nor the university had sufficient funds to expand and modernize their main libraries, SJSU president Bob Caret and San José mayor Susan Hammer brought the two together to build a shared facility, combining the collections and staffing of both the public and university libraries and building an award-winning new facility, completed in 2003. The successive university and city administrations agreed that the collaboration should continue and formed the Beyond MLK partnership. Don Kassing and Carmen Sigler, SJSU's current president and provost, helped ensure that CommUniverCity became a flagship project for the partnership, thus providing top-level administrative attention and support, as well as a regular forum for reports on progress.

Being part of Beyond MLK helped secure the necessary resources to move forward. SJSU provost Carmen Sigler agreed to fund a part-time executive director for CommUniverCity, and the city agreed to match SJSU contributions. Over the summer of 2005, the project steering committee selected an executive director (the first author, Terry Christensen, who served from 2005 to 2007) and presented a menu of projects to the Five Wounds/Brookwood Terrace Neighborhood Advisory Committee (NAC). Based on the preferences of the NAC, five projects involving faculty from five different SJSU colleges were selected for fall 2005: civic engagement, community planning, walkability/mapping, college-going culture for schools, and earthquake safety preparation.

The implementation of these projects and the development of CommUniverCity San José during the 2005–2006 academic year were facilitated by the part-time executive director and two full-time VISTA volunteers supported by the Health Trust (a nonprofit community benefit organization) and the city of San José. The city provided office space and technology support at a community center in the project area. During their first months of service, the executive director and VISTA volunteers secured CommUniverCity San José's first external grant from Pacific Gas and Electric; oversaw the development of the CommUniverCity Web page, developed by students in the SJSU management information systems program; approved the creation of a logo, an in-kind contribution from an SJSU alumna; organized 511 volunteers for a day of community service; and assisted in the completion of several service-learning projects. (See Table 3.2 for a list of CommUniverCity projects from 2005 to 2007.)

In its first two years of operation (the 2005–2007 academic years), CommUniverCity San José projects resulted in a total of 1,459 SJSU students working with 2,871 community residents to complete 21,281 hours of service supported by $433,451 in donations, grants, university expenditures, and city contracts.

SETTING THE GOALS: WHAT'S DIFFERENT ABOUT COMMUNIVERCITY

While collaboration between a community, a university, and a city makes CommUniverCity uncommon, if not unique, other aspects of this effort also set it apart.

GEOGRAPHICAL CONCENTRATION

CommUniverCity focuses multiple projects in a single geographical area. Like many other universities, San José State faculty and students engage in lots of service-learning projects, but they tend to be randomly distributed rather than concentrated. Faculty members organize projects independently, selecting an area where they perhaps have a connection or one with identifiable needs. By concentrating projects in a single geographical area, CommUniverCity hopes to have a greater cumulative impact than scattered, independent projects could achieve.

INTERDISCIPLINARY COOPERATION AND LEARNING

The concentration of projects across a range of disciplines facilitates interdisciplinary cooperation and learning. When projects are not geographically concentrated, it is almost impossible for them to be linked in a meaningful way. But concentration ensures that cross-fertilization between faculty members and students of different majors occurs. While interdisciplinary cooperation and learning are not unique to CommUniverCity, they are embedded in the structure of the organization.

LONG-TERM COMMITMENT

CommUniverCity is distinguished by its long-term commitment to the community and the city. Initially the promise was for a minimum of five years, again in hopes of a more significant cumulative impact than shorter-term projects could achieve. "Most service-learning projects are like one-night stands," one San José city administrator observed, "but what we're hoping for here is more like a marriage—or at least a long-term affair." Many community organizations and institutions have experienced working with universities as one-night stands—they come and go with no long-lasting effect. The assurance that the commitment was for years, not a single semester, gave CommUniverCity credibility with the city, the neighborhoods, the schools, and other local institutions that were mistrustful of short-term relationships.

While five years seemed like a long time to university participants, others take a longer view. "How long is your commitment?" asked an executive of the San José Redevelopment Agency at a meeting of city and university leaders. "Five years," said the CommUniverCity executive director proudly. "Well, ours is for thirty," responded the agency executive, implying that the university needed to think further about its long-term role. CommUniverCity is already doing that, but the promise of at least five years reassured the city and the community that the university commitment was a solid one and that a greater impact could be achieved by concentrating projects geographically and over a long period.

COMMUNITY RESIDENTS: SETTING PROJECT PRIORITIES

CommUniverCity is different in another way too: community residents, not the faculty or the city, set project priorities. This was the founding concept of San José's Strong Neighborhoods Initiative, which CommUniverCity readily adopted but is a very different way of operating for a university. In most cases, faculty interests define projects, albeit sometimes in consultation with community leaders. In this case, residents set the broad priorities for projects through the NAC. CommUniverCity leaders then seek faculty members whose classes and interests fit for the priorities.

Initially, as the community developed its priorities, some projects were directly proposed by CommUniverCity to the NAC and readily approved. Even after the neighborhood priorities were set during CommUniverCity's first year, a process has been developed for proposing projects that are not an obvious fit with the priorities. In fact, the residents would most likely approve almost anything the university proposes—happily welcoming any kind of attention and service for their neighborhoods. But as a matter of principle, CommUniverCity, like the city through its SNI program, is committed to following and facilitating neighborhood project priorities rather than setting its own.

BUILDING SOCIAL CAPITAL

Neighborhood priorities fall into three categories: education, health, and neighborhood environment. CommUniverCity added the encompassing goal of building community (or social capital). According to Robert Putnam (2000), "Whereas physical capital refers to physical objects and human capital refers to properties of individuals, *social capital* refers to connections among individuals— social networks and the norms of reciprocity and trustworthiness that arise from them" (p. 19). Strongly connected communities— those with substantial social capital—are self-sustaining. Social capital allows residents to resolve collective problems more easily, widens awareness of shared fate, and spreads helpful information. People feel better about themselves and their neighborhoods. Among the positive outcomes linked to higher social capital are education and children's welfare, safer neighborhoods, economic prosperity, health, happiness, and higher participation in public life (Putnam, 2000.)

When the CommUniverCity Steering Committee considered building social capital as an objective, the executive director warned that it was a "scary goal" because its achievement is highly uncertain. But the committee unanimously agreed that this was the right goal to strive for, not only for the community but also for the students.

As a consequence, all CommUniverCity projects must include an element of building social capital, which minimally means engaging both residents and students. We discuss the ways we are measuring this and other outcomes later in this chapter.

Case Studies of Selected CommUniverCity Projects

In its first years, CommUniverCity projects have included two days of service in which nearly twelve hundred students and residents carried out physical improvement and school projects; a walkability and mapping project relating to health and providing data for community planning; earthquake preparedness training; intimate violence prevention workshops; chemistry experiments for elementary school children guided by university students; a solar energy project; an ongoing program of physical activity and tutoring in a local elementary school; as well as the projects that will be discussed in more detail in this section. In addition, university students have completed four statistically valid surveys of the neighborhood to assess community needs and views and measure the impact CommUniverCity is having. Residents, city staff, and university faculty and students interacted in all the projects—a new experience for most participants. Residents and city staff had rarely intermingled with students and faculty previously, and because SJSU is a commuter campus, faculty and students rarely interact with one another outside the classroom. The simple opportunity to be together was enjoyed by many participants and surely contributed to community building itself.

Community Planning: Updating the Action Agenda

The flagship project for year 1 of CommUniverCity was a community planning project to update the FWBT neighborhood priorities for both the city's SNI program and CommUniverCity projects. Over the course of the 2005–2006 academic year, eighteen master's students in urban and regional planning, under the leadership of Professor Dayana Salazar and Paul Pereira of the

City's Strong Neighborhoods Initiative, worked with over ninety FWBT residents to update priorities for neighborhood projects. Completing over three thousand hours of service, students assembled research data on the current state of the neighborhood and the progress toward meeting priorities set five years previously, interviewed residents and city staff, and presented their preliminary findings to the community as a basis for subsequent planning. This was followed by three community workshops in which residents, supported by students, professors, and city staff, developed recommendations for future priorities and conducted an elaborate voting process to determine the top ten projects for FWBT. Resident participation more than doubled from the first round of goal setting in 2001—from forty-three to ninety participants—and FWBT was the first of the nineteen SNI neighborhoods to update its action plan. Once the residents agreed on priorities, they became the basis for city and CommUniverCity programming in FWBT.

The final list included capital projects such as streetscape improvements and traffic calming, improved services such as increased law enforcement and crime prevention, concentrated retail development, housing rehabilitation, and other projects that are primary city responsibilities. Other items were not within the city's scope, such as improved access to health care, creating a college-going culture, and developing a community plan for the site of a future rapid transit station. Working with the residents, schools, and nonprofit partners, CommUniverCity was more capable of addressing these needs as well as assisting with housing rehabilitation and other action items. Key projects are listed in Table 3.2.

The community planning project was supported by a grant of sixty-three thousand dollars from the city and university-funded partial release time for one faculty member. The city viewed the project as a prototype for renewing the action agendas of the other eighteen SNI areas and funds included payment for the faculty member to write up not only the FWBT plan but also a procedural manual. The urban planning master's students who participated gained invaluable experience not only in planning but also in working with the community—practical experience that will surely help them in their careers.

TABLE 3.2 Selected CommUniverCity San José Projects, 2005–2007

Project Title	SJSU Department(s)	Number of Students/Hours Served	Outcomes
Civic Engagement	Political Science	98/1,324	Increased voter registration; organized candidate forum
College-Going Culture	Counseling (Department of Education)	34/122	Workshops on attending college for elementary school children and their parents
Community Planning	Urban Planning	32/3,096	Year-long research and workshops for residents to set plans and priorities for FWBT
Annual Community Surveys	Urban Planning, Political Science	105/2,526	Annual public opinion surveys focused on building social capital
Inquiry in Action	Chemistry	140/160	College students guide elementary school students through chemistry experiments
Healthcare Access	Health Sciences	13/30	Outreach and marketing plans for free school health clinics
Neighborhood Walkability	Health Sciences, Urban Planning	151/1,334	Street-by-street survey of pedestrian access and safety
Intimate Violence Prevention	Psychology	28/160	Workshops for teens and adults on intimate violence prevention

TABLE 3.2   (*continued*)

Project Title	SJSU Department(s)	Number of Students/Hours Served	Outcomes
School Support	Education, Sociology	38/3,150	Tutoring and organized recess activities for elementary school students
Days of Service	All university	1,042/5,717	Physical service projects (house painting, neighborhood and park cleanups, mural painting, and others)
Earthquake Safety Education	Engineering	13/278	132 residents attended workshops; three homes inspected
BART/Town Square Planning	Urban Planning	70/2,250	Community workshops to plan major transit-oriented development site
Renewable Energy	Engineering	14/514	Develop and install solar power project at community center

COLLEGE-GOING CULTURE

Although only 8 percent of FWBT residents have completed a bachelor's or more advanced degree, getting the neighborhood children to college emerged early as a strong top neighborhood priority. As a consequence, an ongoing CommUniverCity project brings graduate students in the SJSU Counseling Education program to one of the elementary schools in FWBT, where they conduct in-class workshops and evening presentations for parents and children and staff information tables at parent nights and other school events. Providing basic information about what it takes to go to college, including finance and admission requirements, SJSU counseling education students have so far interacted with nearly five hundred parents who might otherwise have little information about the possibilities of their children going to college.

The college-going theme is also expressed through other CommUniverCity projects in elementary schools. These include high school outreach, chemistry lessons by SJSU students for elementary school students, organized recess and lunchtime activities, tutoring, and more. SJSU students wear CommUniverCity T-shirts or clothing with SJSU logos when they participate in these school programs (this also serves as a sort of dress code), and they are advised whenever possible to plant a seed by simply saying to the children they meet, "I go to college at San José State. Are you going to go to college?"

Civic Engagement

Consistent with CommUniverCity's theme of building social capital, a civic engagement project was implemented during the 2006 election cycle. The project had two components: voter registration and a candidate forum.

During the spring 2006 CommUniverCity day of service, preceding the California primary election in June, SJSU political science students registered sixty FWBT residents to vote. Working Saturdays before the November general election, they registered an additional eighty-three residents. The combined total increased voter registration in the FWBT precincts by 3 percent. In reflection papers, 94 percent of student participants clearly demonstrated learning about voter participation, and 80 percent successfully applied concepts from class texts to their own experience.

In addition, CommUniverCity partnered with eleven neighborhood associations, the FWBT high school, and the League of Women Voters to organize a forum for candidates for the San José mayor and city council. The planning committee of neighborhood leaders, faculty, students, and the league organized logistics, solicited contributions of food, and oversaw outreach efforts. The result was the largest grassroots forum in the November city election campaign, attended by over 240 residents on a Friday night. Candidates were impressed by the organization of the event and community turnout. Residents appreciated access to the candidates and the organization of the event and, for the first time ever, having the spotlight on their community and their concerns during an important election campaign.

Voter turnout in the FWBT precincts was 30.6 percent in the November gubernatorial election in 2002 and 51.6 percent in 2006, the year of our project. Turnout in Santa Clara County, where FWBT is located, was 51 percent in 2002 and 59 percent in 2006. Although most of the dramatic increase in FWBT turnout was surely due to other factors, such as competitive state and local races, the CommUniverCity projects may also have helped.

PENDING PROJECTS

As CommUniverCity approaches its third year, most projects continue, and others, especially those focusing on health, are emerging. The spring 2007 flagship project was a series of workshops to help community residents anticipate development of vacant lands around a proposed rapid transit station. The transit agency proposed mostly surface parking lots, but neighborhood children came up with the idea of a "town square," and residents are advocating for high-density, mixed-use development. The transit agency has responded positively so far. As one participant said, "Most neighborhoods get involved in proposed projects after decisions are already made and it's too late to have an influence. This project is helping FWBT residents get ahead of the curve, so they can help shape the plans before it's too late."

OUTCOMES ASSESSMENT

CommUniverCity San José has been conscious of the need for outcomes assessment from its inception, not only because the university expects it but also because showing outcomes justifies funding by the city and others. For CommUniverCity, outcomes assessment functions at two levels: student learning and impact on community. Student learning is measured for each project through student evaluations and reflection papers. Cumulatively, the evidence points to the power of service-learning. But the long-term impact on students as citizens, an outcome yet to be assessed, is also of interest. Finally, CommUniverCity seeks to assess its short-term and long-term impact on the community, an important outcome but one that is rarely assessed by service-learning projects. We can readily count volunteer hours (21,281!), the number of residents served (2,871!), the number of houses painted, voters registered, parents counseled on going to college, and the like. We can point to city policies that have been changed through the CommUniverCity collaboration. But assessing real change in the community—much less taking credit (or blame!) for it—is more challenging. CommUniverCity has a plan, however, and over the next few years, outcomes will be assessed by the means described in the following section.

DATA COLLECTION

In its first year, CommUniverCity VISTA volunteers set up a system to track statistical data on the Five Wounds/Brookwood Terrace neighborhoods, beginning with the 2000 census data that will be compared with the 2010 data when they become available. We will look particularly closely at home ownership, education, and income. We also have crime statistics, voter participation rates, school test scores, and other data. In addition, CommUniverCity VISTA volunteers created and maintain a "social capital tracker," which records attendance and participation at community meetings and events. If we are building social capital, attendance should improve over time.

FOCUS GROUPS

For more qualitative data, the CommUniverCity outcomes assessment plan calls for focus groups of residents, students, community leaders, faculty, and nonprofit partners. These will occur in years 4 or 5 of CommUniverCity—after participants have had time to put their experience into perspective. We are particularly interested in students' perceptions some years after their service—and whether the experience enhanced their own civic engagement.

SOCIAL CAPITAL SURVEY

To provide a statistically valid baseline against which to measure future outcomes, CommUniverCity conducted a social capital survey in spring 2006 among random samples of residents in FWBT and a similar SNI area called East Valley. (The complete survey report is available at www.communivercitysanjose.org.) The outcomes assessment plan calls for a follow-up survey in year 4 or 5 of CommUniverCity, which will allow comparisons within and between FWBT and East Valley over time. We hope to find that social capital has increased in FWBT due to the concentrated efforts of CommUniverCity there, while remaining around baseline level in East Valley.

With funding from the city, the survey was carried out through the Survey and Policy Research Institute at SJSU. From random samples of two thousand to three thousand residents in each community, 315 telephone interviews were completed with FWBT residents, and 343 with East Valley residents, yielding a 5.5 percent margin of error for the survey. About 25 percent of the interviews in each community were conducted in Spanish.

The survey included a variety of social capital measures: social trust, informal socializing, community involvement, organizational memberships, and volunteerism. We also asked about obstacles to participation, which allowed us to identify busy work schedules, lack of information, and trouble with language as the top three barriers to civic involvement for FWBT residents. In addition, we asked if respondents had contacted the city of San José in the past year and if they were aware of SJSU students working or helping out in the neighborhood. In the 2006 baseline survey, there was no difference between FWBT and East Valley on these measures, but we hope to see significantly higher numbers for both of these indicators of CommUniverCity's impact and visibility in FWBT in the follow-up survey.

The survey also included measures of several outcomes related to social capital, on which we also hope to see more improvement in FWBT than in East Valley over the next few years. Residents were asked to rate both their neighborhood and the city of San José in terms of general quality of life, physical condition, safety, and community pride. They were asked how long they intended to stay in the neighborhood and how much impact they felt they could have in making the community a better place to live. Other outcomes measures included interest in local politics, voter registration and participation, and self-reported levels of health and happiness.

In addition to this social capital survey, SJSU students have conducted door-to-door surveys with randomly sampled households in FWBT in the fall semester each year since 2004. These door-to-door surveys were initially designed and conducted by master's students in urban and regional planning as a service-learning project in their quantitative methods course, and they included questions about issues such as neighborhood walkability and the adequacy of street lighting. Political science undergraduate students taking a class on public opinion joined the urban and regional planning students starting in fall 2006, conducting the survey as a CommUniverCity project.

These annual door-to-door surveys also offer an opportunity to ask more detailed questions about different issues each year as the survey is updated in consultation with the CommUniverCity steering committee and city staff working in the neighborhood. In 2006, for example, questions were added about whether children attended the neighborhood schools or went elsewhere and the adequacy of on-street parking.

Along with collecting valuable data for outcomes assessment, the students involved with the door-to-door survey projects gain hands-on experience designing, conducting, and analyzing surveys. They also learn more about the people living just a few blocks from campus as they develop a sense of connection to the community that is all too rare on SJSU's commuter campus.

Elements of Successful Collaboration, Challenges, and Potential for Replication

A combination of just the right factors is essential for a successful collaboration—conditions that clearly existed for CommUniverCity. But even a successful project faces challenges. In the case of CommUniverCity, these included engaging the residents of a low-income, immigrant community and coming up with funding when all the partners—the neighborhood, the university and the city—face serious fiscal shortfalls. Despite these challenges, it is the hope of the CommUniverCity partners that their project will not be unique but can be replicated in other communities.

COLLABORATION: IT TAKES A VILLAGE

No one element can account for a successful collaboration: it takes a village—or at least a combination of interested and committed partners plus an environment that nurtures and appreciates collaboration.

CommUniverCity benefited in numerous ways from a confluence of elements. The city and university were searching for ways to continue their collaboration. The university had been expanding service-learning and seeking to strengthen community connections—and university leaders were prepared to support these activities with funding, albeit limited. The city had created the Strong Neighborhoods Initiative process to reconnect staff to residents and increase responsiveness, and it had provided substantial funding through its redevelopment agency. The FWBT neighborhoods had a cadre of active leaders and an infrastructure of neighborhood groups that facilitated community connections—and an established Neighborhood Advisory Committee that could work with CommUniverCity. The FWBT area itself was a good choice, underserved but far from hopeless and with great potential.

But even perfect conditions cannot make a project work without the right people, including residents willing to volunteer and faculty ready, willing, and able to listen to the residents and work with them. The leadership and advocacy within their respective institutions of Dean Susan Meyers at the university and Kip Harkness, the city's SNI manager, was essential. CommUniverCity was also fortunate to be working with Paul Pereira (an SJSU alumnus and respected member of the local Portuguese community) as the leader of an excellent team of city workers in FWBT. Having a senior faculty member with a long history of community activism as its part-time executive director also brought a formidable network and deep knowledge of the campus, community, and local government to the project. Two VISTA volunteers, funded by the city and the Health Trust, a CommUniverCity partner organization, maintained the organization on a day-to-day basis, supporting the executive director, the steering committee, and project leaders and initiating projects of their own. All of these individuals and constituencies came together in a dynamic steering committee whose monthly meetings are characterized by nearly perfect attendance and high energy.

Also contributing to the success of CommUniverCity were a catchy name, a cute logo, and even T-shirts. This combination made CommUniverCity visible in a way that most university programs are not. This is simple but true.

CHALLENGES: INVOLVING RESIDENTS AND FUNDING

Turf wars, siloed city and university bureaucracies, institutional self-interest, personal ambition, and the simple failure to produce can all be challenges to undertakings like CommUniverCity, but they have not been for us. That is because the people who have chosen to participate or who have been recruited to work with CommUniverCity—faculty, city staff, residents, and others—through self-selection or by other means have been collaborators. The commitment of top city and university leaders to collaboration has also helped.

The real challenges for CommUniverCity have been getting residents involved and, inevitably, funding. Residents of FWBT are poor and working class; many do not speak English; most work hard and have little free time. Getting them to meetings is tough, but we are learning how to communicate through the schools, by canvassing door-to-door, and by phone tree as well as e-mail, although the last is limited in FWBT. Person-to-person contact always works best, and we have learned when to schedule meetings for the convenience of this community. We also always make sure to have food and translators at meetings and to make everyone feel welcome when they arrive. Involving residents will continue to be a challenge, but we are making progress.

Funding is another matter. Despite the enthusiasm for CommUniverCity, funds are tight for both the university and the city, and a collaborative project is not as important as providing classes or police protection. CommUniverCity does not cost a lot (the executive director's half-time salary, the VISTA, office space, supplies, and, ideally, release time for faculty to develop and implement service-learning projects), but too often we rely on faculty members and others to contribute time on top of their regular duties rather than as part of them.

The prospects for external funding seem good, although many foundations are leery of funding what they think should be the responsibility of universities (teaching) and cities (public services). Similarly, most corporate donors have their own agendas, for which CommUniverCity may not always be a good fit. Whether foundation or corporation, applying for restricted grants or gifts requires advance planning that CommUniverCity has not caught up with yet. Our projects vary from semester to semester, and we have not yet been able to plan years into the future. Fortunately our first and major funder, Pacific Gas and Electric, had the wisdom to see the overall benefits of CommUniverCity and provided an unrestricted grant that, along with university and city support, has provided a solid foundation for our first years.

REPLICATION: YOU CAN DO IT

CommUniverCity may seem like the result of a perfect storm of factors, but it is not beyond replication without such substantial levels of university and city collaboration—without a Beyond MLK initiative or even a Strong Neighborhoods Initiative. A single faculty member could start such a project with his or her own service-learning projects, but it would be best to find a few colleagues with whom to collaborate, simply by concentrating projects in a selected neighborhood. Try to find an existing community or neighborhood organization to work with so that residents can be involved in the selection and implementation of projects. You do not necessarily need to go through the year-long priority-setting exercise that CommUniverCity did. Residents could develop broad project priorities at a single workshop, or faculty could simply take project proposals to the community organization for approval and buy-in. Finding committed faculty and some sort of community partner is crucial. Add at least some level of administrative support from the university (a dean or a department chair or two). Reach out to someone in city government: a mayor, city manager, or district council representative. They will need to provide some staff support, but it does not have to be on the scale of San José's SNI. Then reach out to potential partnering organizations. Ours include the school district and nonprofits that work on health and affordable housing. Like so much else that we do, this can be done with the sweat equity of faculty members, but success is most likely with some staffing, including a part-time executive director and VISTA volunteers or at least interns—but it does not have to cost a lot of money.

Let us know when you succeed. CommUniverCity San José would love to be part of a CommUniverCity network across the U.S.A.—and beyond. And if you would like more information, the Web sites listed in Exhibit 3.2 can provide a great deal of detail on our projects.

EXHIBIT 3.2   COMMUNIVERCITY RELATED WEB SITES

• CommUniverCity San José	www.comunivercitysanjose.org
• City of San José	www.sanjoseca.gov
• Strong Neighborhoods Initiative (SNI)	www.strongneighborhoods.org www.sanjoseca.gov/planning/sni/maps.asp
• Five Wounds/Brookwood Terrace (FWBT)	www.strongneighborhoods.org/fivewounds06.asp

Voices: City and University

CITY: GOVERNMENT PARTNERS

Laura Lam

CommUniverCity (CUC) has expanded the imagination of the Strong Neighborhoods program by aligning diverse academic disciplines and student enthusiasm with neighborhood priorities and city resources. In addition to implementing capital improvements and enhancing city service delivery in the Five Wounds/ Brookwood Terrace Strong Neighborhoods Area, CUC has broadened community improvements to include increasing civic engagement, creating a college-going culture, exploring community partnerships around renewable energy, and beyond.

Neighbors, students, professors, nonprofit partners, and city staff contribute to the comprehensive effort of building community in Five Wounds/Brookwood Terrace. By concentrating efforts in one neighborhood over a period of several years, CUC maximizes the potential for relationships to develop, blossom, and thrive. Collectively, CUC partners work to achieve sustainable change.

In an effort to implement neighborhood priorities effectively, Strong Neighborhoods strives to leverage and align resources whenever possible. CUC has leveraged significant resources to enhance the quality of life within the Five Wounds area, ranging from volunteer labor to neighborhood surveying. Students contribute substantial time and energy through the various volunteer initiatives underway. In return, they gain a keen appreciation of civic responsibility. Residents devote countless hours to planning and implementing their neighborhood priority projects alongside their CUC partners. The resulting community improvements, often inventive and pioneering in nature, are a testament to the creativity generated through CommUniverCity.

■ ■ ■

Laura Lam is the Strong Neighborhoods Initiative manager for the City of San José.

City: Government Partners

Paul Pereira

The CommUniverCity collaboration has helped us in lots of ways. Our contracts with the university have produced survey data and planning documents at a bargain price, and the volunteer hours of SJSU service-learning students strengthened our case when the city applied for a state grant for a planning project. CommUniverCity's focus on social capital also helped inject that value into the work of our Strong Neighborhoods Initiative. CommUniverCity has provided invaluable training for SJSU graduates and helped the city recruit over a dozen into city jobs—at a time when we are doing succession planning for the huge number of retirements we expect in the near future.

But CommUniverCity has also had direct policy impacts by offering fresh perspectives and proposing alternatives to current city policies as student service-learners become acquainted with a neighborhood and gain an understanding of how and why current policies affect the neighborhood, becoming social advocates in the process. One example is the change in the city's house painting program. Previously house painting projects were targeted toward owner-occupied households. Students in the College of Social Work who had been working in the vicinity of several FWBT mobile home parks and had come to understand and build relationships with some of the fixed-income and disabled population in these mobile home parks realized that the house painting program was not regularly extended to mobile park occupants because mobile homes are classified as just that: mobile. The State of California recognizes the mobile homes as vehicles, and for that reason the house painting program did not apply to the inhabitants of these parks. Students pointed out that a large percentage of trailer park occupants are low income and disabled. Made aware of this paradox, city officials worked quickly to revise the policy to include owners of mobile homes who committed to stay on site and keep their mobile homes for a set number of years.

We expect an even more dramatic impact on public policy when residents, assisted by students of urban and regional planning, complete development on an alternative plan for transit-oriented development at the site of a future rapid transit station in FWBT. All signs so far suggest that government planners are listening and responding to the ideas of the residents.

■ ■ ■

Paul Pereira is the Strong Initiatives manager for FWBT for the City of San José.

University: Administrative Perspectives

Susan Meyers

Ideally an urban university enhances and enriches the quality of life in the community. CommUniverCity San José is an exemplar of that ideal: student learning is linked to the service needs identified by the city residents, and the results are mutually beneficial. The challenge (as it is in life in general) is to maintain a balance such that the community service provided by the university students meets authentic community needs, promotes quality learning linking theory to practice, and instills in the student an appreciation for his or her responsibilities as an engaged citizen in a democratic society. The CommUniverCity Steering Committee, composed of representatives from the city, university, and community, works collaboratively to maintain the balance that ensures the benefits of the partnership for the students, city residents, the city, and the university.

■ ■ ■

Susan Meyers is dean of the College of Education at San José State University.

UNIVERSITY: ADMINISTRATIVE PERSPECTIVES

Carmen Sigler

San José State University benefits from its partnership in Comm-UniverCity at many levels. Our students' classroom education is enriched by participation in service-learning, faculty benefit from innovative collaboration across disciplines, and the university as a whole benefits from improved outreach and public relations, as well as the generation of funds through grants and government contracts. CommUniverCity is a wonderful, collaborative vehicle through which the university continues to fulfill its mission of community service.

■ ■ ■

Carmen Sigler is provost of San José State University.

References

Frederickson, H. G., Johnson, G. A., & Wood, C. H. (2004). *The adapted city*. Armonk, NY: M. E. Sharpe.

Putnam, R. D. (2000). *Bowling alone: The collapse and revival of American community*. New York: Simon & Schuster.

CHAPTER FOUR

LEARNING POLITICS AND LEARNING TO LEARN

A Collaborative Service-Learning Project with a Local Government

Jeffrey L. Bernstein, Joseph Ohren

Imagine a financially strapped municipality that desperately needs funding to repair its roads. Local officials could ask residents to vote to approve a tax based on property values (commonly called a millage referendum), but they would want a sense of how to get the millage passed before such an election. Imagine also two university classes, one on local government and one on research methods. Professors in both classes want an engaging way to bring real-world perspectives into their classes to help students bridge what they are learning in class to what expert practitioners actually do.

The marriage of these needs is the focus of this chapter. We describe the work of two groups of students in two separate undergraduate classes at Eastern Michigan University joining together to conduct a public opinion survey about this millage issue. It aims to serve as a guide for those considering developing and launching service-learning partnerships between universities and local governments. We pay particular attention to the challenges of implementing such a plan, particularly with two sets of students in different classes. We assess the impact of those efforts on faculty, students, and governmental partners and discuss the benefits of using such an approach for teaching students political science and for helping them learn how to be better learners.

SITUATING OUR PROJECT WITHIN ACADEMIC SERVICE-LEARNING

Classes that use academic service-learning combine out-of-classroom service experiences with reflective in-class instruction to enhance student learning and build stronger communities. Through active engagement in the community and application of course materials to real-world problems, service-learning aims to excite students while engaging them directly in the learning process, helping them create their own knowledge rather than passively accepting knowledge poured into their heads through less engaging methods. The growth of service-learning programs throughout the academy, and this book itself, is testament to the growing consensus that service-learning is achieving at least some of its lofty aims.

The prototypical service-learning experience might involve students working in a soup kitchen or homeless shelter as part of their work in a course on poverty and inequality. Rather than merely reading about economic disparities and their harmful effects, students might supplement their course work with a few hours a week working directly with those victimized by poverty and inequality of resources. The students perform a valuable service to the community by serving meals or tutoring homeless children. But service-learning is more than community service; students also learn more about the subject they are studying through their immersion in real-world problems, helping them view what they are learning in class in a more realistic way.

We believe that the service, when done right, combines with the enhanced academic experience to create a significant learning experience (see Fink, 2003, for a useful discussion of what characterizes significant learning experiences). A key component of this experience comes from the affective dimension; as students work directly with those who need their help, they are personally affected by what they see and learn. These experiences get their attention and consequently help students engage more in the material. In addition to reaping an enhanced academic experience, students participating in these activities may emerge with a greater commitment to social justice than they had previously.

We applaud such transformations, even as we agree with Strain (2006) that such results may be difficult to achieve within the space of a single project. However, these connections can be even more elusive when the service projects involved do not serve individuals within the community (at least not directly), but rather serve local municipalities from within the classroom setting, as we did here. While we will argue that our project represented a valuable service to the community, we cannot hope to transform students in the same way that working in a soup kitchen might. Still, we argue that service-learning with a local government partner can be a transformative educational experience for students; participants in projects such as this one come away with valuable lessons about local government, political processes, and the learning process in general that would be difficult to achieve using other methodologies.

SERVICE-LEARNING AND LEARNING ABOUT LOCAL GOVERNMENT

Arguments about declining civic engagement among Americans, particularly among younger generations, are ubiquitous in the political science literature today (see, for example, Putnam, 2000; Skocpol, 2003). Leading scholars in the field take note of Americans' distaste of politics (Dionne, 1991) and their low levels of political knowledge (Delli Carpini & Keeter, 1996; Niemi & Junn, 1998), and often they offer dire predictions for the future of the American experiment with democracy (Somin, 2006). What these and other perspectives have in common is a sense that citizens feel disconnected from the political system and believe that their voices are not heard very much within the political world.

As university professors, we have limited ability to change the world on a macrolevel. We can, however, have an impact on our students. On closely examining the messages sent to students, we understand the source of some of this perception of a remote, impenetrable system. The typical emphasis in an introductory political science class is American national government, geographically far removed from students and realistically beyond their ability to influence. (At our institution, like many others, this introductory course is typically the only one students take.) Citizens are bombarded with studies that demonstrate what they do not know about politics (for example, more Americans can identify the Three Stooges than they can the three branches of government) and focus less on what people do know and what they can do. Arguments like Lupia's (1994, 2006; see also Popkin, 1991) that citizens do have ways to reach rational political judgments even in the face of incomplete information are rarely heard by students in introductory classes.

As we have confronted problems of political disengagement, we have both looked increasingly toward local government as an arena in which we can involve students. At the local level, students can talk with officials, get access to budget documents, sit in on public hearings, and experience the give-and-take of deliberations. Indeed, as William Riker (1959) noted many years ago, "Field research on the subject of local politics is particularly attractive for a number of reasons" (p. 12). Local officials are "accessible"; with few written documents explaining local politics in any given community, "the only adequate sources of information are people. . . . Students must use field methods "(pp. 13–14). Riker goes on to note, in a theme that will be evident later in this chapter, that one of the important incidental benefits of such field research is to "banish forever from their thinking our cultural stereotype of the politician" (pp. 15–16). This theme of breaking down barriers and stereotypes surrounding politicians is a common one in many of the other chapters in this book.

When the goal becomes directly engaging students with the system they are studying, academic service-learning classes become an attractive pedagogy. Public administration classes are especially well suited to service-learning, particularly those with a local government emphasis. By its nature, the discipline is applied; studies of budgeting, for example, focus on how the budget is prepared, approved, and executed, incorporating organizational, political, and technical dimensions. The city is right outside the door of our classrooms, and city officials are always happy to receive the services the university can provide (and the university also encourages faculty to work with the city as a way of easing town-gown tensions).

What can service-learning provide to students? One model (Mezirow, 2000) suggests that service-learning experiences can have a transformational experience, leading to "an alteration of our *frame of reference,*" in which the "assumptions and expectations" through which knowledge is filtered are changed. The frames of reference one uses are likely to remain static throughout students' academic career (and perhaps throughout their lives) unless a dramatic event (such as participating in service-learning) upsets these frames and brings the student into "critical reflection" (Mezirow, 2000, p. 18). A second model (Kegan, 2000), known as the "informational model," suggests that service-learning experiences add knowledge and skills but do not fundamentally change the mode by which inquiry is undertaken and knowledge gained. Kegan suggests that this type of learning improves students' abilities and knowledge bases along the dimensions and frames of reference that had existed before.

Summarizing this work, Eyler and Giles (1999; see also Strain, 2006) suggest that while transformative experiences are to be desired, they occur relatively rarely. In research on their students, these two pioneers in the field found perhaps one-third of students claim to have undergone such a transformation. A key element of these transformations comes in the development of deep empathy; often this is characterized by a shift from working "for" people and "helping" them (such as in charity) to a sense of working "with" them (empathy). While this is desired and ideal, it does not always happen this way. Strain's model of "moving like a starfish" suggests that rather than measuring student movement in service-learning on a unidimensional axis, we must remain aware that students will be affected in different ways and may be moving along different dimensions simultaneously as they go through the experience. This suggests that even if a service-learning project does not fundamentally transform students, it can be a successful endeavor.

Active learning pedagogies have a long history of being successful in helping to engage students with course material and improving student learning and understanding (Bernstein, 2008; Bernstein & Meizlish, 2003; Hepburn, Niemi, & Chapman, 2000; Hunter & Brisbin, 2000; Jefferies, 2007; Klinkner & Mariani, 2007; Markus, Howard, & King, 1993; Niemi, Hepburn, & Chapman, 2000; Niemi & Junn, 1998). When students are encouraged to investigate social issues more, they end up with higher levels of knowledge and engagement (Hahn, 1999; Niemi & Junn, 1998). Engaging in debate on controversial issues can have a transformative experience on students, getting them to engage in the political system in ways they previously had not done; learning also increases as these students engage in the process of creating their own knowledge rather than passively accepting knowledge from others (Bain, 2004).

Often, however, the service-learning projects available to students are not of the variety that could be expected to lead to these transformations. For example, while researching the war in Iraq or volunteering on a presidential campaign might lead students to find their own political voice in a meaningful way, how likely is this transformation to occur when the subject of inquiry is a public opinion survey of residents in a small city on how to fund street repairs? It is the rare student who will be transformed by such an experience. But when one chooses to engage in service-learning projects with a local community, for the benefit of both student learning (Riker, 1959) and the municipality (Bernstein, Ohren, & Shue, 2003), these more immediate projects are the ones that need to be done. Is it worth the effort?

We argue, passionately, that such projects absolutely are worth the effort. Strain's (2006) perspective is particularly useful: although we will not move many students a great distance along the dimension of transformation and development of empathy, other lessons are possible. In the section that follows, we describe this project in more detail. We then discuss critical lessons that can emerge from these types of studies for students, focusing on three potentially beneficial outcomes for students that concern course content (how they can gain an enhanced understanding of political science) and two that focus on the learning process in general (how they can become better learners as a result of a service-learning experience). In short, we argue that projects such as this one can make students better scholars.

DEVELOPING THE PROJECT

We had long been convinced of the value of service-learning as a pedagogical tool and shared a strong desire to involve students in the local community. Consequently we both had incorporated fieldwork or service-learning into our courses. On earlier occasions, one of us (Jeffrey Bernstein) had engaged students in a public opinion course in conducting citizen surveys for Ypsilanti on citizen attitudes about funding solid waste disposal. The other of us (Joseph Ohren) routinely required students in undergraduate public administration courses to complete case studies of their own local governments as a vehicle for learning field research techniques as well as linking classroom discussion to their community experiences. Upper-division students were also tapped to conduct special applied research projects in cooperation with local government officials, sometimes enlisting all students for a class project and other times supervising the work of individual students for research on specific topics.

Beyond these classroom experiences, both of us were engaged in implementing grants and contracts with local governments across the region and the state. For example, Bernstein at the time was in the process of conducting a special series of evaluation workshops for staff in the Motor Carrier Division of the Michigan State Police and had undertaken program evaluations for several public sector agencies in the area. Ohren also worked with scores of local government officials in a variety of capacities, including the city of Ypsilanti, for many years through the Institute for Community and Regional Development at EMU, an applied research and service entity.

Open to new opportunities for service-learning and with many community connections, we began discussions about collaborating in the semester prior to the winter term in which the two classes were to be offered. The two classes included Bernstein's research methods seminar, typically a small class of upper-division students, and Ohren's course in municipal government, a lower-division class. Both courses served as electives for all departmental majors; the research methods course was one of two options students had for fulfilling the department's research methods requirement (since it was upper level and the other option was a lower-level course, this course was by far the less popular of the two options). The project on which we settled was to work with Ed Koryzno, the city manager of Ypsilanti, on helping the city understand residents' views on funding road repairs.

The Challenges Confronting Ypsilanti

Before describing the project, it is important to briefly describe the setting in which this work took place. The city of Ypsilanti is

located in southeast Michigan; it is a relatively small community—
about four square miles geographically and a population of twenty-
three thousand—that is home to EMU. It has one of the lowest
per capita property values of all communities in the region, with
over a third of all property exempt from taxation, and because of
those factors, it has one of the highest rates of property taxation in
the region. In addition, median income is significantly below the
average for the county and the region, and population has been
declining over the past two decades.

Like many other older industrial cities in the Midwest, Ypsilanti
has significant infrastructure problems. Faced with a declining
population, limited resources, and numerous demands on those
resources, city officials over a number of years had postponed
capital improvements. This was especially true of road and street
maintenance and reconstruction because of the large cost and
the nature of the funding mechanism required. Beyond annual
commitments from already tight operating budgets, local officials
would have to seek voter approval for bonds to support long-term
rebuilding efforts.

Two years before this project took place, the city council had
appointed a blue ribbon commission to study the condition of
the streets and explore options for addressing any needs identified. After several months of work, the commission reported to
the council and the public a strong recommendation for a significant reconstruction effort, paid for by revenue bonds backed
by three mills on all property in the city subject to property taxation. (One mill would cost property owners $1 for every $1,000
in state-assessed property value, typically half of the actual market value of the property. Thus, the owner of a home valued at
$200,000 would pay $300 a year for this tax—calculated at $3 per
$1,000 on a state-assessed value of $100,000.) This would require
a major campaign to help residents understand the need for the
street assessment and the rationale for the commitment, and ultimately it would require voter approval of the special millage at a
regular election to secure support.

After some months of discussion and debate, the city council
in fall 2000 approved placing the street assessment question on the
ballot in April 2001. Individual members of council and the blue
ribbon commission, along with other community leaders, joined

forces in a campaign-style organization to support the millage question and began developing and disseminating brochures, news releases, and other information to generate interest in, understanding of, and support for the millage. The local government itself, however, could only provide information on the question since, as in most other states, Michigan law forbids the governing body from acting officially to endorse or oppose such a referendum.

As the campaign began to unfold, local officials were interested in knowing to what extent residents understood the issues; this would help in determining the kinds of information residents might need to make a decision on the issue. Similarly, they were interested in knowing whether people supported the proposed millage. At a meeting on another matter between the city manager and Ohren, the question was raised as to whether this would be a suitable topic for student research.

We discussed the proposition and, given the two courses in question, agreed to develop and conduct a survey to help the city council better understand citizen views and engage students in a real-life learning opportunity. Bernstein's research methods class would be learning about developing and conducting public opinion surveys; such applied work offered an opportunity for students to gain real-world experience. However, these students would no doubt lack sufficient substantive expertise on local government to write such a survey. And the students with the substantive knowledge of local government (and the specific case of Ypsilanti) would have no particular expertise in how to construct and administer a survey.

SCAFFOLDING THE EXPERIENCE FOR THE STUDENTS

Once we reached an understanding of what would be done in the project, the next challenge was to develop outlines for both classes, creating several joint learning opportunities to provide the necessary scaffold for the project. A foundation for the learning experience was deemed essential. Working with two classes of students posed some unique difficulties, but the basic problem is the same in all service-learning efforts: how to link classroom discussions and course work to the service-learning experience. Several conscious efforts were designed to provide this scaffold.

Students needed to have contact with local officials to deeply understand the nature and importance of the task facing them. Both sets of students had to be prepared in terms of research methods, especially survey research, and both groups of students had to be familiar with the basic operation of local government. Thus, the two courses were designed to provide that necessary background.

Given that the two classes were scheduled on alternative days of the week during daytime hours, one on Monday, Wednesday, and Friday and the other on Tuesday and Thursday, a collaborative rather than team teaching approach was employed. Both faculty agreed to participate to some extent in the other class, and both courses used the same exercises to provide the scaffold for the survey and report to city council. Our collaborative arrangement had numerous advantages besides these practical ones. We could serve as resources and sources of support for one another (a fact aided by our having worked together many times in the past); this was especially important since it was our first effort at a collaborative teaching project. It also made doing the project more fun for the two of us (and, we think, our students).

The challenge was to prepare all students to be both methodologists and substantive experts on local government. Students in the methods class would play a lead role in the survey, but since all students would be involved, both classes had to have a sufficient understanding of methodology to make a contribution; in addition to interview and observation assignments, this was accomplished by having the methods instructor spend two class sessions with the local government class. And given the emphasis on field research in studying local government, all students had to know more than just how to develop and conduct a survey. Personal observation and individual interview assignments were created and linked to local officials, and all students were provided a primer in local government, assigned readings for both classes, and two days of lectures by the municipal government instructor in the methods classes.

In addition to readings and guest lectures, course assignments were vital in connecting the pure academic side to the applied research task. The first two assignments—observing a local government meeting and interviewing a local government official or citizen activist—helped to scaffold the eventual service-learning project. Both assignments, and the survey, were fair game on tests in both classes as an added incentive for encouraging students to read the material, take the written assignments seriously, and be prepared to address these subjects on exams.

Observation Assignment

Students in both classes were asked to attend a meeting of a local governing body. They were encouraged to attend a session in their home communities as a way of getting to know their own local governments (even most of our residential students live within driving distance of their hometowns), but they were allowed to attend any governing board meeting that was convenient. In advance of attending a session, they were assigned a short reading on observation that addressed some of the methodological challenges associated with this kind of field research. They were assigned Chapter Eleven from Manheim and Rich (1995) and read the appendix of Fenno's (1978) *Home Style* as an example of what can be learned by watching and observing. The research methods instructor complemented the readings in the municipal government course with a class discussion of observation as a methodology.

After attending the session, students were asked to write a description of the meeting—who attended, what was on the agenda, how people interacted, what happened that was striking— and then to reflect on what they observed. The intent was to familiarize them with how local boards act and how members behave in a public setting, and to introduce them to both local officials and people in the community who might have been actively engaged in discussion at the board meeting. With respect to methodology, students were also asked to consider observation as a scientific research method. Were the data gathered in the observations valid, and could data from multiple observations be compared and used to build conclusions about local governing boards?

Interview Assignment

Beyond observing the interaction of residents and local officials at a meeting of the governing board, students were assigned to identify and contact either a local activist or a governmental official and set up an appointment for a personal interview. Again, students in both classes were assigned a brief reading on interviewing, and the research methods instructor again made a presentation in the municipal government class. For this assignment, students read Chapter Eight in Manheim and Rich (1995), as well as a couple of chapters from Lane (1962) as an example of an interview-based study. They were coached as to the kinds of questions to be pursued—the focus was on citizen participation in local decision making from the perspective of either an activist or an elected official—and in the process of setting up and conducting the interview itself.

After the interview, students again were required to prepare and submit a written report summarizing the data from the interview and to reflect on the personal interview as a method for gathering data. As with the observation assignment, students were asked to address the methodological issue. Could interview data across a number of respondents be used to draw generalizations about citizen involvement in local government decision making? We view these assignments, taken together, as important building blocks for the eventual service-learning experience. Once sent out into the field, students had some exposure to what local government really was about (outside the textbook approach), which would help them be better and more perceptive observers.

THE SURVEY

In many respects, the primer on local government and the two methodology assignments were preliminary to the larger learning experience: developing and conducting a survey of residents to ascertain understanding of and support for the street millage that was on the April ballot. To provide students a firsthand introduction to the issue at hand, the city manager was invited to attend one of two joint sessions of students in both classes that were held through the term. The city manager provided background information on the street problems, the budget issues involved, the work of the blue ribbon commission, and the nature of the referendum process required for securing approval of the street assessment.

He indicated to students the kind of information that city officials were seeking and how it would be used in the weeks and days leading up to the election. He also emphasized the importance of timely information: if the survey data were to be of use, the work had to be completed and presented to the council at least three to four weeks prior to the election. The task for students was to gauge public sentiment on the question, identify potential gaps in information and understanding, and provide guidance to the manager and council, and indirectly to the advocacy group formed to support the street millage, on steps to be taken leading up to the April election. They essentially were engaged as political consultants in this real-world exercise.

Given this background and with additional readings and instruction on survey design, students in the methods class began assembling a brief questionnaire and considering the pros and cons of various options on how to conduct the survey. A phone survey was selected as the most expeditious approach, given the time constraints, and a reverse directory was used to select a random sample of residents on city streets. Name and contact number lists were prepared for each student in the two classes as the survey itself was vetted again and again.

Drafting the survey was primarily the responsibility of students in the methods class, although drafts were circulated to students in the local government class as a modified trial run. Were the questions garnering the right information? Did they make sense? Were questions subject to multiple interpretation? Once the survey was in final form, class sessions in both courses were devoted to training students in the survey process: going over the script, capturing information, follow-up calling as needed, and so on.

Students were asked to complete calls in the afternoon or evening hours, with about a dozen names assigned to each student. Once the completed survey forms were submitted, students in the methods course coded and input responses and ran preliminary statistics in preparation of a written report to city council. Although the report itself had to be prepared by the two instructors, given spring break and the need for speed, the students played a significant role in determining what the content of the report should be. Moreover, in early March, the second joint session of students from both classes was held. In attendance were several city council members, the city manager, and several other administrative officials. Students from the methods class (*not* the instructors) presented the report to their peers and to city officials.

POWERFUL OPPORTUNITIES THROUGH A SERVICE-LEARNING EXPERIENCE

In describing what students learned through this experience, we divide the lessons into two categories: lessons that inform student knowledge of how the political system works and lessons that tie more generally to an understanding of epistemological issues and how knowledge is constructed. This division, of course, is somewhat artificial. For example, understanding what we know about the political system is influenced by how we construct that understanding. Still, we believe this distinction is useful as we assess the important lessons that we believe students took away from the class. We do not claim the lessons are novel ones; most students should have entered these upper-level classes aware of them. What should be unique, we believe, is the depth of understanding of such lessons engendered by our project.

BUILDING AN ENHANCED UNDERSTANDING OF THE POLITICAL SYSTEM

"Muddling Through"

One of the first lessons we wanted students to learn about the political system calls to mind Charles Lindblom's (1959) classic article, "The 'Science' of Muddling Through." Lindblom argued political change happens slowly and is often constrained by the status quo on an issue: policy change proceeds incrementally from current policy rather than changing dramatically (but see Schulman, 1975, for an interesting treatment of the circumstances under which nonincremental models can explain the policy process). Since dramatic responsiveness is not a characteristic of incremental policymaking, this provides fuel for the perception that government is unresponsive to what citizens want and incapable of giving them what they need.

In working with Ypsilanti, our students gained experience working with a government that clearly wanted citizen input and took the necessary steps to gain it. Yet they also learned about the constraints that limit government; in this case, something as simple as funding and fixing the roads provoked diverse views among citizens and ultimately became a major project requiring years of discussion, consensus building, planning, and implementation. Like most other public policy issues, council action placing the street assessment question on the ballot did not just happen. This history was shared with students when the city manager visited the class; it was reinforced as students continued to work in this vexing public policy area.

Nobody could have driven on Ypsilanti's roads premillage and not concluded that street repair was needed; even so, particularly for a financially challenged city, moving from problem identification to solution is not easy. In each of the previous five years, the deteriorating condition of the city's streets had surfaced in council work sessions. During budget deliberations, council had weighed devoting general fund monies to street maintenance projects, but declining revenues and the demands of other needs took precedence. Beyond that, there was little consensus on the council or in the community as to whether additional taxes should be levied to support these needs, since the city was already one of the highest tax jurisdictions in the county.

A year before placing the street repair millage on the ballot, the city council had decided to appoint a blue ribbon commission to provide a fresh look at street needs, explore options for addressing those needs, and assess public support for any alternatives. The commission device is a common one in government as a means for both stimulating and delaying action, especially when consensus is lacking. The report of the commission in this instance did prompt action by council, resulting in the ballot question. This was, of course, just the beginning of our story, since successfully passing the millage required that voters be convinced to support it. But at least to this point, the city manager had helped students understand the long gestation period of public policies (Kingdon, 1995).

Political Decision Makers Are Constrained in Their Actions

Most students do not understand the structure of local government and the roles and relationships of the various actors in a city. Our efforts in the American government class leave them with the notion that all democratic governments must have separation of powers, checks and balances, and strong parties fashioning agreements on policy (or creating deadlock, as the case may be). Thus, part of the scaffold in both classes had to include attention to the structure of the city manager form of government, since the principal contact at the start of the discussion was the Ypsilanti city manager. In his class presentation, he explained his appointment by council, his accountability to the council—he can be terminated by a majority vote of council at any time—and his role in enabling the council to make good decisions by identifying issues and providing information and recommendations. He also noted that despite the use of partisan elections in the city, party plays much less of a role in structuring policy debate at the local level than it does at state and national levels. The city manager's presentation emphasized the need to generate consensus among local officials and within the community on the need for action.

Beyond this preliminary discussion of structure and roles, the manager provided the background leading up to the street assessment referendum at the center of attention and then described the constraints facing local officials. Resource constraints limited action on infrastructure needs over several years as the city faced significant budget challenges. The manager provided insight on the budget problems without overwhelming students, noting that revenue sources were limited, revenue levels were capped, and ultimately budget allocations, like other public policies, required broad consensus on council and in the community.

The requirement for a voter referendum on the millage question provided another example for students of the constraints facing local officials. Unlike at the national level, many tax and spending issues at the local level require explicit citizen support registered through elections. The street millage was an example of a special assessment that could be approved only by the people, and for students, this was a lesson in direct democracy. This meant understanding how information is provided to residents, how support is generated, and ultimately how a public policy campaign unfolds. Complicating matters for city officials was the explicit limit in state law on what the city itself could do in this policy debate. The city council placed the question on the bal-lot, but the city could not advocate one way or another for the assessment. Individual officials could take positions, and several council members joined the advocacy group supporting the mill-age question, but council could not formally take a position on the issue.

Students began to understand that the action taken by the council in placing the question on the ballot was, like so many other things in politics, the product of a long and winding road after many discussions in different councils over several years, assessment of the need for action and exploration of alternative approaches to action, and ultimately the grueling task of generat-ing public support for what was deemed a critical need. As efficient (and perhaps desirable) as it might have been for city officials to act as benign dictators and dictate to the city the best solution to the problem, they cannot do so.

Coming to Terms with Public Opinion Presents Methodological Challenges

Once a decision is made that we desire to understand what the people think about a given issue, the next challenge becomes determining how to gain this understanding. Political science professors are trained in graduate school to have a toolkit of methodologies that they can use as necessary based on the prob-lem confronting them. With the understanding of these multiple methods comes an understanding that every methodology has its weaknesses; thus, being able to reach the same conclusion with different methodologies is always a good thing. Finally, profes-sionals in the discipline learn that all conclusions are somewhat tentative and true answers often elusive.

When considering views on a particular issue, the various options in play might include conducting surveys, in-depth inter-views, or focus groups, or observing public meetings and discus-sions. If the decision is made to do surveys, possibilities include doing surveys by mail or by phone (Web-based surveys provide still another option today), or conducting the surveys in person. If the decision is made to do phone surveys, a sampling frame must be developed, methods for calling determined (for example, how many calls to a particular number before giving up), and decisions made on how to train callers. None of these decisions have to do with the content of the survey, including issues of how questions are worded, how answer choices are structured, whether questions are open- or closed-ended, and how nonattitudes are filtered.

Academics who engage in survey research confront these issues all the time; for students, they often represent new problems. Critically, students also learn that the choices they make on these methodological issues can have a significant impact on the answers they receive. As one student wrote to us:

> As a student interested in political science methodology, I was excited to participate in writing a real survey. I was able to take all the book knowledge I had acquired previously and actually apply it. Instead of analyzing examples of good or bad survey questions in a textbook, our class was analyzing words we actually collaborated on and wrote ourselves. I think the challenges of survey writing were made much clearer to us through this process.

One example of this was the powerful learning moment that arose when students tried to write a question asking people what they would think of a three-mill increase in property taxes in order to fund road repairs. How do you explain to residents what a "mill" is (since very few would know off the top of their head) without biasing their responses? Watching students go through successive drafts of a three-line introduction to the question drove home the notion that methods play a critical role in political inquiry. And, powerfully, there truly was no right answer to this question. Like professionals, these students found themselves forced to come up with their best, *educated,* guesses about what would work.

ENHANCING STUDENT CAPACITY AS LEARNERS

In addition to the lessons about how the political system works, in hindsight we believe projects such as these can give students the opportunity to gain a deeper appreciation for how knowledge is constructed in political science (and in the academic world more generally). We believe that the benefits to students from learning these lessons can be extremely broad and go a long way toward making them better learners throughout their college careers and the rest of life in general.

Embrace Messiness

Imagine the standard course syllabus we give our students. With reading assignments, plans for each class, and outlines of what students need to know, the path to enlightenment is presented to students in a somewhat linear manner. Buy the books, read, come to class, study, and learning will occur. Now consider the work we do in our research. Our own knowledge does not come in a linear manner. It is, rather, somewhat circular. We read in order to understand something, form hypotheses and test them, write a draft of a paper and try it out on others, return to where we were to revise our ideas and analysis, share with others, and so on. At the risk of drawing too stark a contrast, the way we learn is dramatically different from the way we structure learning for our students.

When learning does not take place in this neat, clean, linear fashion, it can be described as being messier. A useful way of conceptualizing this might be to compare reading a textbook to reading multiple primary source documents. A textbook takes the accepted wisdom of the discipline and presents it as a fait accompli, with answers given in a tidy fashion. Primary source documents, however, present data in rawest form. Researchers must interpret results, including contradictions among them, in offering a narrative. Students in these classes were much closer to the second approach than the first. The observations and interviews were very much primary source data. The surveys required students to interpret what appeared before them and make sense of the results themselves. They were required to analyze the results and create recommendations on their own (albeit with help from the instructors). While constructing knowledge on their own may not be as efficient, we believe the deeper understanding that it engenders, and the comfort with the messiness of the learning process it provides, is well worth the trade-off.

Embracing messiness is not without cost, however. When an instructor gives up this much control and empowers students to create their own knowledge and drive the class, he or she puts a great deal of trust in students. This trust must be reciprocated: students, for example, will be resistant if the workload is left too unpredictable or the grading rubric poorly developed. Instructors must also find a happy medium between being an expert (and thus earning the respect of students) and stepping back from this leadership role at appropriate times. These challenges must be negotiated with care, and we would strongly suggest that doing so is very much worth the effort.

Bridging the Expert-Novice Divide

A second critical lesson to emerge from this project concerns the divide between experts and novices. Students often view themselves as novices in the political world, often for good reason. They look to faculty and practitioners to be experts. But by exposing them to the mental operations and work products produced by experts, students begin to gain a sense of themselves as experts—or at least people who could possibly become experts (Pace, 2004; Wineburg, 2001). This can have a profound effect on their learning. Demystifying what experts do and showing students the processes experts use to attain their expert judgments empower students as learners across all contexts.

By giving our students close access to how experts such as the city manager, city council members, and their professors approach this sort of a project (in both similar and different ways), students are presented with models for how to think about these issues. Critically, they learn that academics think in many of the terms we have laid out so far; dealing with methodological uncertainty and messiness, for example, are regular features of the experts' jobs. As Randy Bass (2006) said in describing expertise in a keynote speech to the Eastern Michigan University Faculty Showcase, "Experts' ability to speculate expertly is what makes them experts." An awareness of this fact is one of the critical things that separate true experts from novices. Once novices learn that uncertainty and messiness are not failings but rather can be a hallmark of expertise, their own thinking processes typically start to improve.

CONCLUSION: WHAT IS GAINED?

Unlike more traditional approaches to service-learning—participating on local cleanup efforts or working at the community center—the service project described here engaged a group of students in two classes collectively in applied research for the city of Ypsilanti. We had multiple objectives in mind as we designed the course outlines and the survey project prior to the start of the term. We wanted to:

- Augment readings and class discussions with a real-world experience in local government
- Engage students in several different methodologies so they had a better understanding of how researchers study political phenomena
- Develop, conduct, and report on a challenging research assignment that was important to city officials

At a deeper level, however, we wanted to introduce students to the complexity and messiness of the political process. In this conclusion, we reflect on some final lessons of this process for students, faculty, and the local government with which we collaborated.

From the perspective of students in the two classes, the project must have been viewed by some as "just more work." The additional readings across courses and what were perceived as additional assignments were no doubt perceived as demanding. Although we limited the number of joint sessions to two— one with the city manager early in the project and the second for the final presentation to local officials—not all students were able to attend the joint sessions given conflicting class schedules and obligations. For some, conducting phone interviews, even with the training we provided and the detailed script, was outside their comfort zone. These types of challenges are ubiquitous in using service-learning modules.

The project required working with peers, underscoring the point that learning is a collective effort. It also meant interacting with city officials, albeit in a limited way: the presentation by the city manager, observing a governing board, interviewing a local official or activist, and presenting the report to several local officials at the end. Nonetheless, this interaction brings to life the discussions in the texts, emphasizes the humanity of these officials, and, as Riker (1959) noted, dispels the stereotypes of the politicians.

The presentation of the survey findings, not just to peers but to local officials who were interested in and likely to use the findings of the research, also proved to motivate greater student effort. Local officials commended the students for their efforts, providing positive feedback, and used the survey findings to tweak their information campaign. Students also learned from the comments of local officials and the project itself that "politics" matters; they heard about the need to build public support for governmental action, dispelling the belief that local officials are unresponsive or that they can simply ignore the wishes of residents. As one student told us:

> I really liked how this project connected me to the outside world. I felt that my experience in the classroom was made more meaningful because I was completing an assignment that would impact the community. I think our class really took this project seriously because we wanted to produce a workable survey and we wanted to be accountable to the local officials. Most of us had driven on Ypsilanti roads for years, so we knew how important this millage was. It was a challenge to apply what knowledge we had gained in the classroom to write the survey questions and then vet them to make sure that our survey would yield quality data for the city to use.

For the city, the benefits of a project like this are manifold. Small cities like Ypsilanti seldom have the staff capacity to conduct the kind of research undertaken by our students. Rather, officials rely on anecdotal evidence and various expressions of citizen concerns. Our project, if completed in a timely fashion, would provide more reliable and objective information on the views of residents on the proposed millage. Furthermore, city officials also viewed the project as a way of helping students have a more realistic sense of how local governments work. Simply sharing the lengthy history behind the street millage question—the lack of consensus on prior councils, the constraints on local funding, the long process needed to build community support for action—provided a much more realistic picture of how things get done. It answers for students, and potential citizens, more effectively than any lecture could, the question, "Why is it so hard to get government to act?"

We have argued previously (Bernstein et al., 2003) that projects such as this represent win-win situations for all involved. Ypsilanti got a low-cost public opinion survey (which, we add with more than a little bit of pride, almost perfectly predicted the actual millage results—it passed with 63 percent of the vote). Faculty grew as instructors and provided a new, unique opportunity to students, and students were provided an enhanced learning experience that shows significant potential to not only make them better political science students but also to make them better learners across instructional contexts. Through the class project described here, students were able to pierce harmful stereotypes of government and political actors and understand the complexity and messiness of local government decision making and the challenges of applied social science research. While they did not become experts in the process, they certainly emerged with a much greater appreciation of the challenges facing government officials. And, in the end, we believe we did as well.

Voices: The Government Practitioner

Edward B. Koryzno Jr.

It was my pleasure to work with Jeff Bernstein, Joe Ohren, and their students when they did the street repair millage survey in 2001. The students provided a wonderful service to the city, and we are grateful for what they did. This work, however, must also be viewed in a larger context. This is not the first project that the city of Ypsilanti has done with the university, and it will not be the last. As such, my insights on working with the university as a partner reflect on a broader experience than just this project.

When the road millage issue arose, the city was in a difficult situation. The streets clearly needed to be repaired, but we were already one of the highest tax jurisdictions in the state. We had a limited budget, few readily available sources of new income, and numerous needs. Working with Joe and Jeff at the university allowed us to solicit feedback from the community, in a cost-effective manner, about what really amounted to an aggressive proposal for solving the problem. The students provided a service for us that we would have been in no position to obtain on our own; we certainly could not have afforded to hire an outside firm to gather these data. And given how accurate the actual poll was compared to the results and how much useful qualitative information it provided, I don't think we skimped much on quality.

Beyond simply predicting the final vote, the survey provided valuable feedback for the group that was working on getting the millage passed. This group, YES (Ypsilantians Enhancing Streets), used the information from the surveys on their Web site and in publicity material they put together. It is impressive to me that we got over 60 percent of the voters to approve a fairly expensive (but necessary) road millage even though we have a relatively poor community with a small tax base. I credit the community organizers and, by extension, the students for helping us make this happen.

From a personal standpoint, I very much enjoyed working with the students in the political science classes. As Jeff and Joe point out, local government is closest to the people, and local government officials can play a role in helping to demystify the process and helping students to see that they can play roles on local issues. I had similar experiences when I was a student and very much enjoy the opportunity to work with students during their time at EMU. I believe strongly in the power of local governments to help communities and enjoy having the chance to encourage others to consider this as a career.

In the larger picture, the university remains a major player in the city's development and operations. With the closing of so many of our industrial plants in recent years, our largest property owners are now rental housing complexes, most of which rent to students. People know Ypsilanti through their involvement with the university, as alums, parents and friends of alums, or just through knowing that a large university is located here. And while constitutionally EMU functions somewhat as a city within a city, we always recognize the need to cooperate and collaborate with the city.

This cooperation and collaboration can take many forms. As a smaller example, we worked together with the university last year to jointly purchase salt for the roads, saving each organization some money. On a larger scale, we are working with the university on a range of beautification projects around campus, hoping to help make the city look more attractive and attract more commerce. Each of these projects is facilitated by the work that has come before it.

Over the almost twelve years I have been city manager, we have developed strong relationships with numerous vice presidents of the university. We are currently engaged in some grant work with the College of Business and with the Institute for the Study of Children, Families and Communities. We have had numerous student interns from the university working in our finance and planning departments over the years, and have an ongoing relationship with the program in historic preservation—EMU has one of the country's top historic preservation programs, and we have the third largest historic district in the state. We are well aware that the fate of the university and the city are intertwined.

And as Jeff and Joe allude to, a project such as this one does not develop out of thin air. The surveys followed by a few years some focus groups Joe had run with a former faculty colleague and also after Jeff had done a survey of our residents on mechanisms for funding solid waste disposal. Joe continues to do annual goal-setting retreats with members of the city council. These relationships have been very positive, making it easy to add this survey to our list of joint ventures.

It is important, of course, for the city to maintain positive relationships with the higher administrators in the community. But much of the real work, particularly the work involving students, gets done at the level of the departments and programs. While not neglecting the administration, I would recommend to other city administrators near colleges and universities that they spend time getting to know the faculty and students, with an interest in getting involved with local governments. The rewards can be tremendous. Based on our experiences, I would encourage colleagues in my line of work to explore ways to form mutually beneficial relationships with the universities in their communities. Students, faculty, and the community all gain a great deal from them.

■ ■ ■

Edward B. Koryzno Jr. is city manager of Ypsilanti, Michigan.

References
Bain, K. (2004). *What the best college teachers do.* Cambridge, MA: Harvard University Press.

Bass, R. (2006, April). *Getting started in the scholarship of teaching and learning.* Keynote address presented at the Eastern Michigan University Faculty Showcase, Ypsilanti.

Bernstein, J. L. (2008). Cultivating civic competence: Simulations and skill building in an introductory government course. *Journal of Political Science Education, 4*(1), 1–20.

Bernstein, J. L., & Meizlish, D. S. (2003). Becoming Congress: A longitudinal study of the civic engagement implications of a classroom simulation. *Simulation and Gaming, 34*, 198–219.

Bernstein, J. L., Ohren, J., & Shue, L. (2003). A collaborative teaching approach to linking classes and community. *Journal of Public Affairs Education, 9*, 117–127.

Delli Carpini, M. X., & Keeter, S. (1996). *What Americans know about politics and why it matters.* New Haven, CT: Yale University Press.

Dionne, E. J. (1991). *Why Americans hate politics.* New York: Simon & Schuster.

Eyler, J., & Giles, D. E., Jr. (1999). *Where's the learning in service-learning?* San Francisco: Jossey-Bass.

Fenno, R. F. (1978). *Home style: House members in their districts.* Boston: Little, Brown.

Fink, L. D. (2003). *Creating significant learning experiences: An integrated approach to designing college courses.* San Francisco: Jossey-Bass.

Hahn, C. L. (1999). Citizenship education: An empirical study of policy, practice, and outcomes. *Oxford Review of Education, 25*, 231–250.

Hepburn, M. A., Niemi, R. G., & Chapman, C. (2000). Service-learning in college political science: Queries and commentary. *PS: Political Science and Politics, 33*(3), 617–622.

Hunter, S., & Brisbin, R. A., Jr. (2000). The impact of service learning on democratic and civic values. *PS: Political Science and Politics, 33*(3), 623–626.

Jefferies, P. S. (2007). *The effects of community service experience, student attitudes, and class climate on the level of political knowledge.* Paper presented at the American Political Science Association Teaching and Learning Conference, Charlotte, NC.

Kegan, R. (2000). What "form" transforms? A constructive-developmental approach to transformation theory. In J. Mezirow & Associates, *Learning as transformation: Critical perspectives on a theory in progress* (pp. 35–69). San Francisco: Jossey-Bass.

Kingdon, J. W. (1995). *Agendas, alternatives, and public policies* (2nd ed.). New York: HarperCollins.

Klinkner, P., & Mariani, M. (2007). *The effect of a campaign internship on political efficacy, trust and responsiveness.* Paper presented at the American Political Science Association Teaching and Learning Conference, Charlotte, NC.

Niemi, R. G., & Junn, J. (1998). *Civic education: What makes students learn?* New Haven, CT: Yale University Press.

Lane, R. E. (1962). *Political ideology: Why the American common man believes what he does.* New York: Free Press.

Lindblom, C. E. (1959). The "science" of muddling through. *Public Administration Review, 19,* 79–88.

Lupia, A. (1994). Shortcuts versus encyclopedias: Information and voting behavior in California insurance reform elections. *American Political Science Review, 88,* 63–76.

Lupia, A. (2006). How elitism undermines the study of voter competence. *Critical Review, 18,* 217–232.

Manheim, J. B., & Rich, R. C. (1995). *Empirical political analysis: Research methods in political science* (4th ed.). White Plains, NY: Longman.

Markus, G. B., Howard, J. P., & King, D. C. (1993). Integrating community service and classroom instruction enhances learning: Results from an experiment. *Educational Evaluation and Policy Analysis, 15,* 410–419.

Mezirow, J. (2000). Learning to think like an adult: Core concepts of transformation theory. In J. Mezirow & Associates, *Learning as transformation: Critical perspectives on a theory in progress* (pp. 3–34). San Francisco: Jossey-Bass.

Niemi, R. G., Hepburn, M. A., & Chapman, C. (2000). Community service by high school students: A cure for civic ills? *Political Behavior, 22,* 45–69.

Niemi, R. G., & Junn, J. (1998). *Civic education: What makes students learn?* New Haven, CT: Yale University Press.

Pace, D. (2004). The amateur in the operating room: History and the scholarship of teaching and learning. *American Historical Review, 109,* 1171–1191.

Popkin, S. L. (1991). *The reasoning voter: Communication and persuasion in presidential campaigns.* Chicago: University of Chicago Press.

Putnam, R. D. (2000). *Bowling alone: The collapse and revival of American community.* New York: Simon & Schuster.

Riker, W. H. (1959). *The study of local politics.* New York: Random House.

Schulman, P. R. (1975). Nonincremental policy making: Notes toward an alternative paradigm. *American Political Science Review, 69,* 1354–1370.

Skocpol, T. (2003). *Diminished democracy: From membership to management in American civic life.* Norman: University of Oklahoma Press.

Somin, I. (2006). Knowledge about ignorance: New directions in the study of political information. *Critical Review, 18,* 255–278.

Strain, C. R. (2006). Moving like a starfish: Beyond a unilinear model of student transformation in service-learning classes. *Journal of College and Character, 8,* 1–12.

Wineburg, S. (2001). *Historical thinking and other unnatural acts: Charting the future of teaching the past.* Philadelphia: Temple University Press.

CHAPTER FIVE

LINKING ADVANCED PUBLIC SERVICE-LEARNING AND COMMUNITY PARTICIPATION WITH ENVIRONMENTAL ANALYTICAL CHEMISTRY

Lessons from Case Studies in Western New York

Joseph A. Gardella Jr., Tammy M. Milillo, Gaurav Sinha, Gunwha Oh, David C. Manns

In August 2003, twenty students and community members collected thirty soil samples for lead testing from areas surrounding a New York State Superfund site on the east side of Buffalo, New York, that formerly housed a lead smelter. The site bordered a church and school, public housing and residences, along with small businesses in a poor, urban, minority neighborhood. Owned by the

---

We gratefully acknowledge support for the work reported in this chapter from the National Science Foundation Analytical and Surface Chemistry program, the vice president for public service and urban affairs at the State University of New York at Buffalo, the University of Buffalo Environment and Society Institute, the William and Flora Hewlett Foundation, and grants from the Lewiston Porter Schools and Kenmore Tonawanda Schools.

city of Buffalo, the lot was an open and overgrown field where children regularly played. Although the site was contaminated with lead waste at levels thousands of times higher than that which would trigger U.S. Environmental Protection Agency action, a lawyer for the city initially refused to recommend a fence and warning sign, citing the need to protect "property values." In response the church pastor posted a sign pointing to the lot, identifying it as a toxic/contaminated site. Within a week, the city relented and put up a fence.

Following that effort the community asked state agencies and the city to test soil adjacent to the site. Community members simply asked whether the lead contamination had spread beyond the property line. The state agencies and city refused to do additional testing; the result was an unusual opportunity for public participation with service-learning students in environmental chemical analysis. Using geographic information systems (GIS) analysis of state, federal, and community data, a cleanup plan submitted by the community was accepted by the state of New York. In the end, this resulted in remediation during summer and fall of 2007 of an area five times larger than the original Superfund site, all because the residents insisted that the contamination was not limited to the small area and had their own data, gathered by students in a service-learning course, to prove it. The residents received a planning grant from the state to plan further redevelopment on land now safe for residential housing.

University-community partnerships involving service-learning or clinical fieldwork in environmental science, engineering, public health, and law and policy have become common. National evidence of this is the examination of environmental justice in the 1990s, which led the National Institutes of Environmental Health Sciences (NIEHS) to incorporate public participation and community partnerships within major grants for environmental public health studies (National Academy of Sciences, 1999). The experiences of these projects and others provide lessons about the complexities of government involvement in service-learning partnerships from the environmental sphere.

The cities of Buffalo and Niagara Falls in Erie and Niagara counties in western New York, along with many other municipalities, are a fertile region to explore environmental service-learning opportunities. In this chapter, we review case studies to illustrate interactions with government partners at multiple levels. Environmental work in the area is heavily influenced by the history of Love Canal (Deegan, 1987; Levine, 1982; see below for some details). The projects developed here have brought together multiple universities and colleges, academic schools, departments, and disciplines, as listed in Table 5.1.

One important service-learning vehicle has been the efforts of the lead author (Joseph Gardella Jr.) in developing service-learning within an advanced undergraduate chemistry course,

TABLE 5.1 CONTRIBUTORS TO ENVIRONMENTAL SERVICE-LEARNING IN WESTERN NEW YORK

Faculty	Students	Government Partners
Science: Chemistry, biology, geology, geography	Undergraduate: Chemistry, chemical engineering, geology, geography, environmental engineering, planning	Local: City of Buffalo, Erie, Niagara County Department of Health, local towns School district: Lewiston Porter Schools
Engineering: Environmental engineering, chemical engineering, civil engineering	Graduate: Chemistry, geology, geography, environmental engineering, planning	State: New York State Department of Environmental Conservation, New York State Department of Health, New York State Office of the Attorney General
Biomedical: Public health, epidemiology, social and preventive medicine	Professional schools: Engineering, law, architecture, planning	Federal: U.S. Environmental Protection Agency, U.S. Army Corps of Engineers, Agency for Toxic Substances and Disease Registry
Professional schools: Law, architecture, and planning	Biomedical sciences: Medicine, public health	

Analytical Chemistry of Pollutants (Gardella et al., 2007). Beginning in 1994, course revisions for service-learning built on the existing academic chemistry framework, which involved students working in teams to design and execute field studies, including sampling, analysis, and reporting. These were married to structure and action based on common models of public service-learning (Eyler & Giles, 1999; Ritter-Smith & Saltmarsh, 1998). The resulting years of work have had a broad impact on teaching, research, and service in environmental analytical chemistry at the University of Buffalo (UB) and in western New York State.

We focus this chapter on the multiple complex relationships between these environmental service-learning projects and the host of sometimes overlapping government agencies with regulatory and policy responsibilities in the field. Environmental and public health agencies operate at all levels of government: federal, state, school districts, towns, cities, and counties. These agencies' interactions with service-learning initiatives from the university, faculty, and students are interesting, are sometimes successful, and many times are fraught with difficulties.

BACKGROUND

Mindful of George Santayana's famous dictum that those who do not study history are doomed to repeat it (Santayana, 1905), many lessons from Gardella's own undergraduate experiences in environmental pollution analysis in service to community needs have informed our projects. In this sense, what we are doing is not really new. In the 1970s, undergraduates in chemistry worked on research programs that responded to community needs and interacted with local elected officials. Working from this history, we set out to modify this UB chemistry course to align it to community needs and include the developing pedagogy of service-learning in the sciences. Service-learning in undergraduate chemistry classes has had a distinct environmental focus (Fitch, Wang, Mellican, & Macha, 1996; Kesner & Eyring, 1999), often taking on projects analyzing lead contamination in communities. Others have developed innovative field courses in environmental analysis examining environmental indicators of pollution (Shachter & Edgerly, 1999; Ward, 1999; Wiegand & Strait, 2000). A fuller description of our course development process can be found in Gardella et al. (2007), which emphasizes the content development and implementation of the course. Key features of these processes include alignment of the curriculum with government regulatory testing requirements, training for service-learning and community involvement, and sustaining long-term collaborations with communities regarding environmental issues in air, soil, water, and sediment.

ISSUES AFFECTING GOVERNMENT ENVIRONMENTAL EFFORTS

When service-learning courses focusing on environmental policy are designed, several challenges must be kept in mind and discussed with students to help them understand contextual factors. First is the community's environmental history, which in our area is dominated by Love Canal. At Love Canal, buried toxic waste began leaking into residences, causing community concerns about public health and resulting in the first instance of federal (indeed, presidential orders for) emergency relocation and demolition of housing (Deegan, 1987; Levine, 1982). Love Canal also led to the development of so-called Superfund legislation, where a tax on industry was used to create an emergency relocation and remediation fund. In New York, both the federal EPA and the state Department of Environmental Conservation (DEC) have funded Superfund programs that identify toxic sites with potentially significant health impacts on surrounding communities.

Locally, Love Canal's impact has been to provide two lessons for residents, agency professionals, and faculty doing service-learning, and these have become the underlying assumptions that inform much of the community's perspective on environmental issues:

- Community activism is required to get industry and government to respond to environmental pollution problems, regardless of the regulatory regime.
- Some local, state, and federal health and environmental agency representatives lack respect for and may actually fear

community activism. They see activists as lacking knowledge about chemical exposure, toxicology, and relative risk, and thus not understanding the complexities of their jobs.

It is important to identify the impact of this community context when preparing students for public participation in the course as students will be operating within this set of beliefs.

Second, there is great complexity in the responsibilities of different agencies. In Table 5.1 we illustrate a range of government agencies involved in environmental issues at all levels of government. At the federal level, the U.S. Environmental Protection Agency and the U.S. Army Corps of Engineers are involved in a variety of ongoing projects and provide first-line environmental work. For public health issues related to the environment, the Centers for Disease Control's Agency for Toxic Substances and Disease Registry is often a resource on public health impacts of environmental issues, and it is involved in studies of health impacts in cooperation with EPA. At the state level, as is typical of most other states, New York has an active environmental function in the state Departments of Health and a fully functional Department of Environmental Conservation, along with an environmental action bureau in the Office of the New York State Attorney General. At the local level, city and county health departments and environment and planning functions are common, along with school districts, which often are involved in environmental issues from the perspective of protecting children and staff. Students need to be given some understanding of these differing and overlapping agencies and their jurisdictions to know how what they do will be used by these agencies.

Third, agency staff at all levels tread a fine line in responding to community involvement and encouraging public participation, including from college students and professors. Often they try to balance a tension between listening and answering questions and demands from community groups, which can range from long-established interest groups to hastily constructed neighborhood groups, with responding to the sometimes conflicting priorities set by elected officials. Agency officials often grow impatient with attempting to validate the relevance and credentials of what constitutes a community stakeholder and often choose instead to answer to elected officials as the appropriate "representatives of the people."

Students must be made aware of these tensions and how the dilemma agency officials face can be detrimental to their attempts to engage in service-learning and community involvement. This is not unique to environmental community controversies, however, and is a longstanding tension in American democracy. Wilentz (2005) describes the roots of the tension between public participation in government decisions and elected officials' making decisions for the public, locating its origins at the earliest stages of American democracy. As Foner (2005) notes, even in the earliest days of the American democracy, the so-called Democratic-Republican societies were formed outside government to criticize George Washington's administration. While these groups claimed a right of the people to debate public issues and organize to affect public policy, Washington himself saw the elected government as the voice of the people and condemned the societies as "self-created." Wilentz (2005) insists this was precisely what made them democratic: unlike most previous political groups, they were not formed by political leaders, yet they claimed the right to scrutinize and criticize the conduct of elected officials. This work on the rise of American democratic structures is directly relevant to the contesting between community groups as stakeholders and elected officials as representatives that is played out in many environmental issues. An understanding of this dilemma can help frame community involvement in service-learning, where government agencies and their staff juggle multiple interests and constituencies.

THE COURSE

Chemistry 470, Analytical Chemistry of Pollutants, has been taught at UB since the 1970s. Initially the course involved a lecture component focused on environmental statistics and analytical methodology for detection of pollutants in air, water, soil, sediment, and solid wastes. A field study project involved students in writing a proposal and work plan for field sampling and analysis, plus the execution and reporting of a sampling, analysis, and reporting project.

The revision of the course in the mid-1990s included new content, and training in community involvement as service-learning was introduced (Gardella et al., 2007.) This supported the transformation of the field study into projects that respond to community requests and concerns. Students in the course are organized into groups of four or five, focusing on a particular analytical project within a neighborhood. Projects in these neighborhoods can extend over several years and through multiple sets of students. Ultimately this means that even in a course-oriented environment, we can sustain collaborations with communities beyond semester-based experiences. The course, as it has been modified, has also served as a vehicle for recruiting students into longer-term undergraduate and graduate research projects. This creates unique opportunities to expand the development of the course materials and sustain the interactions with communities.

Grading in the course has several components. First, there are the traditional problem sets and midterm and final exams on the class lecture and case study material. The service-learning project itself is summarized in a fully documented report with data tables and a presentation that students make to the community, another graded component. In addition, students are asked to prepare self and group evaluations. Using methods of self-assessment, journals, and self-reflection common in service-learning courses (Eyler & Giles, 1999; Ritter-Smith & Saltmarsh, 1998; Wiegand & Straight, 2000), students are required to review their contribution to the project and their team members in a narrative essay. That material serves as a means to assign the distribution of credit in the project and to have the students reflect on and critique their participation in the project.

PUBLIC PARTICIPATION

One important feature that has defined the work on this course over the past twelve years has been evolving approaches to preparing students for the process of community participation, especially when it involves collaboration and interaction with government agencies. Students quickly learn that it is not simply a matter of providing "expert" advice as a consultant to people who do not know what questions to ask. In fact, our observation is that community members ask sophisticated, complex, and difficult questions. At the same time, while on the surface our efforts are generally welcomed by all involved, there are clear tensions that can develop among professionals from industries, agencies, and elected officials. Gardella has been involved in many pitched political battles as an outcome of these rules of engagement experiences. This has allowed us to develop some clear advice and training for students participating in these studies, the key ideas of which are captured in the six in Table 5.2. Open communication is critical, obviously. But more than that is needed for science and engineering students, many of whom have not been prepared for the process of political debate and public communication. Much of what is developed for students must be guided by the research in community engagement and public policy. For public participation (as opposed to public notification), the International Association for Public Participation has particular relevance for environmental decision making; its core values are given in Exhibit 5.1.

It is interesting to note that the IAP2 framework has been used by the state Department of Environmental Conservation's environmental justice training. It is also worth noting that the training appears to have had a limited effect on day-to-day operations of agency officials. While some of the staff who have been trained in environmental justice and public participation view it as a tool to engage the public, the tension between public engagement and elected officials has not been overcome. Furthermore, the demands of the IAP2 core values are quite high: asking that communities engage in planning and execution of work and that they be given the right to influence the work that is done. In practice, regulatory compliance-driven efforts often limit the involvement of community groups.

Role of Research

Environmental issues are complex, and ways need to be found to engage the public by simplifying data and presenting them in forms that foster public understanding and interest. Geographic information systems (GIS) and geographic information analysis (GIA) can serve this role, and a special effort to create GIS

TABLE 5.2 RULES OF ENGAGEMENT

Rules of Engagement for Academic-Community Interactions	Key Questions and Comments for Students and Faculty
Define the problem.	What does each stakeholder want to achieve?
Define the players.	What are the specific roles and responsibilities of all participants and stakeholders?
	Which are driven by statutory or regulatory concerns?
Consult the community (listen).	How can all voices be heard and respected?
	Learn to develop collaborative methods for agendas, meetings, and hearings.
	Do not accept conventional wisdom from agency, industry, or community experts without listening to all voices.
Get the data.	What are the relevant measurements?
	How do these measurements relate to regulated measurements?
	What information is not being collected by standard measurements and monitoring?
	Can the community design the measurement strategies?
Interpret, and make decisions.	Define the results of the measurements to the community.
	Use collaborative techniques to answer further questions from the community.
Make recommendations.	Make clear reports that address specific recommendations to the community, industry, elected officials, and government agencies.

information useful for public consumption is a major effort in the GIS community.

Environmental data, which have a strong geographical underpinning, are often hard for those without training in geography to make sense of whether for the public or for policymakers.

EXHIBIT 5.1.   PUBLIC PARTICIPATION IAP2 CORE VALUES

- The public should have a say in decisions about actions that affect their lives.
- Public participation includes the promise that the public's contribution will influence the decision.
- The public participation process communicates the interests and meets the process needs of all participants.
- The public participation process seeks out and facilitates the involvement of those potentially affected.
- The public participation process involves participants in defining how they participate.
- The public participation process provides participants with the information they need to participate in a meaningful way.
- The public participation process communicates to participants how their input affected the decision.

Source: International Association for Public Participation, www.iap2.org.

GIS holds the key to multidisciplinary solutions of many socio-environmental problems that have been inadequately addressed within a nongeographical framework. As Seiber (2002) writes, GIS can "present a visually compelling image of an issue and quickly analyze data from disparate sources" (p. 153). GISs are such flexible systems that they can assume different roles (cartographic tools, spatial databases, decision-making tools, education assets, and others) depending on the context of use. For the purposes of the work presented here, GIS is primarily used as a portal to spatial awareness: teaching the general populace to appreciate that "where-ness" matters in most social and environmental investigations.

Taking advantage of the university's research strengths in GIS and GIA complements government agency efforts to do data analysis, provides a level of data analysis for the community that is often better than agency capabilities, and empowers the community with information that government or industry may not even have.

CASE STUDIES IN ENVIRONMENTAL SERVICE-LEARNING WITH GOVERNMENT PARTNERS

As the course has developed over the years, we have built long-standing relationships and collaborations with the six communities identified in Table 5.3, which summarizes the studies that have taken place in each neighborhood:

TABLE 5.3 COMMUNITY PROJECTS WITH LONG-TERM SUSTAINABLE COLLABORATIONS

Community Name	Studies Underway or Completed
Seneca Babcock (Buffalo)	Air emission of indigo dye–related pollutants
	Soil study of neighborhood park with lead emissions
Hickory Woods (Buffalo)	Soil studies of metals
	Polycyclic aromatic hydrocarbons source apportionment by multivariate statistics
	GIS studies of soil contamination, location, and sources
Bellevue (Cheektowaga) (Eastern Erie County)	Air emissions from quarry
	Comparative study of autoimmune disease prevalence and asthma prevalence
East Ferry Street (Buffalo)	Lead contamination outside the Superfund site
	GIS analysis of lead hot spots
	Comparative public health studies of blood lead level, lupus prevalence, and asthma prevalence in community
Tonawanda (northwestern Erie County)	Soil contamination at school adjacent to uranium processing plant dating back to the Manhattan project
	Air emissions from multiple industries
Lewiston Porter (northwestern Niagara County)	Soil contamination at school adjacent to World War II TNT plant, radium storage site, and hazardous waste landfill
	Community GIS evaluation of publicly accessible soil and groundwater pollution

• In Seneca Babcock, airborne emissions from chemical plants and soil contamination from local industry directly affect residents living in the poorest neighborhood in Buffalo, where per capita income is about seven thousand dollars a year.

• Hickory Woods is a community of federal and state subsidized new housing built adjacent to a former steel mill and coke plant, now a New York State Superfund site under remediation. Some of the housing was built on contaminated land with city knowledge, and high levels of soil contaminants dominate the neighborhood.

• Bellevue/Cheektowaga is a community surrounded by an active quarry, emitting hydrogen sulfides and crystalline silica in air emissions, and three landfills, one cited for illegal dumping of hazardous waste.

• On East Ferry Street in Buffalo, a lead smelter operated from the 1920s to 1972, when it was torn down. Extensive lead contamination in the soil exists over a large area, adjacent to a growing church congregation and public housing. Twenty-three cases of lupus have been documented in the neighborhood, and the New York State Department of Health (2004) reports the highest childhood blood lead levels in the state in surrounding areas (Haley & Talbot, 2004).

• In Tonawanda, an elementary school was built in the 1950s adjacent to a site where uranium was processed for the Manhattan Project. Subsurface groundwater testing on the site shows significant uranium contamination, and several radioactive contaminated buildings have been demolished in the past six years. The community also suffers from airborne emissions of carbon disulfide and petroleum products, and one of New York's highest emissions of mercury generated by a coal-fired power plant.

• In Lewiston-Porter, schools were built on a buffer zone from the Lake Ontario Ordnance works, a World War II munitions plant later used to store high-level nuclear material, which is now stored at the Niagara Falls Storage Site on the adjacent land. A portion of the "remediated" land was sold to create New York State's only hazardous waste landfill.

■ ■ ■

The community concerns that exist because of this history and these issues are significant, and not without reason. The discussion of the three cases that follows focuses on a number of key issues for including community participation in study design and execution, the need to identify preparation for students doing community work, the advocacy that follows a commitment to the long term, and the impact of the work in urban environments.

SENECA BABCOCK

The Seneca Babcock community, a one-square-mile area within the city of Buffalo just north of the Buffalo River, was built as employee housing for the first chemical plant in western New York, the Schoellkopf Dye Works, later known as National Aniline Corporation. In 1972, National Aniline was acquired by Allied Chemical and split into three companies, the Allied (now Honeywell) Buffalo Research Laboratories, Buffalo Color Corporation, which retained the indigo dye manufacturing components, and the PVS chemical corporation, which acquired the portion of the chemical facility that produced sulfuric acid and derivatives. Buffalo Color operated until 2002, when it went bankrupt due to overseas competition, leaving a federal Superfund site that is now being remediated by the EPA. Chemical workers and their families still reside in the neighborhood, which is among the poorest in Buffalo. Like many other industrial neighborhoods, housing is interwoven with industrial sites, some operating, some abandoned. In the 1950s, the New York State Thruway Authority built the southern portion of the U.S. Interstate 190 ring highway for Buffalo through this neighborhood. Extensive railroad lines also crisscross the neighborhood.

In 1995, PVS Chemical emitted an extensive sulfur dioxide release, an air pollution event that stayed in the area for five days. In 1996, Gardella was asked to join the Good Neighbors Environmental Committee to bring his expertise to bear in providing the neighborhood with a better understanding of environmental contamination and air quality monitoring and to help facilitate communication between the companies and the community.

For the first four years of collaboration, a series of air and soil monitoring studies was undertaken with collaboration from the community. Driven by concerns from residents about unusual odors, this began with development of personal air sampling badges to monitor for volatile organic compounds and specifically for formaldehyde. Using these badges, residents collected samples, which students extracted and analyzed at the university. A series of studies showed volatile organic chemicals from a variety of industrial and transportation sources, with data supplemented by extensive sample notebooks kept by the residents. The residents also implemented personal air sampling pumps to develop better sensitivity to and detection of smaller amounts of compounds than the badges could reveal.

The most important study was one involving the chemical formaldehyde. Residents, industry representatives, and local government were working with data from the U.S. EPA Toxic Release Inventory (TRI) for Buffalo Color Corporation, the company that had the most extensive air emissions. Formaldehyde was often cited by industry representatives as a compound present in household indoor air pollution coming from a variety of sources, and their plant emissions, mainly part of a sewer permit, could not be the source for community exposures. To test the notion that community involvement works, we tested for formaldehyde using a specific test badge (Miksch et al., 1981; National Institute of Occupational Safety and Health, 1994). The results of over eighty badges were developed and reported by students to the community. The main finding was that high formaldehyde exposures were limited to those who lived with or were two-pack-a-day cigarette smokers. Thus, the residents collecting their own data were able to validate what industry experts had told them. But they believed it only when they had independently developed the same conclusion in collaboration with our faculty and students.

This was a powerful lesson for both the community and industry, and on this basis, Buffalo Color industrial hygiene staff began a closer collaboration with us on these projects. Working with chemistry faculty and students, the community developed a sampling plan for aniline (an important chemical in dye production and a known human carcinogen) and ammonia, two pollutants emitted with the highest risk for exposure. Buffalo Color designed the sample points to be near their point source of emissions. The community was relieved about aniline emissions when extensive air sampling over several months did not detect aniline in the area. Thus, the conclusion that cigarette smoke and other exposures were more significant than that from TRI-reported releases was made by the residents and students. This of course confirmed the hypothesis and claims of government and company representatives, but it was done by the residents collecting the data themselves, not based on the claim of industry representatives with no data. The lessons from Seneca Babcock helped us see the potential for building trust by helping industry communicate with the community and empowering citizens to collect their own air samples, with students providing the chemical analysis.

HICKORY WOODS

In 1988, construction of a few modest homes (selling for fifty to sixty thousand dollars each) in a small neighborhood that bordered an abandoned Republic steel mill and the Donner Hanna coke plant was begun as part of a novel public housing program using federal and state housing funds to build subsidized homes. In addition, grants were made available to purchasers of older homes to make improvements. This public housing strategy had been used successfully throughout Buffalo by the leadership of the (then) mayor and his housing and planning offices. The mayor, whose parents had never owned their own home, sought to find a location for this development in his own home district of South Buffalo, and thus Hickory Woods was developed bordering an abandoned industrial site. As the housing program was developing, the steel mill and coke plant next door were being demolished, leaving 219 acres later designated as a Superfund site. In 1992, building on his predecessor's successful home ownership strategy, a newly elected mayor began a second phase of home construction in Hickory Woods. These were more expensive homes (selling for one hundred thousand dollars) on a large strip of land that was given to the city by LTV Steel, the owners of the Republic Steel/Donner Hanna plant, along a street that bordered the Superfund site.

Concerns about potential soil contamination from the Superfund site were identified immediately, but despite a letter from the New York State Health Department in 1993 and continued requests by the developer, the City of Buffalo refused to conduct an environmental assessment of the land. The original developer backed out, and a new developer was engaged, with homes constructed until 1999, when a city inspector was called to Abby Street to identify construction problems with a home foundation. The inspector identified liquid coke wastes on the site, high in carcinogenic contaminants. Soil testing was pursued, and high levels of the carcinogenic coke waste were detected in nine lots: five undeveloped and four with housing completed, three of which were occupied. The residents were moved out of their homes, and those lots were remediated. However, residents in the neighborhood began to raise other concerns, such as the identification of contamination hot spots (an elevated level of concentration of contamination within a related geographical area, not restricted to property lines, and depth), the sources of contamination found elsewhere in the neighborhood, and the use of city trucks and city employees to transport soils from empty lots at two in the morning. They also wanted to know why the remediation was limited in scope, asking why the fence lines of lots used to define remediation areas were "magic." In other words, how could an extensively contaminated site five feet away be dangerous but the lot next door be safe?

In 2000, the city asked for help from EPA staff. Upon reviewing the data and information, EPA conducted a substantial soil study of the neighborhood (about seventy homes over just a few city blocks), taking six hundred soil samples at the surface and at multiple depths. The results clearly showed elevated levels of arsenic, lead, and coke wastes in various regions of the neighborhood. At this writing, seven years later, no official comprehensive remediation plan exists. Although several individual lots and a public park were remediated by the EPA, residents are still left with their fundamental questions about hot spots and magic fences:

- What are the contaminants, and how dangerous or toxic are they?
- Where are the hot spots in the neighborhood?
- Why are cleanups restricted to fence lines or property lines?
- What is the source of contamination?

With this background, in the spring of 2001 we began to develop a GIS and GIA approach to categorizing and analyzing the soils data from the EPA studies and all previous studies that were publicly available. A key feature of the project was the lack of willingness of federal or state agencies to undertake a geospatial analysis of the data. Citing confidentiality issues, the agencies declined to address neighborhood concerns. To overcome this problem, our students went door to door to obtain permission to use individual data sets from each residential lot to create the GIS database and provide mapping to answer fundamental questions about hot spots. This work has involved master's-level students as well as three Ph.D. students, several of whom started work by taking the CHE 470 course as undergraduates and two of whom then served as teaching assistants. The GIS-GIA approach has yielded a substantial, independent analysis of the soils data so that the community has been able to prepare its own remediation plan for the neighborhood. Even so, the neighborhood remains in negotiations over their "three Rs": relocation, remuneration, and remediation. This approach to GIS-GIA played a significant role in this neighborhood and now underpins all other public participation projects we undertake (Coffey, 2002; Milillo, Case, & Gardella, 2007; Milillo, Coffey, & Gardella, 2007).

The controversy about the source, level, and effects of the contamination found in the Hickory Woods neighborhood is continuing as residents attempt to develop a plan for remuneration, relocation, and remediation. In 2006, a newly elected city administration began working to develop a comprehensive cleanup plan and relocation and remuneration plan for those affected. Finally, after six years of effort, the City of Buffalo is using the GIA first developed in 2001.

In this case, students were extensively involved in the use of the GIA, along with the design of soil sampling and testing, interpretation of results, and working directly with residents on interpreting the results. This is an exciting example of new research-driven results having a direct impact on a continuing political and environmental controversy. Residents as well have learned a great deal about soil sampling, soil chemistry, contaminant toxicology, and GIA.

East Ferry Street Superfund Site

The East Ferry Street lead smelter site was first identified as a hazardous site in 1997 by the City of Buffalo. The contamination resulted from an abandoned industrial complex housing a zinc and lead smelter and refining operation from the 1920s through the early 1970s, when the smelter building was demolished. The original site at 858 East Ferry (the name the community knows as the site), a 3.3-acre empty lot, was used by the smelter to dump waste ash and slag. A 2.3-acre adjacent site at 856 East Ferry Street was the location of the smelter facility, according to the city's 1939 Sanborn maps. Site investigations showed extensive lead contamination: subsurface soil values for lead content were as high as 96,000 parts per million (ppm), or 9.6 percent. Furthermore, the true geographical extent of this lead contamination was not defined in the early studies. Not surprisingly, residents in this community were concerned about a variety of environmental health issues and their proximity to this Superfund site.

In the late 1990s, a local Baptist minister and community leader purchased an abandoned supermarket site across the street from the smelter site. He converted it into a growing church community (now forty-three hundred members), the True Bethel Baptist Church. Concerns in the community about environmentally related illnesses led to the establishment of the Toxic Waste Lupus Coalition (TWLC) in 2000. The TWLC was awarded a five-year National Institutes of Environmental Health Sciences grant in 2001 to study the incidence of lupus and other autoimmune diseases and asthma in environmentally affected communities, in collaboration with the University at Buffalo. Due to a lack of action by the New York State legislature and governor, funding for the New York State Superfund program was depleted in the late 1990s, and reauthorization took several years. Since the initial studies indicated that the geographical extent of lead contamination was not clearly delineated, residents, church members, and the TWLC approached us in 2003 to consider developing additional lead soil data to provide answers about the extent of pollution.

Students first created GIS maps of the existing environmental data from New York State DEC analyses from the neighborhood. These maps, which included overlays of high-resolution aerial maps, allowed the community to visualize where samples had been taken and the geographical extent of lead contamination (along with other contaminants). Using these maps, residents and members of the community, along with ten students, planned and collected thirty soil samples in summer 2003. These samples, taken from private residences, nearby public housing, and the True Bethel Church property, were analyzed by an EPA-certified commercial laboratory for heavy metals. Data showed elevated lead levels (500 to 1,000 ppm) in surface soil samples outside the 856 and 858 East Ferry sites.

As a result of this study, the DEC planned a much more extensive site sampling plan in 2003, and it reported in 2004 that the geographical extent of elevated lead contamination spread farther to the west than first identified (New York State Department of Environmental Conservation, 2004, 2005). Three additional industrial properties at 810 East Ferry showed elevated lead levels and were targeted for cleanup. The residents worked with a newly funded New York State Superfund planning process to propose their own remediation plan, which the New York State DEC accepted in 2005. Work began in late 2006 and is continuing to excavate and remediate the entire area, with significant cleanup to residential standards at 858 East Ferry.

Students worked with community members for several years on the development of maps that summarized and explained report data. These maps were used to plan where to take samples from the community in areas that had not been sampled previously. The community learned about sample collection, chain of custody processes, data analysis, and comparison of soil data from surface samples and subsurface data. Furthermore, they had data that were outside the public agencies' control, which allowed them to learn how to use their questions and data to prepare their own remediation plan. NYS DEC representatives noted that this was among the few sites where community involvement created the accepted remediation action plan.

CONCLUSION

In all the cases, the government interactions with service-learning made for complex relationships and tensions among service-learning collaborators, the community, and government agency staff. Some tensions were resolved positively, as in East Ferry. In addition, the use of GIA has evolved into a serious research and public service effort. The outcome of this work is a different view of the role of analytical chemistry in environmental public policy for students; rather than simply interpreting or implementing regulations, students see the limits of policy and regulation and the ability to influence new public policy and regulations. A key example is the use of GIA to set remediation and cleanup limits rather than property line or fence line decisions. UB students and faculty have contributed to a broader discussion of remediation where pollution exists rather than on specific sites within boundaries decided by a street or fence. As is the case for most other environmental work, science, public policy, and regulation intersect with economic and political decisions. For the students and faculty who have been involved, immersion in political processes can only be healthy, as more science should be used in public policy and environmental decision making.

Voices: The Community Organization

Judith M. Anderson

In many instances, citizens of small communities have identified social or environmental problems that plagued their neighborhoods but do not have the expertise or workforce to address them in a manner that ensures a viable outcome. This was the case in the remediation of 858 East Ferry Street, a class 2 Superfund site in the heart of the predominantly African American east side of Buffalo, New York. The community felt that a recently discovered cluster of seventeen lupus patients in close proximity to the East Ferry Superfund site might somehow be related. They tried desperately for over a year to get someone to fence in the site and post signage stating it was a hazardous waste site. But without the knowledge of how government works or the technical details of the problems, community residents were stymied.

The talents and expertise of service-learning students and faculty from Buffalo University were a perfect complement to what neighborhood residents already knew, allowing us to build capacity to address the environmental issues that have plagued our community. Citizens are familiar with the history of their neighborhood. They know what businesses and industry were there and why they left, what the concerns of the residents were at the time, and if there were any negative impacts on the community. Their stories can be researched by students and verified with data that can then be translated into sound recommendations and actions for change. This is exactly how we addressed the community's fear that lead, mercury, and PCBs were migrating from the 858 East Ferry Superfund site onto the adjacent church, school, and public housing complex. Although the community was concerned, the state environmental agency had assured us that such toxins could not migrate, and there was nothing to worry about, but the community remained unconvinced, and we had no first-hand knowledge of our own.

We called on Joe Gardella, a UB chemistry professor, and his students to assist and show the community how to take their own soil samples. In working with the students, residents developed a level of understanding that allowed them to connect their awareness of the community to the science that was needed to make a case to the state for mitigation. Together Gardella, his students, and community members took the samples at the fence line, across the street from the site, in front of the housing complex, and two blocks downwind of the site. The results showed that toxins had indeed migrated nearly everywhere we had tested, though fortunately, the levels were low enough to assuage most of the concern. Yet the community learned that it could not just take the word of others that everything will be all right. It was important to have the skills or be connected to someone who does so the community could have facts to build on.

Working with service-learning students is a tremendous benefit to both parties. The students learn the different cultures and nuances of the community and how to develop relationships based on respect and support for each other's differences. The community gets a level of expertise that would otherwise be unavailable, or at least quite costly. Together, goals are set to meet everyone's objectives and to work toward a win-win outcome. And sometimes what the students learn and what the community learns comes together in unexpected ways.

Our first service-learning student was an environmental study major who had done an internship with the New York Department of Environmental Conservation. His knowledge of the workings of the department showed us how to access important public information and helped us understand their process for identifying hazardous sites. We learned about the permitting process and toxic release inventory lists and how these can affect our community. Following his graduation, we hired him as the community's first environmental specialist. One of his first paid assignments was to write a grant to get more funding to continue the environmental justice work in the community. Our relationship with UB has strengthened our ability as a community organization to work with local and state government to deal with serious issues that face our neighborhoods.

■ ■ ■

Judith M. Anderson is community health coordinator for the Environmental Justice Action Group of Western New York.

References

Coffey, E. (2002). *A study of arsenic contamination in Hickory Woods, Buffalo, NY, by development of analytical methodology, background determination and GIS contamination modeling.* Unpublished master's thesis, State University of New York at Buffalo.

Deegan, J., Jr. (1987). Looking back at Love Canal. *Environmental Science and Technology, 21*(4, 5), 328–331, 421–426.

Eyler, J., & Giles, D. E., Jr. (1999). *Where's the learning in service-learning?* San Francisco: Jossey-Bass.

Fitch, A., Wang, Y., Mellican, S., & Macha, S. (1996). Lead lab: Teaching instrumentation with one analyte. *Analytical Chemistry, 68*(23), 727a–731a.

Foner, E. (2005, October 31). The American political tradition. *Nation.* Retrieved January 12, 2009, from www.thenation.com/doc/20051031/foner.

Gardella, J. A., Jr., Milillo, T. M., Sinha, G., Oh, G., Manns, D. C., & Coffey, E. (2007). Linking community service, learning and environmental analytical chemistry. *Analytical Chemistry, 79*(3), 811–818.

Haley, V. B., & Talbot, T. O. (2004). Geographic analysis of blood lead levels in New York State children born 1994–1997. *Environmental Health Perspectives, 112*(15), 1577–1582.

Kesner, L., & Eyring, E. M. (1999). Service–learning general chemistry: Lead paint analyses. *Journal of Chemical Education, 76*(7), 920–923.

Levine, A. G. (1982). *Love Canal: Science, politics and people.* Lexington, MA: Lexington Books.

Miksch, R. R., Anthon, D. W., Fanning, L. Z., Hollowell, C. D., Revzan, K., & Glanville, J. G. (1981). Modified pararosaniline meted for the determination of formaldehyde in air. *Journal of Analytic Chemistry, 53,* 2118–2123.

Milillo, T. M., Case, C. M., & Gardella, J. A., Jr. (2007). *Indicator Kriging analysis of surface and subsurface soil contamination: Arsenic and lead.* Unpublished manuscript.

Milillo, T. M., Coffey, E. S., & Gardella, J. A., Jr. (2007). *Use of geostatistical interpolation methods in the study of lead contamination in soil.* Unpublished manuscript.

National Academy of Sciences & Institute of Medicine Committee on Environmental Justice. (1999). *Toward environmental justice: Research, education, and health policy needs.* Washington, DC: National Academies Press.

National Institute of Occupational Safety and Health. (1994). *Method 3500, NIOSH Manual of Analytical Methods (NMAM)* (4th ed.). Atlanta, GA: Centers for Disease Control and Prevention.

New York State Department of Environmental Conservation. (2004). *Pre-design investigation report, East Ferry Site, City of Buffalo, Site 0-15-175.*

New York State Department of Environmental Conservation. (2005). *Record of Decision (ROD) Amendment, 858 East Ferry Street Site City of Buffalo, Erie County, New York, Site Number 9-15-175.* Retrieved January 12, 2009, from www.dec.ny.gov/docs/remediation_hudson_pdf/915175.pdf.

New York State Department of Health. (2004). *Promoting lead free children in New York State: A report of lead exposure status among New York children, 2000–2001.* Retrieved January 12, 2009, from www.health.state.ny.us/nysdoh/lead/exposure_report/index.htm.

Ritter-Smith, K., & Saltmarsh, J. (Eds.). (1998). *When community enters the equation: Enhancing science, mathematics and engineering education through service-learning.* Providence, RI: Campus Compact.

Santayana, G. (1905). *Life of reason: Reason in common sense.* New York: Scribner.

Seiber, R. E. (2002). *Geographic information systems in the environmental movement.* In D. Weiner, T. M. Harris, & W. J. Craig (Eds.), *Community participation and geographic information systems* (pp. 153–172). New York: Taylor and Francis.

Shachter, A., & Edgerly, J. S. (1999). Campus environmental resource assessment projects for non-science majors. *Journal of Chemical Education, 76,* 1667–1670.

Ward, H. (Ed.). (1999). *Acting locally: Concepts and models for service-learning in environmental studies.* Washington, DC: American Association for Higher Education.

Wiegand, D., & Strait, M. (2000). What is service learning? *Journal of Chemical Education, 77*(12), 1538–1539.

Wilentz, S. (2005). *The rise of American democracy, Jefferson to Lincoln.* New York: Norton.

CHAPTER SIX

PANDEMIC FLU PLANNING SUPPORT FOR THE COMMONWEALTH OF MASSACHUSETTS

Charles Hadlock, Jennifer Infurna, Peter Koutoujian, Jennifer Ricci

In this chapter we discuss a project that was originally designed as an experimental alternative to the traditional senior thesis requirement for our honors students. By way of background, Bentley College is a large, independent business school with relatively high rankings at both the undergraduate and graduate levels. About 90 percent of our students major in one of the business disciplines, but all students also pursue an ambitious and well-rounded curriculum in arts and sciences intended to prepare them for leadership positions in society. When we instituted a collegewide honors program in 1999, we included a traditional one-semester academic thesis requirement. Over time, student and faculty feedback suggested that for many students, the traditional disciplinary thesis did not serve as the best vehicle for a senior capstone experience. We would like such a capstone experience to tie together many of the diverse academic disciplines they have been studying and to help the students develop a sense of independence and empowerment as they move into the world of practicing professionals.

Since most of our students directly enter the workforce on graduation, we redesigned the capstone experience to include as an option participation on a team-based research project, working on a problem for an outside client organization. We intended to seek out research problems that were interdisciplinary in nature and would enable students on the team, representing a number of distinct academic majors, to see how their own disciplinary background could make an impact on a real-world project. We recognized that numerous valuable projects could be found within the public sector and could be used to give the students direct experience on the diverse interactions that take place continually among government, business, and the public. This would all take place while the students were making an important contribution to a government organization's mission.

The various groups involved in a service-learning project may each have their own primary objectives. Figure 6.1 suggests the major objectives pertaining to this project. As we discuss this project from the viewpoint of the various participants, we will show how these various objectives have been addressed. Not all of our capstone project courses follow the service-learning model; some, for example, are carried out for corporate clients with specific business objectives. There are typically about twelve students on each such team, and the project carries three course credits.

TEAM-BASED SERVICE-LEARNING PROJECTS

While the focus of this chapter is on a project for the Massachusetts legislature concerning planning for a pandemic flu outbreak, we have pursued other similar team projects at our institution, such as a support mission for a medical clinic in Alabama seriously damaged by Hurricane Katrina, an evaluation of alternative state bottle bill enhancements carried out for the Boston mayor's office, and an investigation of the feasibility of modifying school demolition contracts in the city of Waltham to include specific deconstruction requirements. Not all of these have been in the context of an honors program capstone experience, but they carry many of the same characteristics.

FINDING THE CLIENT AND DEFINING THE PROJECT

Given our multiple objectives, it will come as no surprise that identifying a client and a project can be quite challenging. Figure 6.2 suggests the general outline of our process for carrying this out.

FIGURE 6.1 STAKEHOLDER OBJECTIVES FOR THE PANDEMIC FLU PROJECT

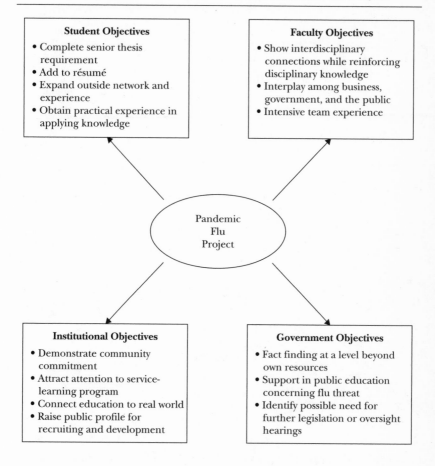

An especially important constraint is timing because a project that is likely to be of high interest to a client organization is generally not one that can be planned far in advance. After all, if the client really needs the kind of assistance that could be provided through the service-learning project, he or she will probably seek it out from other sources unless a student team is ready to go to work at the time the need is recognized. A key strategy therefore is for the university to establish dialogue with potential clients on an ongoing basis, independent of the selection of a topic for a particular semester's project. Thus, much of the activity associated with the upper boxes in Figure 6.2 can indeed be carried out well in advance.

Figure 6.2   Client-Project Identification Process

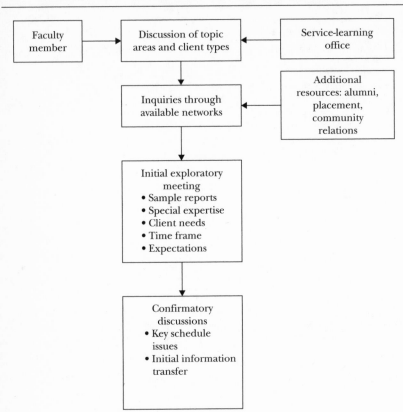

A second complication related to timing is the fact that students are asked to register for these group capstone research projects well before the selection of a topic has been made. (Of course, there can be registration changes at the beginning of the semester.) While this leaves the students in a state of some uncertainty as to whether the topic will match their interests, it gives the professor a better idea of the composition of the class, such as the academic majors and minors represented. It also gives the professor a chance to contact the students soon after registration in order to learn more about their interests and career direction. This information can then all be taken into account in seeking a suitable project.

With respect to the pandemic flu project, initial discussions between the faculty member and the service-learning director identified the threat of a pandemic flu outbreak as a matter of considerable public interest and one that involved a number of public agencies, and hence potential client organizations. We learned that Peter Koutoujian, the state representative for the city in which our college is located, was in fact the chairman of the Joint Legislative Committee on Public Health, which had oversight responsibility for pandemic flu planning on behalf of the state legislature. He became the first potential client we would approach with the idea of such a project. We also were personally acquainted with the representative, and an initial inquiry by our service-learning director led to an encouraging invitation to pursue this initiative through a discussion with his staff.

The committee staff met with the first author, Charles Hadlock, at the statehouse in the summer months prior to the fall semester when the course was scheduled to begin. During the initial meeting, Hadlock described the conceptual foundation for the project and the kind of relationship that would be fostered between the committee and the student team. He presented the committee staff with background information about the nature and goals of the honors class and the general idea of a project related to pandemic flu planning, and he demonstrated a novel computer model that could simulate pandemic flu spread within communities.

Chairman Koutoujian perceived the collaborative project with the Bentley honors class as an opportunity to support his role in researching planning issues regarding pandemic flu and obtaining an independent assessment of the overall level of preparedness. He had, in fact, devoted considerable resources over the previous legislative session to increasing public awareness and coordinating state and local efforts to more effectively prepare for a pandemic. Thus, he saw the opportunity to work with the Bentley students as a chance to not only assist in the educational development of students from a local college, but also to harness much needed resources to keep working on the issue. The computer modeling tool was perceived to have the potential to be used to educate and increase awareness by the public and various government leaders about the importance of taking action to improve pandemic planning.

Although the topic of pandemic flu planning was agreed by all parties to be a viable basis for the project, it was recognized that the chairman and committee staff would need to further define the objectives of the project in terms of their specific interests and needs. This ultimately led to a primary focus on the role of nongovernmental organizations (including businesses, nonprofits, and traditional nongovernmental organization) in preparing for a flu pandemic. A further natural refinement was to focus on Massachusetts Health Services Region 4 (a geographical region containing districts that the chairman represents), although it was recognized that an in-depth research project even with this specific focus would inevitably lead to considerations on a broader state or national level. The project underwent further refinement once the semester started and the students became directly involved, and this process is discussed in a later section.

INITIAL STEPS IN GETTING THE PROJECT UNDERWAY

Table 6.1 presents an overview of the main sequence of activities in this project. Since this is a student-run project, it is essential that in very few meetings near the beginning of the semester, both the professor and the students develop a good sense of the capabilities of the various participants and, in particular, identify those students who seem to have the talent, energy, and leadership skills that will be essential in managing individual tasks and leading the overall project. The professor's principal role is as coach, not as project leader, and developing the skills associated with effective team processes is one of the learning goals for the project. In addition, the professor, who is generally not an expert in the subject matter of the project, can also model the role of "professional learner" and thereby help the students develop analytical learning approaches that will be of long-lasting benefit.

If the students are to create a favorable impression in their initial kickoff meeting with the client, it is important that they quickly develop some background in the subject matter of the project. In this case, even during the first class meeting, after

TABLE 6.1 OVERALL PROJECT PROGRESSION

Time Line	Activity
Week 1	Background presentation by professor; initial student research
Week 2	Client kickoff meeting
Week 3	Scoping of project; identification of interests; selection of student project manager
Week 4	Selection of task teams; detailed scope of work; baseline report outline; other preliminaries
Weeks 5–9	Research, writing, presenting, revising; formulation of findings
Weeks 10–12	First complete draft report; intensive student review and revision cycle
Week 13	Final report completion; presentation design
Week 14	Final public presentation and report delivery at statehouse

receiving some background from the professor, students decided how to divide up what appeared to be the most important issues related to the project so that each could acquire some detailed background before meeting the client. The professor set the informal target that each student should bring something to the initial client meeting in their designated area that would be likely to provide new information that the client had not previously known. This would help build client confidence from the start, a key ingredient for developing a productive relationship during the course of the project.

In the pandemic flu project, the focus of this early research was on the program plans of a number of other states that had obtained federal Centers for Disease Control funding for preliminary planning purposes. By having the students submit an initial research paper by the beginning of the second week, the professor was able to know what kind of background they had developed, and he was able to use this to coax some additional participation out of the students during the initial client meeting, and thus make the meeting more interactive than might otherwise have been the case.

The chairman and committee staff met with the class during the third class meeting, which was late in the afternoon, and the visitors stayed on campus so that the students could host them at dinner in a campus dining hall. (The professor does not generally attend such dinners so that the students and clients can be entirely engaged in discussions with each other.) This meeting served as an opportunity for the clients to be introduced to the students and to talk about the objectives and anticipated outcomes of the project. We note that, as is common in the initial interactions between consulting groups and potential clients, there is a certain inevitable uncertainty on the part of all participants. The students find it hard to believe that they will actually be able to offer something of value to the client over the course of a single semester since they are beginning with essentially no specialized knowledge of the subject matter. The clients do not yet have any good sense of the capabilities of the students, and thus they are uncertain about what to ask for from the students and what to expect. The professor, who also has limited prior experience with these particular students, shares some of the uncertainties held by the client. Although he would likely be able to structure the project more efficiently in preparation for the initial client meeting, he wants the students to have the learning experience of trying to do that largely on their own even if it makes the project a bit less efficient in converging on the client's objectives. In the end, this meeting is the best opportunity for the client to sell the project to the students and to begin to develop the kind of rapport with the students that is an essential motivating factor in their wanting to deliver a superb result at the end of the semester.

Very soon after the initial client kickoff meeting, we had to put in place a student leadership team that would have the confidence of the entire class and the professor. We have a fairly standard procedure for carrying this out. The professor asks each member of the class to submit a confidential recommendation of that person's three highest choices, in rank order, for student project manager, along with any supporting comments or rationale. They can of course nominate themselves. Independent of whether they include themselves on this initial list, the professor also asks each student to address his or her own capabilities and interest in the role of project manager. The responses tend to be very thoughtful, and they provide considerable insight that would not otherwise be available to the professor. Based on these responses the professor then interviews two or three of the leading candidates, explaining to them in the process the magnitude of the responsibility associated with taking on this role. Some well-qualified students are eager to be the project manager, while others may be reluctant due to the press of other responsibilities. (There is no remuneration or other tangible benefit to being project manager, but it is an attractive leadership opportunity for good students and can also be used quite strategically on a résumé.) The professor makes the final decision and explains it to the class in a way that helps to solidify support for the designee. The students are also asked to identify the areas within the project scope of most interest to them. Given this input and knowledge of their academic major and minors, the professor and the student project manager identify task leaders. For the pandemic flu project, there were four task teams: (1) organizational resources, (2) financial resources, (3) informational resources, and (4) modeling. The first three had three students on each team, and the modeling team had two students.

The last key organizational step was the definition of a detailed scope of work, which in a commercial consulting practice would be the central core of the consulting contract. Based on the initial kickoff meeting with the client as well as the early research being carried out by the class, the task teams were asked to draft a detailed scope of work that would serve as an agreement between them, the client, and the professor of the deliverables to be expected from their portion of the project. This agreement among the various participants or stakeholders is vital for a successful project.

The students were somewhat surprised to see how common such scope statements were and how easily they could find examples online. However, it still took several class sessions for the students to converge on scope documents that were both practical and unambiguous and contained sufficient detail to serve as a clear target for the work in the remaining part of the semester. In addition, a working draft of the scope of work was reviewed at a planning meeting between the project manager and the client, and this led to greater understanding of the client's needs. The students found this exercise to be somewhat frustrating, but they were considerably buoyed when the client responded that the results were comparable to the core of a professional consulting contract and helped clarify what the team thought they would be able to accomplish. This scope document offered a further advantage when team members were questioned by various agencies about the nature of the project. They could point to the project's public Web page, which was also set up and maintained entirely by the students, including obtaining an appropriate domain name.

Although the scope of work is detailed, an overview of the work performed by the students is reflected in the organizational structure described and included the following four tasks: (1) analyzing the roles and interfaces among the various public and private organizations involved in the pandemic planning effort and identifying areas of ambiguous responsibility, weak lines of communication, or untapped resources; (2) analyzing the way in which state and federal funds have been used in preliminary planning, comparing this to the approaches taken in other states, and identifying inefficiencies or areas for improvement; (3) evaluating the communications instruments being used to educate the public about the risk of pandemic flu and assessing their overall ineffectiveness; and (4) developing a computer simulation model for the spread of a flu epidemic under various countermeasure strategies, such as antiviral drugs, vaccination, and quarantine. These tasks made good use of the wide variety of academic majors represented in the student group.

KEY ELEMENTS IN THE ONGOING PROGRESSION OF THE PROJECT

As any project progresses, it is important to ensure that interactions among students and between students and clients stay on track. Students need guidance on carrying out their projects, and clients need to be kept up to date. We have identified six key elements to keeping projects on track: writing the reports, assessing progress in and out of class, monitoring interactions with clients, monitoring interactions with outside organizations, guiding the formulation of research findings, and preparing the final report.

A Novel Report Writing Strategy

Based on personal experience in the consulting industry, Hadlock made two suggestions to the students that were intended to facilitate the development of a final report, which was envisioned as a document of about 150 single-spaced pages. First, a final report can actually be started on the day the scope of work is settled. In particular, a good scope of work can lead directly to a tentative outline of the final report, and the outline can even be converted into a contents page. The process of naming the individual sections and giving a title to the report itself helps to provide further focus. The contents page can then be used to provide section headings for a master document, and then the semester's main task is simply to fill in the spaces between the headings with appropriate text and figures. Naturally there will be some modifications along the way as the task areas become better understood, but they become minor modifications within a solid framework.

Second, figures and tables can be used as a valuable organizing theme for individual sections. Rather than focusing on the task of writing text for each section and then introducing an occasional figure or table where necessary, the students were encouraged to design their sections around a sequence of graphics that they would produce before writing any text. This is an approach and a skill that is not commonly cultivated in college writing courses, but it can be invaluable because the graphics will be the main elements that many readers will focus on as they browse through the report and decide what sections to read in detail, and also because the writing task then simply becomes the task of describing or elaborating on the story told by the graphics. This can make the writing task much easier. Professionals often use this strategy in writing consulting reports, and the students came to appreciate its value as they tried it out.

Ongoing Research Progress and Class Meetings

The student project manager and Hadlock met frequently to discuss the status of the project and plans for upcoming class meetings. The team met twice a week for an hour and fifteen minutes, and it was determined that the first meeting of the week would be a time to share research updates from each team member and that the second meeting of the week would be a time where task teams could break away and work on their own. This time was also an opportunity for the student project manager and the professor to circulate and meet with each task group to address any issues or problems. By closely monitoring the advances made by the class, the student project manager and the professor were able to adapt the timetable to the pace and needs of the class. Because the timetable was built with each task team's input in mind, their response to the evolving timetables, even if the timetable was quite ambitious, was positive. The client was flexible with any adjustments made and offered ideas and suggestions whenever their help was sought.

Nevertheless, the expected length of the final report and scope of the research sometimes appeared overwhelming, given the time constraints placed on the team by the ambitious project schedule, which needed to allow multiple rounds of review and revision. The key ingredient in managing this intense project along the way was the effectiveness of the student project manager, who exhibited three important characteristics: excellent people skills, high personal standards, and a real dedication to the goal of satisfying the client's needs. Her own energy was enhanced by the fact that she developed a close working relationship with the client, including regular communications by telephone, e-mail, and in person, throughout the project.

Client Interactions

The support that the chairman and staff showed for the project, even though they were not quite sure what the quality and comprehensiveness of the final product would be, was a major factor in energizing the entire class. The committee staff interacted regularly with the student project manager in order to evaluate and revise the scope of work and receive updates regarding the progress of the project. The chairman and committee staff provided input regarding contacts and resources within Massachusetts Health Services Region 4 to help support the students' research endeavors and put them in touch with professionals and experts in relevant fields. Interactions between the committee staff and student project manager occurred at least weekly and consisted of in-person meetings, telephone conversations, and e-mails. Regular interactions with the student project manager also provided opportunities for the chairman to involve the students in relevant state government events.

The students participated in several events related to pandemic flu and local public health emergency preparedness, which provided valuable educational and networking opportunities.

Interactions and in-person meetings with the student project manager and other members of the student team provided students with valuable experiences in participating and assuming leadership roles in professional settings. The poise and professionalism they displayed from the beginning of the project engendered a sense of confidence in the client, who thus harbored no reluctance to refer them to additional contacts throughout the public and private sectors. These communications skills were enhanced further as the project progressed, and the students were able to respond confidently and appropriately to inquiries about the project from other agencies, even in situations posing considerable professional or political sensitivity.

The student team was composed almost entirely of business students, and they were not always familiar with the political landscape and governmental structure. Fortunately, committee staff were always readily available and willing to fill in political background for the team. This not only contributed to the success of the project but enhanced the learning experience for students. Some of the key aspects of government that were made real through this project included the specific role of the legislative branch in focusing on the need for new legislation and in monitoring the overall success of various initiatives, the roles of particular agencies within the executive branch and their sensitivity to budget planning and availability of funds, the interaction among government agencies at the state and local levels, the level of access to detailed government information by members of the public and the general openness of government agencies to communications with the public, and the general pacing of government decision making and program implementation, which can be quite different from the corporate environment in which the students had had much greater experience during internships.

Contacts with Outside Parties

This project required class members to be in contact with many outside organizations since a key focal point of the project was to assess the extent to which diverse resources had been effectively integrated into pandemic flu planning. In addition, the class's parallel investigation of the distribution of funds within the pandemic flu planning effort involved tracking the budgets of government agencies at the state and local levels. The client for this project was an arm of a Democratic-controlled legislature, while much of the pandemic flu planning effort was being led by the Department of Public Health in the Republican-controlled executive branch. All this was taking place at the time of a heavily contested gubernatorial election. Since the class's responsibility was to make an overall assessment of the quality of certain portions of the planning effort, it was essential that inquiries along these lines be handled in the most sensitive and professional fashion.

The student project manager made the coordination of such contacts a high priority and received valuable advice in this respect from the client. In particular, it was crucial for her to be fully informed about which outside parties were being contacted and the content of the exchanges between the parties and the team members, to share this information with relevant parties (the client, the rest of the team, other outside parties who were interested, and the professor) and to determine which tasks needed more outside contacts. At our class meetings, there was time for all team members to share updates on their research, including any interviews with outside parties or contact leads they had come across. This information enabled other members of the class to extract value from the contact as well. By sharing plans for approaching contacts in advance, one contact might serve the needs of several groups within the team, thus avoiding redundant conversations or multiple calls from different task groups. In addition, when multiple contacts were invited to campus to participate in a focus group discussion, representatives of each task team were able to participate in order to pursue their own interest areas. The students were careful to present their interview questions in an unbiased manner and to express gratitude to the interviewee for their willingness to speak with the team. As the extent of contacts with outside parties increased, the class became more aware of potential areas of sensitivity. This was quite a good experience for them. Knowledge of such concerns enabled other team members to take a more strategic approach when they interviewed their contacts, and thus they were better able to avoid certain issues and anticipate discussion surrounding such concerns.

One aspect that the students did not anticipate was the level of interest in our research project on the part of many of the outside parties whom they contacted. Because the project was largely involved with assessing situations and activities that the contacts were dealing with on an everyday basis (and working hard at) and because many of the contacts felt strongly about the importance of flu pandemic preparedness, they took great interest in the final outcome of the research. Therefore, the team received several requests from such parties to update them on our findings and share preliminary results with them. To enable outside parties to follow the project, the class developed a dedicated Web site, with the Web site creation, design, and maintenance done internally by the project team. We also created a set of business cards for the student leadership team in order to facilitate subsequent communications with outside contacts.

Formulation of Principal Findings

One of the most challenging aspects of a research project, in which there are many participants even when organized into task teams, is the integration of all their contributions into an easily understood set of findings that can be featured in an executive summary. In fact, in the midst of the inevitable cycle of multiple revisions under tight time frames at the end of the semester, it is practically impossible to devote an adequate amount of time to identifying and properly articulating the most important outcomes of the research. Therefore, a key strategy is to push the task teams to begin to formulate their most important findings, even if in a preliminary way (as hypotheses, say), during the course of the research. We did this during the class meetings at which the teams reported on their weekly accomplishments. By asking them to tell the class what they thought might be emerging as important observations, we added an extra element of focus to their ongoing research. In addition, other members of the class were able to inquire about the basis for their conclusions and help identify additional data that might be necessary to obtain an adequate level of confidence in the potential finding.

This process served an additional important goal as well. As the class started to see specific findings emerge, it increased their confidence that they would be making a useful contribution to meeting the client's needs. While it would be easily imaginable that the pace of this project could lead to psychological exhaustion in the last few weeks of the semester, the articulation of meaningful findings (together with the enthusiastic cheerleading of the student project manager and the professor) helped to keep the energy level high right through the final report and presentation.

The Final Report and Presentation

The final report prepared by the class was a well-written, acetate-bound document of over 150 pages, with numerous original tables and figures and about seventy references. In the client's opinion, this report provided valuable insight into emergency preparedness measures currently underway in Region 4, as well as gaps in emergency preparedness and opportunities for strengthening preparedness measures. Pandemic influenza planning in Massachusetts is not yet highly centralized; therefore, data collection on state, regional, local, and other organizational initiatives has always been complex and time-consuming.

Unfortunately, policymaking is often reactive and not proactive, due in part to limitations in resources. Legislators and the communities they represent benefit most from prospective identification and resolution of community and public health deficiencies. However, often legislators do not have the resources to identify such shortages. The final report and data provided by the student team provided resources, not usually available to legislative committees, for the identification of public health deficiencies that can prevent unnecessary difficulties if they are addressed prospectively.

More specifically, the research presented in the final report included detailed descriptions of federal, state, and local funding mechanisms for pandemic flu, as well as state comparisons of alternative funding mechanisms, valuable for legislators when considering prospects and impacts of infrastructural changes. The report also included data collected from interviews and focus groups conducted with local municipal leaders as well as members of nongovernmental organizations within Region 4.

Data collected from the constituencies of legislators' districts often play a pivotal role in policy and legislative initiatives. Having access to such information as compiled in the final report provided tangible evidence of the needs of the community, as well as material that can be referenced in the future. Data presented in the final report also highlighted new leaders and professionals involved in pandemic planning within and outside Region 4 that the chairman and committee staff would be able to access for further support in the future.

The final report was introduced in a PowerPoint slide presentation given by the student project manager and other team members. The event took place in a traditional committee hearing room at the Massachusetts State House, and individuals who had volunteered their time and participated in the research, as well as key legislators and staff, were invited to attend the presentation. The chairman presided and introduced the team members and the background on the project. Hard copies of the final report were made available at the statehouse presentation, and electronic copies were made available on the chairman's Web site and by e-mail. The chairman and committee staff expressed intent to use key components of the report in order to develop and validate recommendations in areas of pandemic planning, such as organization of public health regional infrastructure, funding of pandemic planning, and best practices in public education and awareness. The student project manager and members of the team distributed the report by e-mail to all of those third parties with whom they were in contact during the research stages of the project, along with an additional message of thanks.

GRADING AND OTHER COURSE MANAGEMENT ISSUES

Hadlock told students at the beginning of the course that he did not intend to use grades as any kind of motivational issue. He would be monitoring the work of the class members on an individual basis and meeting with them periodically to give feedback on their work and writing. In addition, he asked all members of the class to maintain a course portfolio of their contributions throughout the project. At the end of the semester, he collected and reviewed these portfolios and assigned grades. The portfolios, in combination with the students' participation in class, were evaluated using a worksheet that allowed the accumulation of points in various categories, such as research depth, analytical strength, quality of writing, participation in class discussions, assistance with logistics (hosting client dinner, collating final report, and so on), and contributions to final oral client presentation. This was an outstanding team effort by a group of the strongest seniors in the college, and no one received a grade lower than B+. The overall energy of the class, derived from several factors described previously, made it virtually impossible for anyone to make less than a reasonable contribution to this project. Nevertheless, this problem does arise occasionally with similar projects and is usually addressed by means of direct discussions with either the project manager or the professor, with any hint of grading impact being used only as a last resort, since that can serve to change the tenor of the class.

An important component of any service-learning course is a reflection experience. This provides an opportunity for the students to process the broader implications of their participation in the project. One entire class meeting near the end of the semester was devoted to such an exercise, and it led to interesting exchanges of viewpoints about government, business, the dedication of people to a better society, and the opportunity to make a difference. Naturally these observations were also raised periodically throughout the semester in a more spontaneous fashion. The students particularly noted the human face of government in the many people with whom they interacted during the semester. For example, they saw impressive knowledge and professionalism, bureaucratic frustration, ideological dedication, political effectiveness, and various forms of hierarchical relationships. They also compared and contrasted these observations with some of their experiences in the corporate world.

OVERALL PROJECT IMPACT ON THE FOUR STAKEHOLDER GROUPS

In keeping with the theme of this book, it is clear that there are multiple perspectives on the impact that service-learning projects might have. Clients, of course, are the key consumers of the results of the project and want to see that their own time has been well spent. Students find that working on these real-world projects strongly complements their in-class learning. Faculty who work with capstone service-learning projects can see students learning to make the transition out of school and into the workplace. And academic institutions themselves may find that the connections developed from service-learning projects benefit them as well, beyond the obvious pedagogical gains.

CLIENT PERSPECTIVE

The project provided valuable tools that legislators and legislative committees can use in the future to improve public awareness and education regarding pandemic planning and preparedness. For example, the final report compiled data from public surveys that indicated that the public may not be concerned enough about pandemic flu to maximize preparedness either at individual levels or across sectors. The evaluations of various media channels such as Web sites highlighted opportunities to strengthen state public educational resources. Identifying what types of information motivate action by the public is essential for tailoring communications and public service announcements accordingly. Other state and local agencies would greatly benefit from having access to research that identifies best practices for public communication and education.

Another valuable tool that will have an impact on budget and infrastructural changes needed for more effective pandemic planning is the FLUSPREAD2 modeling tool, an agent-based simulation model delivered as an adjunct to the final report. FLUSPREAD2 graphically simulates the spread of pandemic flu and can be manipulated in order to depict flu spread under various conditions or types of interventions. This tool is vital for communicating to the public, the business community, and state and local leadership the positive impact that interventions can have when responding to pandemic influenza. The chairman has already showcased the FLUSPREAD2 tool as part of a conference convened to promote continuity of operations planning within the business community. The conference, convened at a regional hospital, included participating members from local chambers of commerce, local boards of health, and hospital emergency planning coordinators, and the model was run live by the student modeling group while the chairman explained the points that could be learned from it, such as the mitigation effects of quarantine and travel restrictions or the administration of antiviral medication to persons in the immediate social network of flu victims.

This kind of project also benefits government agencies in the long term by introducing students to public service careers and state and federal government processes. Service-learning projects with collaboration between students and government agencies increase the pool of well-qualified candidates interested in government public service positions. Through regular interactions with the student project manager and other team members, it was clear that such students would be ideal candidates for staffing many positions at governmental organizations. Government organizations often attract candidates who have majored in political science; however, policy development requires individuals with a broad range of strengths, interest, and knowledge, and this experience showed all parties how a group of students with diverse majors and strong business orientation were able to make important contributions to the governmental mission.

STUDENT PERSPECTIVE

Student feedback (on standard college forms and informally) on this capstone experience was quite positive, except several noted that the workload turned out to be more than they had bargained for. The opportunity to write a capstone report as a team effort was much more energizing than the relatively isolated experience they observed some of their peers having in writing an individual thesis. There was a very high level of pride in the final project report, and several students requested additional copies to carry with them to job interviews. Since some of the students are pursuing careers in the consulting industry, this experience gave them a realistic opportunity to test the consulting environment firsthand. Students were unanimous in commenting that the opportunity to work for a real client was highly motivating.

Although students typically work on team-based projects in many courses in our institution, the teams are never as large and rarely as structured as the one they participated on in this case. For example, they had to coordinate closely and share their research data with the rest of the team. Therefore, they learned and practiced critical teamwork and communication skills. Gathering data from outside parties was a necessity in accurate completion of the report. Students learned how to develop a concise set of interview questions and properly conduct interviews with outside parties. And throughout the course, they had to continually present their research findings and their written drafts for review and critique by other members of the class, all of whom had quite high standards.

The students noted that one of the most important impacts that this project had on the team was improving their knowledge of the political sector. As business students, they often do not have as much exposure to politics as other students may. Through this project, they learned about the intricacies and nuances of government in a way that is not easily reproducible in a basic government course. This is an experience that they recognized as particularly valuable as they enter the business world, since government and business are so closely intertwined in our social and economic systems.

FACULTY PERSPECTIVE

From a faculty perspective, the kinds of impacts described above from the points of view of the client and the students would be enough in themselves to justify service-learning projects of this nature. But there are additional impacts that an educator would like to see result from a capstone undergraduate experience.

Students who participate in field trips, such as company visits, plant tours, or museum programs, often comment that they wish such experiences were more commonly integrated into their courses. Except for particular applied technical skills, such as accounting methods, the connections between much of their academic work and the real world appear to be somewhat tenuous. Projects such as this pandemic flu capstone course serve an important role in bridging this gap between the academic disciplines and the real world. In addition, this kind of experience also helps to demonstrate the connections among the disciplines themselves. Such fields as marketing, information design, economics, accounting, and mathematical modeling all came together in this project to render advice about a public policy issue being managed within the constraints of our governmental structures. The perspectives from the different disciplines opened people's eyes to the complexity of societal decision making well beyond the much narrower perspectives they are likely to have had on this issue at the outset of the project.

The time when students make the transition from the academic world to the world of work is a challenging one for many because they have to change their self-image from that of a relatively passive student to a person who is expected to exert independent initiative and leadership. While some are hungry for this new role, even many very good students approach it with more trepidation than gusto. This kind of project helps students to see themselves in a new light. They begin the semester thinking that the concept of actually helping an outside client is a foolish illusion, and they finish feeling empowered and appreciated. Along the way, they have learned valuable strategies for organizing their writing; they have strategized with their colleagues about the most effective structure for a major oral presentation; they have dealt with numerous issues of complex team dynamics that they will continue to encounter in their future careers; and they have learned to be resourceful to a degree that they might not previously have felt capable of.

INSTITUTIONAL PERSPECTIVE

Service-learning programs with government partners offer outstanding institutional benefits that too often are not fully appreciated by the individual faculty members who may consider offering them. For this reason, faculty members also may often overlook the valuable institutional resources that are available for supporting such endeavors. While not a unique offering for our institution, the pandemic flu project represented an expansion of our activities in what might be called "high academic level" service-learning. It has certainly opened the eyes of other faculty members to the possibility of projects of this type and has shown them that service-learning programs can extend their impact well beyond the needs of local community service organizations. This does not mean that one kind of contribution is better than another, only that the range of contributions may be wider than one might initially think, and thus a wider range of faculty members and courses may be able to have a service-learning connection.

Aside from this contribution to the vitality of our service-learning initiative, the pandemic flu project provided excellent visibility for our institution throughout the halls of the statehouse and in all the public agencies, businesses, and organizations with which we interacted during the project, and in the press. These are all potential employers of our graduates and hosts for student internships, and if not potential employers themselves, at least new networking opportunities. For some observers who may have thought of a business-oriented college in narrower terms, their awareness of this initiative surely expanded their image of our institution. At a time when we are trying to attract more top-quality high school graduates, who often plan to attend liberal arts colleges even though they will ultimately enter careers in business, such public exposure as a broader-based institution contributes to our recruiting success. A special feature article on this project in our alumni magazine has similarly raised our image among an alumni population consisting of potential donors to the college, parents of future students who may attend, and possible employers.

CONCLUSION

Service-learning is an important educational movement that helps to inculcate in students a higher awareness of their responsibility and empowerment to effect change. When carried out in association with government partners, it has the additional advantage of educating students about how to effect such change within the framework of our governmental systems. The pandemic flu project discussed in this chapter appeared to achieve excellent success in reaching such objectives, as well as accomplishing a number of additional educational goals. We have pursued other similar team research projects at our institution in the form of honors capstone experiences and otherwise. Every such project presents its own challenges. It is important to keep in mind that each of these challenges also presents a teaching opportunity, and a flexible faculty member and well-matched client generally find considerable satisfaction in working together on this kind of valuable educational venture.

Voices: The Academic Institution

Service-Learning at Bentley College

Franklyn Salimbene

Since its inception in 1991, Bentley's service-learning program has built a number of partnerships with community-based organizations in Waltham and the greater Boston community. Every semester, approximately six hundred Bentley students engage in a number of projects where they use information and skills learned in their classes to render service and where the service they render reciprocally informs their learning. Projects range from conducting marketing research, developing Web pages, and writing grant proposals for local nonprofit organizations to working directly with elders, the disabled, children, and those whose native language is not English. With the pandemic flu project and others like it, however, we have expanded our project range to a more sophisticated level in terms of the kind of work being carried out by the students and the type of client organization involved.

My involvement with the flu project began when my colleague Charlie Hadlock, who was teaching a capstone course in the honors program, asked me to brainstorm with him about a service project that he wanted his students to undertake with a high-profile client in the public sector. As director of service-learning at Bentley, my role and that of my office is to support faculty, students, and community partners in developing and implementing service projects that enhance teaching and learning and have a meaningful impact on the community.

During our conversation, it was clear that Charlie wanted a project that would have a significant environmental or health impact beyond the local community. As I listened to him, I was immediately drawn to the idea that state government would be the perfect project partner. And because our local state legislator, Peter Koutoujian, was also cochair of the state legislative committee on public health, we had a readily available opportunity to make something happen. We were right. We contacted Peter, and the flu project came into being.

As I consider the range of service projects that my office supports, I find those like the flu project particularly appealing. For faculty and students alike, working with an important government client that applies the service rendered in developing or implementing public policy adds an element of reality and excitement to the learning process that is not easily matched by other project types. It motivates students. Furthermore, and more important from a service perspective, such projects place students, faculty, and the university itself in the unique position of truly making a difference and having an impact on the critical issues of the day. It is what engaged citizenship is all about.

Faculty are engaged as they contemplate the project issue and bring their academic and pedagogical expertise to bear in working toward a solution. Students are engaged as they endeavor to apply their newly acquired knowledge base and skill set to public problem solving. And finally, the university is engaged as it responds in a way that only it can: as a well-respected public resource adapting its widely applicable research and technological capabilities to public policy issues at no cost to the public.

For universities to make service-learning an effective means of assistance to the public, however, they must be willing to make an internal investment. At Bentley that investment is a system of support for service-learning stakeholders. It begins with a heartfelt belief at the very top of the administrative structure that the university must meet its duty as academic citizen. From this belief flows support for service-learning students that comes in the form of academic credit and, in some instances, federal work-study funding. For service-learning faculty, that support comes in the form of course development grants, stipends, and university-wide recognition. For community partners, support comes in the form of a campus office that coordinates community outreach, collaborates with them in the allocation of Bentley's service resources, provides trained student project managers to troubleshoot and address logistical issues at the service site, and nurtures the relationship over the long term.

Bentley's internal investment in service-learning made the flu project happen. Its promise for similar future collaborations enlivens teaching and learning at Bentley while providing meaningful service to the public sector.

■ ■ ■

Franklyn Salimbene is director of the Bentley College Service-Learning Center in Waltham, Massachusetts.

CHAPTER SEVEN

LET'S GET IT STARTED

Leadership, Civic Engagement, and Service-Learning

Kendra A. King

In the fall of 2005, the Black Eyed Peas, a multimillion dollar recording group, released the popular song, "Let's Get It Started!" The highly infectious hip-hop/pop tune introduced listeners to the power of the possible when an individual or group tries something new. According to the song, getting started can ignite a movement of positive innovation that can change what is commonly accepted as the norm.

In 1994, Oglethorpe University, a small, private liberal arts university located in metropolitan Atlanta, decided to "get it started" and implemented a one-of-a-kind leadership program designed to connect the campus with the greater metropolitan Atlanta business, civic, and neighborhood communities. Through a balance of courses, workshops, and various on- and off-campus experiences, students in the Rich Foundation Urban Leadership Program (RFULP) are prepared to meet the challenges of responsible citizenship and civic engagement in local, national, and international arenas. RFULP provides a variety of structured experiential and service-learning opportunities to address community problems.

In 2006, building on some of the momentum of the RFULP, Oglethorpe opened its Center for Civic Engagement (CCE), which coordinates the university's service and service-learning activities for students, faculty, staff, and alumni. The CCE also works closely with the RFULP and provides it with programmatic support and resources. In return, the RFULP has helped the CCE serve as the university's clearinghouse for service-learning and hands-on experiential opportunities on campus and in the community.

OGLETHORPE UNIVERSITY: A HISTORICAL OVERVIEW

The "old" Oglethorpe University was founded in 1835 near Milledgeville, Georgia, as a southern ministerial training institution for Presbyterians. Prior to the establishment of the university, many southern Presbyterians had sent their sons to Princeton College in New Jersey to obtain theological training. In establishing Oglethorpe, it was hoped that the same rigorous training, development, and liberal free thinking would transpire in the South. The university was named after the founder of the state of Georgia, James Edward Oglethorpe—an emancipator, philanthropist, and educator.

During its early years, Oglethorpe was home to several well-known scholars and alumni, including university president Samuel Kennedy Talmage (an eminent scholar and theologian), Joseph LeConte (best known for his work in optics and geology), and its best-known son, Sidney Lanier, an antebellum poet, critic, and musician. Some of the early course offerings of the university included theology, classical literature, natural sciences, Greek, and Latin. At the height of the Civil War, Oglethorpe was forced to close its doors when it was overtaken by the triple burden of student soldiers, Confederate war bond debt, and the use of its buildings for barracks and hospitals. Although the university soon reopened and made history as the first institution in Georgia to offer evening degree courses, it again closed its doors in 1872, and this time for much longer.

In 1913, Oglethorpe was rechartered and relocated to its current north Atlanta residence. A drastic change from its early inception in the rural community of Milledgeville, the new street address placed the university within arm's reach of the vibrant downtown area. Oglethorpe's Peachtree Street location made the university ripe for a renewed focus on citizenship, leadership, and civic engagement.

As part of this renewed focus and vision, the university received nationwide attention in the 1940s for the "Oglethorpe Idea," an effort to create a curriculum to encourage students to "make a life and make a living," as well as foster community living and interaction. Today this mission continues in the form of the lauded core curriculum program that engages first-year students right away in critical thinking that helps build active citizens. While the predominant makeup of the twelve hundred member student body at Oglethorpe hails from the South, under the leadership of the university's sixteenth president, Lawrence M. Schall, the class of 2011 is the most diverse yet and represents thirty-one states and twelve countries.

As the university embraces the challenge of educating in the twenty-first century, it has adopted a two-prong model of service-learning (initially articulated as experiential learning) and civic engagement that is deeply rooted in the university motto: "Make a Life, Make a Living, Make a Difference."

MAKE A LIFE, MAKE A LIVING, MAKE A DIFFERENCE

Many liberal arts colleges say they prepare students for lives of leadership and citizenship, and Oglethorpe is no different. It seeks to develop students to have a "willingness and ability to assume the responsibilities of leadership in public and private life, including skill in organizing the efforts of other persons on behalf of worthy causes" (Oglethorpe University, 2006). One vehicle that sets Oglethorpe apart from other schools in the pursuit of these goals is the Rich Foundation Urban Leadership Program, the brainchild of Vicky Weiss, a faculty member turned administrator who grew increasingly concerned about the rising cynicism and distrust among students in the late 1990s. Weiss explained:

> I attended a seminar on developing a minor in leadership. When I returned to campus, I spoke to the provost about what we could do as a campus community. He gave me the green light to try to

come up with a solution. I called a meeting on a Friday afternoon, and to my surprise, more than half of the faculty showed up. We discussed our collective concerns that if we did not find a way to effectively engage our students that we would bear partial blame for their lack of involvement in the real world. . . . . [During] the meeting, a colleague reminded all present of the rich and generous spirit of the school's namesake—James Edward Oglethorpe—and his commitment to serving others. The consensus was that we owed it to our namesake to begin to foster an environment whereby students could gain more than an education and a pathway to middle-class living. [All quotations from Weiss are from a personal interview with the author in 2007.]

The next step was to determine the structure of the program. According to Weiss, it

was decided that the leadership program would be a certificate that culminated with a special designation on a student's academic transcript and diploma as well as special recognition at graduation. We also agreed that the program had to be experiential in nature. In other words, students had to do more than just read a book and acquire a theoretical understanding of the phenomena being studied. We felt it was extremely important for our students to be able to spend time in the actual communities and industries being examined in order to integrate the classroom and real world together in what we hoped would be a pragmatic nexus of lifelong civic engagement, leadership, and other-centeredness.

THE BIRTH OF RICH FOUNDATION URBAN LEADERSHIP PROGRAM

After the initial faculty meeting, a cross-disciplinary leadership committee representing a variety of divisions, including the natural sciences, English and literature, theater, politics, business, and public administration, worked on implementation of a program. In 1994, with the support of a majority of the faculty, the administration, and a generous grant from the Rich Family Foundation, Oglethorpe's Rich Foundation Urban Leadership Program was launched with the mission of providing experiential learning and leadership development opportunities to students in the metropolitan Atlanta community.

To meet this mission, the RFULP uses the triangulated approach of academic course work, on- and off-campus leadership, and structured experiential and service-learning as a means of promoting civic engagement and participation. The RFULP also seeks to develop social capital–conscious intellectuals who are active members of the community well beyond their undergraduate experiences. These intellectuals are individuals who understand that "intelligence is not enough," as Martin Luther King Jr. (1947) wrote in calling for intelligence *and* character. Put another way, social capital–conscious intellectuals are those who realize that intelligence coupled with humanity (our hearts in action) is what produces change in our communities and the world.

Nearly a century ago, Hanifan (1916) defined social capital as "those tangible substances that count for most in the daily lives of people: namely good will, fellowship, sympathy, and social intercourse. . . . The community as a whole will benefit by the cooperation of all parts, while the individual will find in his associations the advantages of help, the sympathy, and the fellowship of his neighborhoods" (p. 130). Even given the new focus on social capital driven by Putnam (2000), this definition seems as current. The fundamental mission of the RFULP has social capital at its heart. Students in the program engage in holistic, meaningful, and transformative leadership training and development through hands-on service and experiential education as a means of producing students who become lifelong participants in the community and the world around them.

RICH FOUNDATION URBAN LEADERSHIP PROGRAM ADMISSIONS PROCESS

Students interested in becoming members of the RFULP are required to fill out a program application, submit a two- to three-page essay detailing prior leadership and service, and provide a high school or other academic transcript. In order to successfully earn the certificate degree in urban leadership, students are required to complete four courses: The New American City, Moral and Political Leadership, The Urban Leadership Elective, and the capstone Community Issues Forum: Principles into Practice (see Exhibit 7.1). In addition, students must complete a Leader in Action paper each semester that details and provides reflection of their involvement and service both on and off campus and a final senior portfolio that includes written work from their leadership courses, reflection journals, experiential and internship opportunities, and any programmatic events that they participated in as part of the program.

EXHIBIT 7.1 RICH FOUNDATION URBAN LEADERSHIP PROGRAM COURSES

POL 350. Special Topics in Politics: Moral and Political Leadership—4 hours
In this course, the lives of a number of leaders are examined and a series of questions are addressed. In what did or does their greatness consist? With what issues or moral dilemmas did they wrestle? What challenges did they face? How did they understand and perhaps overcome the constraints of their situation? Upon what moral, intellectual, and "characterological" resources could they rely? What were their strengths? What were their weaknesses? Prerequisite: Permission of the instructor.

ULP 303. The New American City—4 hours
The purpose of this course is to examine the problems and prospects of politics and policymaking in the new American city and its environs. Consideration will be given to the political and sociological significance of a number of the factors that characterize this new development, including extremes of wealth and poverty, the mix of racial and ethnic groups, and the opportunities and challenges provided by progress in transportation and technology. Offered annually.

ULP 304. Community Issues Forum: Principles into Practice—4 hours
This course is taught as a weekly seminar focusing on a particular community issue and accompanied by an issue-related, off-campus internship. Together with faculty, students analyze issues confronting stakeholders, collaborate on solutions, and present findings derived from their internship assignments. Students have interned with the state legislature, local and state chambers of commerce, community food banks, arts organizations, corporations, non-profit organizations, and a number of other community groups. Topics covered in previous years include: community development, education, transportation, health care, and the environment. Prerequisite: Permission of the instructor.

Urban Leadership Elective—4 hours
With the approval of the Rich Foundation Urban Leadership Program
Director and the academic advisor, the student selects an appropriate
course to satisfy the fourth course requirement of the program. Ideally,
the elective course will be part of the student's major or minor, or in
an area of vocational interest. The principal objective of the elective
requirement is to look for intellectual or applied leadership in the
student's chosen field or profession.

In addition to the required academic course work, students demonstrate leadership on and off campus by their participation in University,
civic, and community endeavors in Atlanta. Students organize and participate in conferences, workshops, and symposia on and off campus. At
the end of each semester, students submit a brief memo to the director
detailing their leadership challenges and opportunities that semester.
In the final semester, students prepare a paper reflecting on their leadership experiences during college. The final portfolio contains written
work drawn from the student's leadership courses and experiences.

Admission to the Rich Foundation Urban Leadership Program is
competitive. Students may apply in the freshman, sophomore, or junior
year. The director and a selection committee evaluate candidates on
the basis of commitment to leadership-related study, the desire for leadership understanding and application, extracurricular participation,
academic record, and other experience.

THE CAPSTONE: COMMUNITY ISSUES FORUM

The capstone course of the RFULP is the Community Issues
Forum (CIF), a semester-long course designed to provide students, faculty, alumni, and friends of the university a forum to
engage in collaborative thought, action, and service centered on
a particular issue. Together with community, business, and civic
leaders, students analyze situations, collaborate on solutions,
engage in service-learning projects, and present their findings
and reflections from the experiential assignments and internships to the university community at the end of the semester. The
power of the CIF is its ability to bring students together in small
work groups with community leaders, alumni, and university
friends to study the intricacies of metropolitan area problems
and research solutions.

The first CIF was conducted in 1994 and focused on the Summerhill neighborhood in Atlanta. The residents of this community were being displaced by the 1996 Olympics development (more specifically, Turner Stadium, which now is the home of the Atlanta Braves baseball team). According to Weiss:

> The Summerhill CIF was the best experience we had in the early days because we were able to effectively connect students to an issue that really mattered and they did not just throw up their hands and do nothing; they actually rolled up their sleeves and worked in a variety of government, community, and civic agencies and did something. I remember one young lady who was doing an experiential learning program at the Atlanta Department of City Planning coming into my office frustrated about the spin being put on an issue and asking if the truth would ever be made known. I thought, *Wow! the light bulb is going on now.* The key was not that we were going to solve all the problems of urban displacement, but that everyone was engaged in real work, problem solving, and genuine reflection about a community issue and what, if any, difference one person could make.

The students who participated in the Summerhill neighborhood CIF were placed at a variety of local community sites, including the Summerhill Neighborhood Development Corporation, the Non-Profit Resource Center of the Metropolitan Atlanta Development Corporation, the Atlanta Community Food Bank, the Department of Planning of the City of Atlanta, NationsBank Community Development Corporation, St. Luke's Church Kitchen Ministries, City Council, and the City of Atlanta. While the majority of these placements have been identified in the historical record as internships, it must be noted that the purpose of these placements as identified in the initial structure of the program was to provide vehicles whereby students in the RFULP were able to "assimilate and reflect upon their academic study and its application in experiential learning activities in order to do profitable self-assessment" related to long-term civic engagement. These placements may have been called internships, but they were outstanding examples of service-learning.

One of the greatest rewards of implementing a triangulated approach to learning is that it has the potential to inspire, awaken, and redirect student interest and concern. In the case of the Summerhill CIF, one student was so moved by the ability of a single person to make a difference that he dedicated his life to serving others. He had grown up on a farm in rural Georgia and was seemingly the most unusual suspect to become passionate about urban education and education reform. However, after his CIF, in which he supplied books to the Lynwood Park Community Development Corporation for its after-school program, he decided to focus his career on addressing educational disparities. He is currently working on his doctorate in urban education reform at Columbia University.

This story is far from unique. The CIF, as well as courses such as the New American City, have inspired many students in the RFULP to make a difference, if even on a small scale. For example, one student redoubled her efforts to work with underserved communities. In the spring of 2004, she was one of a small group of students who participated in a CIF that I taught. The forum dealt with the issues of community development, displacement, and gentrification in Oglethorpe's long-standing community neighbor, Lynwood Park, a predominantly African American neighborhood outside our back gates. The student was so moved by the senior citizens' positive response to the formulation and distribution of a monthly communitywide newsletter that she stayed on at the Lynwood Park Community Development Association well after the CIF was over.

The relationship between Oglethorpe and Lynwood Park has been a special one because the university and Lynnwood Park residents have interacted in several leadership and service-learning projects. In 1997 the first official RFLUP service-learning project took place in Lynwood Park, with the DeKalb County Clean and Beautiful Commission as the government partner. During the spring of 1998, the RFULP students continued their service-learning initiatives in Lynwood Park and helped evaluate the aesthetic and physical conditions of the neighborhood. The students documented their evaluations in site surveys that were distributed to DeKalb County government and federal agencies by the Lynwood Park CDC in an effort to secure community development assessment and redevelopment grants.

In addition to the involvement of the RFULP, Oglethorpe has been connected to the Lynwood Park community through one of its service fraternities, Alpha Phi Omega (APO), a national coed volunteer service organization that has worked with the Lynwood Park Community Center for the past eight years. The members of APO provide tutoring and arts and crafts programs. In addition, they were instrumental in the donation to the center of several refurbished computers. And they helped with a communitywide cleanup.

COMMUNITY ISSUES FORUM: THEN AND NOW

During its first decade, the RFULP conducted a host of CIF seminars that examined a variety of urban issues including education, transportation, architecture, ethnography, and immigration. In more recent years, seminars have examined faith-based initiatives, local government annexation and expansion, neighborhood empowerment, and community development.

While the RFULP and CIF have been involved in many important activities over the years, there have been some significant challenges that have rendered the CIFs a bit less effective than in the early days. The major challenge the RFULP and CIFs face has been the constant turnover in the directorship of the program. Since its inception, the program has been under the leadership of seven different directors. This turnover has had a direct impact on the CIF structure, mission, and implementation. Whereas some directors have been strongly in favor of service-learning, other directors have focused their attention on more theoretical and technical aspects of the program. The result has been major changes in the makeup, requirements, and programmatic elements of the capstone course. Under some directors, the course has fit the service-learning model, but under other directors, it has taken on a different focus. Another challenge of the CIF has been student participation and interest. The responsibilities of students today often include work as well as school, which makes it difficult for some students to fit the necessary courses into their busy schedules.

Another challenge facing the CIF has been the scheduling of guests. The course depends on guest speakers, and it has been difficult to find times that accommodate the wide variety of guests invited to every CIF. In addition, there have been problems in student placement at experiential learning sites. Unfortunately, where a student is placed has not always been based on the best service-learning opportunity. Often factors such as transportation play a more important role than the quality of the experience. There have been, for instance, a few students so afraid to ride public transportation that they have refused to participate in certain service activities.

On a more positive note, the CIF has provided the university with a host of excellent government, community, and business partners. As an example, during spring 2004, the DeKalb County government, under the leadership of Karl B. Williams, provided an invaluable opportunity for one of our students to work closely with the Department of Senior Services to organize service delivery focus groups, customer satisfaction surveys, on-site home visits, and implementation of a senior citizen neighborhood location finder database that the county continues to use. In addition, the CIF has been a superb facilitator for student reflection, a hallmark of service-learning. Toward the end of each semester, students spend substantial time reviewing their work, including e-mail updates and journals, both required in the Moral and Political Leadership course and the final portfolio project. Also, the CIF has been effective in motivating some members of the Oglethorpe community to become civically engaged. Other positive programmatic activities are the policy forum breakfasts, the public policy exploration week, the fall urban leadership retreat, and the Society of Urban Leaders. The policy breakfast forum was one of the most successful initiatives of the program. The early morning (7:00 A.M. to 9:00 A.M.) speaker series hosted Atlanta community and business leaders representing a variety of industries, including the Georgia Public Service Commission, the Metropolitan Atlanta Community Foundation, and the Southern Center for Studies in Public Policy at Clark Atlanta University.

Where Do We Go from Here: Chaos or Community?

In 1967, Dr. Martin Luther King Jr. wrote his last book, *Where Do We Go from Here: Chaos or Community?* It is a prophetic offering in which King challenged his readers to step outside their selfish ambition to realize that "what affects one directly, affects all indirectly." Moreover, King pleaded for an end to man's inhumanity to man. He argued that if we did not begin to build a world house where the contributions of all people are recognized, we would soon self-destruct as materialism, selfishness, and greed triumphed over humanitarianism, other-centeredness, and unconditional agape love.

What does this have to do with service-learning, the RFULP, and Oglethorpe University? Everything. What King called for in 1967 is no different from what James Edward Oglethorpe actuated in 1732. He laid a blueprint for transformative change through hands-on service that is still a central part of the university. In looking to the future, it appears that this message will continue to guide the school for years to come, just as Oglethorpe would have wanted. The current president, his administration, the faculty, and students are committed to serving the greater Atlanta metropolitan area. As President Schall stated in his 2005 inaugural address,

> Oglethorpe University, I believe, does have a unique obligation in American higher education, derived from the intersection of three conditions: the visionary ideals and call to action of our namesake, our tradition of education in the liberal arts, and our place in the city of Atlanta. . . . John Dewey wrote 100 years ago that the measure of the worth of any social institution is its effect in enlarging and improving the human experience. That is how I would like Oglethorpe and my presidency to ultimately be measured.

To some, this address may read as mere words—the words that college presidents are supposed to say, especially at their inauguration. The litmus test, however, has been in the positive action of the university in a variety of areas. The ongoing RFULP and CIF— and their commitment to service-learning—are part of this action.

Oglethorpe's commitment to others goes beyond the local community too. It has certainly served the people of Atlanta, but it has also been involved outside the city and even outside the state. It has partnered with Angel Flight to get food and supplies to the victims of Hurricane Katrina. In the first two years after the tragedy along the Gulf coast, more than fifty students, faculty, staff, and administrators dedicated winter, spring, and summer breaks to rebuilding efforts. And under the leadership of President Schall, Oglethorpe has moved closer to building the community of Dr. King's dreams by establishing the university's Center for Civic Engagement, which seeks to engage students and the greater Atlanta community in collaborative service-learning. Thus, the center provides additional programmatic support for the RFULP as the two initiatives work together to serve the university, alumni, friends, and partners.

Oglethorpe is a service-learning-rich liberal arts institution that many feel is on the precipice of national prominence and greatness. The university's vast institutional and privately funded experiential and service-oriented initiatives—the RFULP, the CIF, and the new Center for Civic Engagement—are natural incubators for service-learning. Indeed, service-learning has already been part of what these programs deliver, and the current directors are committed to expanding service-learning opportunities. Service-learning at Oglethorpe will continue to develop and flourish as a foundational building block of civic engagement training that will make our namesake, James Edward Oglethorpe, proud for many years to come.

Voices: Government Partners and University

Karl B. Williams

I partnered with Oglethorpe University, and I would do it again. The partnership was good for many reasons, but two stand out. First, it gave my department [the county Department of Senior Affairs] a student with fresh insight and reflection—someone who was not overly influenced by the bureaucratic red tape that can make what we do difficult and limit our thinking. The student became our one-person focus group, allowing us to bounce ideas off her and get reactions that were not influenced by years of working in the department. Along the same lines, the addition of a college student to the office provided lots of opportunity for inquiry, dialogue, and inspiration. Her presence sparked curiosity and reunited dreams, and some of my staff considered returning to school to complete a degree or starting one. Second, the partnership gave the student the experience necessary to decide whether this area of clientele service was a direction she wanted to pursue as a career.

If there was a downside to the partnership, it was that my office was at the mercy of the student's schedule. At times, this could be a little uneasy as I was unable to demand the same things as I could from paid staff. A minor inconvenience was that my office had to provide the student the same security details (an ID badge, information technology clearance, and access to the department's data) of a full-time employee. Similarly, but not necessarily a weakness, is the fact that with the addition of a new person to the office, there are real needs that must be provided if the service-learning opportunity is going to be meaningful. Whereas in the days of old, all we needed to provide were a pencil and a desk, in our modern world, the necessities are a telephone, computer, and access to a printer—some of which may not be easy to come by.

The greatest lesson I learned came during the Lynwood Park Summit held in conjunction with the service-learning semester. This event brought a variety of key players from the government, business, community, and university together to reflect on the issues of community development related to the work that many Oglethorpe students were doing that semester. While there, it hit me that my greatest challenge is in making a decision when everyone involved is right, as was the case with Lynwood Park issues. The summit provided a valuable opportunity for personal reflection, which has shaped my decision-making process ever since. I encourage any government partner in a service-learning initiative to ask the college or university they are partnering with to have a culminating gathering as a means of dialogue, discussion, and, most important, reflection.

■ ■ ■

Karl B. Williams is deputy director of human services in the Department of Senior Affairs, DeKalb County, Georgia.

THE UNIVERSITY PERSPECTIVE

Peter M. Rooney

The Rich Foundation Board, along with its board chair, Joel Goldberg, wanted to contribute resources to a worthwhile and meaningful endeavor that would make a difference. They felt that the grant would make a difference to our students, the university, and the community friends that the Rich Foundation Urban Leadership Program sought to partner with to foster civic responsibility, leadership, volunteerism, and service-learning. They were right. The gift has touched student, faculty, alumni, and our target communities. Moreover, the generosity of the Rich Foundation has enabled the urban leadership program to lay a foundation of triangulated learning and interaction that has been instrumental in developing a cadre of students who reflect the best of the liberal arts tradition.

■ ■ ■

Peter M. Rooney is vice president of university relations at Oglethorpe University.

References

Hanifan, L. J. (1916). The rural school community center. *Annals of the American Academy of Political and Social Science, 67*, 130–138.

King, M. L., Jr. (1947). The purpose of education. *Morehouse Maroon Tiger, 10*.

King, M. L., Jr. (1967). *Where do we go from here: Chaos or community?* New York: HarperCollins.

Oglethorpe University. (2006). *Oglethorpe University bulletin, 2006–2008*. Retrieved March 16, 2009, from www.oglethorpe.edu/Admission/TUBulletin_2006_2008.pdf.

Putnam, R. D. (2000). *Bowling alone: The collapse and revival of American community*. New York: Simon & Schuster.

Schall, L. M. (2005). *Inaugural address*. Atlanta, GA: Oglethorpe University.

CHAPTER EIGHT

WHEN SERVICE-LEARNING MEETS GOVERNMENTAL INERTIA

Lessons from an Oklahoma Town

Christine Pappas

How effective can service-learning be when, instead of working with a government partner, one is working against it? This chapter is somewhat of an anomaly because it seeks to address that question. Most of the time when a professor sets out to design and implement a service-learning project, a variety of supportive and enthusiastic stakeholders join her at the table: students, relevant government agencies, and the served community, for example. In this case, at the beginning of the project, most of the stakeholders were absent. In fact, the only thing that was really present was the table itself. Literally.

There are many ways to foster relationships among university, governmental, and community groups that lead to successful service-learning projects. Many times when an idea for a civic project is born, meetings are called among the interested and affected parties, and the group moves forward consensually. Leadership is usually undertaken by the most powerful parties. This case shows how

---

An earlier version of this chapter was presented at the American Political Science Association's Third Annual Conference on Teaching and Learning, Washington, D.C., February 18–20, 2006.

a relationship between two people—a student and a professor—can grow to encompass a city government, a neighborhood, a university administration, and hundreds of students.

A WHITE WOMAN WITH A NOTEBOOK

In late 2004, on the heels of a lecture on civic engagement, one of my students at East Central University, Barbara, asked me if there was anything she could ask the City of Ada to do for her neighborhood. She was particularly worried about the long-abandoned house next to hers. Why wouldn't the city tear it down? Ada is a community of about sixteen thousand located in southeastern Oklahoma. Barbara lived in Hammond Heights, a neighborhood about three blocks by five blocks, mainly populated by African Americans, although some whites and Native Americans also live there. It is barely located within city limits, and its isolation and high minority population cause most white Adans to not consider it part of their town. Most Adans have never visited there.

After several conversations, I agreed to meet Barbara on a Saturday afternoon to tour the neighborhood. As we drove, we saw asphalt streets without curbs and open drainage ditches clogged with limbs and leaves. There seemed to be very few fire hydrants and streetlights. We counted more than twenty abandoned homes, some being used as crack houses. Many abandoned cars and other large trash filled the empty lots. Although other parts of Ada may have poor infrastructure, the Hammond Heights neighborhood was the only place in the city where it was consistently subpar. Only one street in the neighborhood had concrete construction with curbs.

Barbara stopped her car at Eddie Weaver's house. Mr. Weaver, one of the old-time lions of the neighborhood, sat on his front porch in a rocker, wearing overalls and holding a cup of coffee in one hand and a fly swatter in the other. I felt that I had gone back fifty years in time. He let me ask him questions about the history of Hammond Heights and why the neighbors had not approached the city council for services. He was patient with my naive questions, and told me that he and others had been to the city council and had even participated in federal grant

applications several times and nothing had ever changed. According to Mr. Weaver, many promises had been made to the people
of Hammond Heights since the neighborhood was established,
but they had never been kept. The neighbors had been promised
new streets, sidewalks, a community center, and a storm shelter,
and for a variety of reasons, none of these things had been delivered. I wrote down what he said in my notebook.

As Barbara and I were leaving, he chuckled at me and said,
"We'll see how much you and that notebook get done out here!"
I laughed, but felt that a gauntlet had been thrown down. White
people with clipboards and notebooks had been to Hammond
Heights before, yet nothing had changed.

Service-Learning Without Government Partners

When confronted with a social problem, such as the lack of governmental interest in Hammond Heights, one might speak truth to
power by imploring political leaders to take heed, or perhaps even
by running for office. However, the complex challenges Hammond
Heights presented seemed to suggest another path. I did not want
to paint dilapidated houses that were rotting on their foundations
or trim trees that would only grow back. I wanted to be a part of
a fundamental change that could bring the neighborhood back to
life and empower the neighbors politically. People needed jobs and
economic development, faith, community, and civic engagement.
Infused with a Freirean approach (Freire, 1972, 1995), Rosenberger
(2000) writes that service-learning "helps develop a critical consciousness in those participating in service" (p. 29), and through
this work, students and neighbors can make connections that can
move a city toward the structural change needed to achieve a more
just and equitable society. Through our work, I wanted to help
foster this critical consciousness in Hammond Heights. By working
together, we could build civic engagement, a commonly cited goal
of service-learning.

It seemed to me that one of the roadblocks in the way of successfully addressing the issues in Hammond Heights was racial
prejudice. According to the 2000 U.S. Census data, Ada is 3.5
percent black, and many of these roughly five hundred people

live in Hammond Heights. Most of Ada is white, and most of the students at East Central University are white. Given the history of the de facto segregation in Ada, racial prejudice was enabling the city and its residents to label Hammond Heights as the "other" to the point that the residents no longer saw it as part of their community. Service-learning scholarship is inconclusive on whether participation reduces racial bias (Hepburn, Niemi, & Chapman, 2000; Hunter & Brisbin, 2000), but Marullo (1998), a sociologist, found in comparing a service-learning section of his Race and Ethnic Relations class at Georgetown to a non-service-learning section that attitudes supportive of diversity actually did increase slightly. Erickson and O'Connor (2000) use contact theory to lay out some preconditions for lessening prejudice through service-learning, stating that not all projects will have a positive result. Within the service-learning context, several factors will improve chances for reducing prejudice: pursuit of common goals, equal status contact, contact that contradicts stereotypes, long-term contact, and social norms that favor contact.

Forging relationships is critical to meeting these goals based on contact theory. Langseth (2000) writes that "designing service-learning without high-investment, high-trust relationships won't result in a lasting collaboration" (p. 250). Marilynn Boyle-Baise (2002) echoes this call for quality relationships, stating that one needs "equal, reciprocal, and mutually beneficial partnerships" (p. 17) in order to build community. Although racism cannot be quickly undone, friendship is "one of the ways that we can work to end racism and classism" (Green, 2003, p. 294). Designing projects that enable neighbors and students to work together in coequal relationships is an obvious best practice.

THE HAMMOND HEIGHTS PROJECT

Resolving to apply what I knew about service-learning to the problems in Hammond Heights, I urged our chapter of Pi Sigma Alpha, the political science honor society, to apply for a chapter activity grant we could use as seed money for a project. We received thirteen hundred dollars from the national office. The officers of Pi Sigma Alpha served as the organizers of the Week of Work, which would be an intensive work week in Hammond

Heights. The student-learners were students in my American Government classes. The course objectives I sought to meet by bringing these students to Hammond Heights included learning about the duties of citizenship, civic engagement, and racism in America. Many of the students were afraid to come to the neighborhood after hearing for years that it was a dangerous place where they would probably be shot at by drug dealers.

THE WEEK OF WORK

In preparation for the Week of Work, the president of Pi Sigma Alpha, Thomas Pack, and I purchased rakes and lawn bags, and we lined up lawn mowers and ladders we could borrow. The vice president of Pi Sigma Alpha, Renee Waters, had an internship with the local newspaper, so her contribution to the week was to write a front-page article announcing the beginning of the Week of Work. The idea of publishing an article seemed harmless enough, but in a town where change comes slowly, the masthead "Work Begins in Hammond Heights" turned out to be a shot across the bow to Ada's established leaders. I was quoted as saying that Hammond Heights was "underserved," but Renee quoted Thomas saying, "We have a couple of years' worth of work just in Hammond Heights. Proposition One money [a three-quarter cent sales tax levied by the city to pay for infrastructure repair] has been used to effect so much change in the city, but nothing is being done in Hammond Heights even though the people who live there pay the tax, too" (Waters, 2005, p. 1). City of Ada officials took umbrage at Thomas's characterization. The mayor personally called him to refute his statement about Proposition One funds, although no public documents seem to support the mayor.

This service-learning project began not with stakeholders coming to the table to set parameters and share strategies, but instead with just the table itself. We kicked off the Week of Work that first morning sitting at a folding table in an empty lot. A sign on the front read, "Let us work for you!" We had spoken to several other student groups and expected other hands to be appearing any minute. My student had circulated flyers around the neighborhood stating "community volunteers needed."

People walked by wondering if we were having a junk sale. After about an hour, a young woman named Myrtle Walker drove up to us and stopped. She said that she and her husband Mitchell would help us do our work. We explained that we did not have any work to do yet. She said that we should come over to her house and paint it. She drove me over a couple of blocks to their house. We walked through, examining the broken porch, peeling paint, and missing steps. I was grateful to have a project to work on, and they were grateful that we could provide materials so we could improve their house.

As people watched us work, many approached us, and each had a project to tell us about. Many of the neighbors joined in to work side by side with us as we laid flooring and painted. Suddenly we had more work than we could complete in a week. I started to tell people that I would put them on my list. Many were wary of that. "I don't just want to be on some *list*," they grumbled. Thinking back to my conversation with Mr. Weaver, I did not want to be another white person with a notebook making promises that would not be kept.

Other students from the university came on their own to Hammond Heights, either from student groups or from my other classes. I heard many complaints from these students, many of whom were born in Ada but who had never been in Hammond Heights. These students had heard many stories and were worried about "gangsters," drugs, and even getting shot. They thought the black neighbors would not want them there. To tell the truth, I was a little worried about that too. In all, about a hundred university students and a few others from the community participated in about twenty projects. Students and neighbors worked side by side painting and clearing brush.

We started making piles of trash and limbs by the street as we worked because the city had agreed to pick up large trash. By the end of the week, almost every house was hidden behind limbs, discarded appliances, and trash. It was in fact all picked up by the city within two weeks, and as spring grass sprouted and trees greened, Hammond Heights began to feel like a new place. I had been leery of a service-learning project that would just mask problems or paint over houses that were rotting on their foundations. Although we did occasionally paint houses without addressing the underlying structural issues, our mere presence in the neighborhood and our willingness to work created synergy in the neighborhood that helped those issues get attention.

THE CITY RESPONDS

City officials, especially the city council member representing Hammond Heights, seemed irritated about Renee Waters's article in the *Ada Evening News*. They summoned her to city hall for some wrist slapping, and subsequently she produced a new article: "Sweeping Repairs Made: Improvements to Hammond Heights Area Under Way," which appeared on April 4, 2005, a week after the first article. In the article, the city pledged over $1 million for a street and sewer project. A public meeting was held on April 25, 2005, at the National Guard Armory. The day before, another story ran about Hammond Heights, this one in the statewide paper, the *Oklahoman*. The new streets project was again mentioned, and this time the price tag was upped to $1.5 million. Mayor Darryl Nemecek urged people from Hammond Heights to come to the public meeting because "they're a part of this city" and "we want to hear their concerns also" (Coppernoll, 2005, p. 9).

The armory seemed like neutral ground because it is located near Hammond Heights, but the din of seventy angry neighbors from Hammond Heights and their children drowned out a lot of the speeches. Several of my students and I watched as city officials, sitting with their arms crossed, defended their inaction in Hammond Heights over the years. One official stated that Hammond Heights improvement was a priority because we "don't want people coming into Ada to get a bad impression." New streets for Hammond Heights had been on the list of projects since 2003, but no action had been taken by the city engineer. He quite simply said that he was sorry but that he had not pursued getting an engineering firm to design the project. The neighbors began to get agitated and ask some pointed questions. "What's so different about these streets than other streets?" one man yelled. "Why do we have to come to a meeting like this to get our ward observed?" another asked. "We want the same things everyone else wants," another man told the representatives from the city.

Paying attention to the response of the city became a focus of my classes until the end of the semester. One student wrote in a reflective essay, "I was a part of a very big shift in the city officials' attention to the area of Hammond Heights. . . . When all of this came together, I was there in the action fighting for democracy."

Two years have passed since that first Week of Work. The Pi Sigma Alpha chapter has been back at work in Hammond Heights three more times (spring 2006, fall 2006, and spring 2007), completing dozens more projects, including building several porches, patching roofs, painting, clearing lots, and working with children. During the most recent work weeks, one of our greatest allies in Hammond Heights has been Sheila Sturgeon, a woman who has lived in the neighborhood off and on for ten years. She worked with the students tirelessly and directed our efforts to where they would do the most good. At the same time, the City of Ada seems to have exerted a greater presence in Hammond Heights, including more code enforcement and abatement of abandoned houses, although there are still complaints from the neighbors that the police presence is not robust enough.

Since that noisy night at the armory, there have been several public meetings between the Hammond Heights citizens and city officials regarding the infrastructure improvements, now estimated to cost $5 million. In an editorial, the *Ada Evening News* wrote, demonstrating a turn in public opinion, "Previous promises of paved roads failed. . . . Taxpayers have waited for progress and reasonably expect the leadership to provide adequate services to their area." The newspaper concluded, "Serious public service to the parts of our city where basics are lacking is a necessity for our beautiful small city. We applaud city leaders and residents for spreading this vision to Hammond Heights" ("Improvements Get to Heart," 2006). In a town where things change slowly, if at all, this public endorsement for changing the way business is done is quite remarkable.

WHAT HAS BEEN GAINED BY THE WEEK OF WORK SERVICE-LEARNING PROJECT

In the following sections, I identify what has been gained by the five relevant constituencies through the Week of Work service-learning projects. I contacted representatives of each constituency to assess these relationships. In the process of conducting this research, it occurred to me that I, the principal faculty member involved in this project, am the only actor who has interacted substantially with every other actor in the web in the context of this project. Because I must be their voice in this project, I strove to keep their voices intact, using many long quotes from each constituency, thereby letting them speak for themselves.

ECU STUDENTS: CITIZENSHIP TRAINING, TOLERANCE, LEARNING

Over the past three years, approximately two hundred ECU students have worked in Hammond Heights. Some work just an hour, and others make a point to be there as long as possible. Many come to the project begrudgingly. Most of my students are from low-income backgrounds and do not understand why they should be assisting someone else when they or their families are equally in need of assistance. The attitudinal growth my students exhibit during the scope of the project is substantial. For example, the current president of Pi Sigma Alpha, Shiloh Renes, wrote a paper on her experiences in Hammond Heights for a regional political science conference: "I can say that the experience has changed the way I look at things. It affects the way I vote, who I support as a candidate, and how I view people as a whole. Now when I look at a problem in the community I see it as something I can help fix. . . . It is a unique experience and many students leave as better and more active citizens" (Renes, 2006, pp. 6–7). Rappoport (2001) posits that the best way to learn how to become a force in local government is to "practice," a conclusion that Shiloh's experience demonstrates very clearly.

The service-learning literature holds that long-term contact is ideal for engendering affective change in our students (Erickson & O'Connor, 2000; Langseth, 2000), although cognitive change takes place more quickly. Hepburn et al. (2000) found that service-learning projects lasting only one year do not result in increased racial tolerance; two-year programs are more effective. Frankly, I wrestle with these findings. As someone interested in experiential learning, I know that learning is facilitated by enacting the material. Therefore, it is hard for me to believe that it would take two years of interactions to change my students' attitudes about civic engagement, political efficacy, or racial toleration. In a reflection paper, a student wrote, "By merely spending a few hours to help out a community, many students met people that have left a lasting impression." I hate to think that the week would not indeed make such an impression.

To solidify the importance of our Week of Work, we continue talking about it in all my classes. I took photos during the barbeque and the community meeting to show my classes and to discuss what was getting done. I photocopied the articles that appeared in the school paper, the city paper, and the statewide paper to show them what they had been part of. Although the Week of Work lasted only a week each spring, it was an experience that we relived until the end of the semester, so perhaps this extension of the experience helped solidify it in their minds.

Beyond citizenship education, one of my patent goals for the Hammond Heights project is racial prejudice reduction, so we discussed the racial aspects of the project both before and after the Week of Work. As Green (2003) notes, it is often not "nice" to talk about race, and Novek (2000) explains that barriers of race and class are not usually addressed in higher education. People often do service-learning to feel good about themselves, and discussions of race can be uncomfortable, especially in southeastern Oklahoma. However, unless the professor models ways to break through the "culture of niceness," to talk about race herself, students will not know how either. In my case, in preparing my students for going to Hammond Heights, I talked about the history of blacks being strongly encouraged in the 1960s to move from the downtown area of Ada to Hammond Heights to avoid racial integration of the public schools. I also told them anecdotes that shaped my own racial consciousness, for example, what it was like to be the only white person in public spaces in Atlanta or New York. These conversations reduced barriers between me and my students, and they also gave my students permission to discuss their own feelings about race and the possibility of full racial integration.

My mainly lower-income students are aware of their whiteness, but they seem not to know the extent to which they enjoy white privilege because they do not feel privileged in their own lives. Trying to get them to see how different it would be for them to walk around white in southeastern Oklahoma instead of black is an uphill battle, but an important one.

I witnessed several events during the Week of Work that made me uneasy. Some of my students played on stereotypes and pretended to be rappers or gang members. I did not stop them, although I wondered what the neighbors would have thought if they had seen my students. Would they have thought it was harmlessly funny or disrespectful? It showed me that these students needed more "contact that defies stereotypes" (Erickson & O'Connor, 2000) to have their racial attitudes affected.

At another time, I was painting with a member of a student organization who happened to know the family whose house we were painting. "What do you think of a bunch of white people working for you?" he asked, half seriously. The women just laughed it off without answering. This exchange demonstrated that Robbie, the student, did not see his service as "equal-status contact," another condition under which racial prejudice is lessened (Erickson & O'Connor, 2000). He saw himself as some sort of missionary who was working *for* and not *with* the people he was standing shoulder to shoulder with, painting their house.

As a white person, I must struggle against the invisible norms of power that my culture affords me, namely, my "privilege of whiteness as a white woman professor" (Goodburn, 1999, p. 83), as well as assist my students in understanding their own raced positions. Unless racial relationships are recognized as powerful, we can never overcome racial discrimination. Forming meaningful relationships between the serving and the served can also help to this end. When we workers—both neighbors and students—sat down to a meal together, I felt that we were truly equals.

Finally, any discussion of service-learning's impact on students would be incomplete without acknowledging its status as a superior way to teach. Many proponents of experiential pedagogies quote Confucius, who supposedly wrote, "Tell me; and I will forget. Show me; and I will remember. Involve me; and I will understand forever." Service-learning is the ultimate way to involve students in their own acquisition of knowledge.

ECU FACULTY: APPRECIATION OF SERVICE-LEARNING, CONTACTS, AGENCY

What did faculty members gain? The provost of ECU, Duane C. Anderson, writes, "Quite honestly, faculty who did not participate may have learned the most because the Hammond Heights project was the first such service-learning activity at ECU and heightened both knowledge and interest on the part of many faculty to learn more about service-learning." He continues, "Faculty gained a new appreciation for the value of out-of-class service as a vehicle for learning."

Truthfully, I was the only ECU faculty member who was substantially involved in the Week of Work. As I stated above, I was the only person in the web of connections who had contact with every other actor. Through the Week of Work, I met and formed working relationships with many people I may not have met otherwise, especially City of Ada officials and residents of Hammond Heights. In fact, I have been contacted by candidates running for city council who seek to court my vote and support. Through service-learning, I have also had an opportunity to get to know my students better as we worked side by side on projects. This increased familiarity helps them as well as me.

A lesson from this project is to recognize how political service-learning projects can become. I became an agent for substantial political change during the course of this project, which placed me in direct conflict with political actors who preferred the status quo. Tony Robinson (2000) challenges political scientists' undertaking service-learning to push for real change, which only enhances our political roles. According to Robinson, instead of painting "decaying houses," we should be searching for the structural roots of inequality and eradicating them. Socratic gadflies promote social transformation through political advocacy, and healing nurses help perpetuate a "glorified welfare system" (p. 607). Taking such a political stand may be uncomfortable and may not fit with the aims of all service-learning projects, although it seems particularly apt for political science. Math tutors might not care why some children are behind in school, but it makes sense for political scientists to take their engagement in social and political issues to the next step, agitating for systemic change.

In the case of the Week of Work, I started out envisioning the project as service or volunteerism, but the deeper we got involved, the more obvious it became that we could really make a difference. We were not there just to paint some houses, but to become advocates for folks who had been shut out of the political process. Their city councilman did not seem to respond to them or visit their ward, but when we threw light on the lack of attention to Hammond Heights, changes started. The Socratic gadfly role was both one that I could not turn from and one that I felt very uncomfortable in. As a supposedly detached scholar, I was supposed to stick to facts and research, not political advocacy.

Another lesson for professors is to anticipate that service-learning may take over their lives. With the Week of Work, because I did not have any clear boundaries delineated, the project could have taken over my entire life and all my time. I suspect that all professors conducting service-learning projects are asked for more than they can give—a new roof, a reliable babysitter, or a community center. Should I have allowed this reshaping of my role to occur? While being a political agent and responding to seemingly endless need, I risk status at my university and fail to protect my time that I need for other things like research, teaching, and other service. Plater (2004) writes that "civic engagement is an explicit or implicit part of every institution's mission" (p. 7), but that does not mean that service-learning projects will get total support or any support at all. It is possible that professors will find themselves out on a limb, not supported by their universities, especially if the service-learning project is politically contentious.

ECU ADMINISTRATION: BEST PRACTICES, RESPECT, PUBLICITY

Throughout the media firestorm during the first year of the Week of Work, I was never confronted or reined in by my university. In fact, institutional support for service-learning has continued to grow at ECU during the past several years as we have moved first to appoint a director of service-learning, and, more recently, to create a university-wide service-learning requirement for all students. Service-learning has been recognized as a "best practice" of college teaching, and the Week of Work has been held up as an example of what a university can do. The ECU service-learning director, Pat Fountain, reports, "From the Week of Work project the internal gains include proof of the service-learning outcomes indicated in the S-L research, motivation to expand/push service-learning efforts and a critical mass that may well serve to keep service-learning going on the campus."

As most colleges struggle with town-gown relationships, service-learning can serve to improve a university's reputation with a community. Duane C. Anderson, provost of ECU, writes, "The Hammond Heights project was a ground-breaking experience for East Central University students and faculty, and for the Ada Community. . . . Perhaps, most important of all though was that ECU, an institution of higher learning, gained respect from a part of the Ada community that had never before had such a direct and positive impact from the university community." Although folks from Hammond Heights have both attended ECU and worked here, the community has been isolated from the full impact of the university on the community at large. The Week of Work has forged relationships that have even brought neighbors to campus for planning meetings.

Finally, good press cannot be ignored. Fountain writes, "This project has received favorable publicity in several media outlets and has the potential to be highlighted in many more media. If the university had to pay for space and time that have been devoted to this project in the various media it would certainly take a good portion of the communications budget. Advertising like this is hard to buy given the limited financial resources of the university for such purposes."

CITY OF ADA: RELATIONSHIPS, BEAUTIFICATION, NEW FOCUS

After my rocky start with city officials, I was a little worried about whether the City of Ada would be willing to provide information for this project. However, the City of Ada spokesperson Mark Bratcher responded quickly to my e-mail. What did the City of Ada gain? "From the City's perspective," he wrote, "it is encouraging to see East Central University interact more with the Ada community. This project helps grow the relationship between residents and students."

Any city is interested in becoming as inviting as it can be, and if the Week of Work did anything, it beautified Hammond

Heights. Bratcher wrote, "The work done by the volunteers and neighbors has improved the physical appearance of the Hammond Heights neighborhood. . . . The City of Ada provided more of a support role for the private property improvement projects, as City employees are only allowed to work in public areas. However, the City certainly supports the efforts of volunteers and the organizers of this worthwhile project." Indeed, over the years, my students have participated in removing much trash from Hammond Heights and have even worked to dismantle and discard whole houses. They have stacked trash and yard waste along the side of the roads in Hammond Heights, waiting for the city and its large trucks to pick all of it up. We consider the project finally finished for the year when the streets are cleared.

Finally, it is the opinion of the neighbors of Hammond Heights that without the Week of Work, the City of Ada would not be planning to spend $5 million on a street project. Bratcher describes the imminent construction: "This project will involve street rehabilitation and reconstruction, new drives, new sidewalks, as well as new signing and striping. The project also includes drainage and storm sewer improvements to remediate flooding issues in the neighborhood. City of Ada crews will replace water and sewer lines that were identified during the design phase and through public meetings. The Hammond Heights renewal project is massive and will be completed in phases over several years. The project is being made possible by Proposition One, a three-quarter cent sales tax dedicated to infrastructure improvements around Ada." This new focus, provided by the Week of Work and the students of ECU, will allow the City of Ada to meet its obligation to be a good government to all of its citizens.

Citizens of Hammond Heights: Stimulus, Renewal, Community

Vivian Whitney, a woman who has roots in Hammond Heights and is a grants research specialist at ECU, states that one of the things the Week of Work has accomplished is "stimulus for community-based involvement and initiatives." She wrote, "In a neighborhood, long ignored, senior citizens and others now anticipate the arrival of Dr. Pappas and her students to assist with projects that would possibly remain 'un-done.'" Pat Bush, a Hammond Heights resident, expressed a similar sentiment to me: "Thanks to the Week of Work, the city has now started the projects they said they had on their agenda." According to her, the project had created better working relationships between the neighborhood and the city. She even felt prompted to attend a city council meeting for the first time in her life to let the city know that she supported the infrastructure projects.

I am proud of the impact we all have had on the community, but I am aware that the Week of Work participants' involvement in Hammond Heights has not been without controversy. In trying to understand some of the animosity directed at me and the project, I turned to Maxine McFalls, a respected member of the Philemon Baptist Church in Hammond Heights who works with Upward Bound at ECU. She wrote, "I am opposed to communities being treated like third-world countries and that someone has to come in and take care of them. I am sure everyone does not share my opinion. I am for residents maintaining their own neighborhoods and being proud of themselves for doing such. Hammond Heights needs leadership from within which I don't feel has existed, not at least since I have been here (thirty-plus years). There is potential there, but for whatever reason, it has not been realized."

For Hammond Heights to truly thrive, leadership must come from within the community. I am hopeful that the Week of Work may spur some leadership. Sheila Sturgeon, who has worked more closely with me than any other person in Hammond Heights, has been a good spokesperson for the neighborhood. She also has helped me by storing supplies in her shed, including a community lawnmower and other tools donated by Wal-Mart. She too has been distressed by the lack of neighborhood participation. "The community can't come together unless everybody pulls together. I would like for everyone to participate," she told me.

Although Barbara and I—a white neighbor and a white professor—began the project, I hope it will be embraced by the neighborhood. One of my students noted, "A newfound sense of ownership has seemed to arise—residents are doing more on their own and seem to have been inspired by the work of the volunteers." Maybe she is right, and leadership will soon follow.

In a service-learning project, the major stakeholders are typically the students, the faculty, and the people being served. Bringing all three of these groups to the table as equals for the planning and implementation of the service-learning project will result in a decrease of the professor's power with students and probably those being served as well. Students should be involved in the planning and preparation of the service project (Fertman, 1994). The Pi Sigma Alpha students and I spent hours discussing the Week of Work, and I listened to their ideas for what we should do.

Much service-learning seems to engage white middle- or upper-class students to serve with low-income people of color, a situation Novek (2000) calls "being tourists in the land of service-learning" (p. 24). That was the case in Hammond Heights, except that most of my students are lower income. This systematic inequality has caused scholars to ask whether "service-learning is just another way for those who have power and privilege, even if only by education, to name the problems and the solutions for the less privileged" (Rosenberger, 2000, p. 24) or whether service-learning is just an updated version of "noblesse oblige" (Boyle-Baise, 2002, p. 1). Recognizing everyone's power in service-learning relationships can help mitigate accusations that elites are sustaining their own hegemony by preserving unequal relationships.

The achievement of intersubjectivity may feel uncomfortable to those used to being in power. For example, it takes the university out of the expert role (Langseth, 2000) and also puts the served, the serving, and the professor on an equal plane. However, our work in Hammond Heights would not have been a success without trusting relationships. The neighbors had to trust me; they did, but not because I was a professor but because I knew Barbara; indeed, most neighbors just assumed that I was another student and not a professor at all. My students had to trust that they were safe in a neighborhood they had always perceived as dangerous. The neighbors also had to trust my students, sometimes letting them inside their homes to paint or clean.

As one of my students put it in an e-mail, "I do think some of the people there might have felt apprehensive about us helping them, a bunch of whiteys from the higher ed community."

During that first year, we tried to design our actions so that cooperation would be easily achieved between students and neighbors. Barbara hand-delivered flyers to many houses explaining the project and stating "community volunteers needed." Neighbors responded to the flyers both by working with us and mounting parallel projects on their own, and that added to the synergy of the week's work. However, I think we made a mistake when we set up our table with the sign, "We will work for you." There was no hint of partnership in that sign, and neighbors may have concluded that they were not supposed to try to work with us. In reflecting on the experience, one student wrote, "The only thing that bothered me was with some of the people we were helping they didn't help us even though some were able to." The proper trusting context must be developed for beneficial coequal relationships to develop.

CONCLUSION

Many things have changed in Ada since we began our first Week of Work service-learning project. There have been meetings at ECU and in Hammond Heights about the future of the neighborhood, and real synergy and new relationships have been created. Members of the Hammond Heights community have worked with me and others at ECU to plan Black History Month events, and a new community choir has been formed. Perhaps most important, three years after the first Week of Work, mounds of red dirt and road construction signs now dot Hammond Heights: the City of Ada seems to be forging ahead with its street redevelopment project. The project is now estimated to cost over $5 million.

Late last spring, I stopped by Mr. Eddie Weaver's house again. I wanted to talk to him about his impressions of the Week of Work over the past three years, but I was nervous about it. I did not want to find out that he thought the service-learning project had been a mistake or that our work had actually damaged the neighborhood. I talked to him in his kitchen—he was still wearing overalls, I was still carrying my notebook—while his wife, Betty, fried pork chops. I asked him what he thought of the project. "We do appreciate Dr. Pappas coming out with the kids. Painting, working inside of homes, sheetrock, cutting grass. You aren't carpenters. You aren't cement finishers. We the people living out here aren't doing anything. That hurts us. We need more neighborhood involvement," he told me. "The city's more interested now that you all and the young kids started coming out here. Been doing a lot more, they sure have. You all and the college kids caused the city to pay attention. We as a community need to do more."

What was gained by this service-learning project? It enabled ECU to fulfill the highest mission of a university: build understanding among diverse people and inspire people to be and do more. We did not work *with* a government partner, but we worked toward building relationships that will allow us to work together in the future.

Voices: Students Make a Difference

Barbara Seals

When I was in American Government class, my professor was talking about how we should all get involved in community projects and that government leaders could help. This made me laugh because there were never any leaders at Hammond Heights. Getting involved in projects? There were none! How can we get involved in the projects if there aren't any? Even though we might be the neighborhood with the greatest need in the city with rickety houses and trash along the road, we do it for ourselves out here!

I decided to ask my professor, Dr. Christine Pappas, the question, "What can we do to help our communities when we are being ignored by the city?" We were being taught about the need for community action, and as a social work major, I was eager to become involved but wasn't sure how to start the process. Looking back now, it was harder than many thought, but definitely worth the effort.

The Week of Work service-learning project involved taking groups of college students from East Central University to Hammond Heights, a neighborhood lying on the outskirts of Ada, which was comprised of mainly African American families. We were to offer ourselves as free labor to do any improvements within our means for those residing in the community. Community service at its finest! Social work heaven . . . almost.

It was hard to get started, because no one seemed to want our help. In the beginning, they slowed down to look at us, but didn't stop to see exactly what we were offering. Being a resident of the community myself, I received several phone calls that week with curious questions about the "white kids" sitting at the roadside by my home. As the project went on, there weren't enough workers or financial means to meet the needs of those being served.

Many of the properties were in sore need of some attention. Abandoned cars and overgrown yards were only a few of the tasks that the students faced. It wasn't because the families didn't value their properties, but when the town in which you live gives your neighborhood lower property values than most other communities in the town, you sometimes feel a little hopeless. Neighborhoods all over Ada were being revamped and "tidied up" by the City of Ada, but Hammond Heights was never mentioned as being in need of city funds. There seemed to be little interest in economic development for this poverty-stricken neighborhood.

It was invigorating being a part of this effort. Several news articles were written in the local paper, and the City of Ada began to take notice of the things being done by a small group of students. For once, it seemed that they were keen on listening to the needs of a long-neglected group. Some work has been done by the city, but there is much more work that needs to be done. Promises of development funding have been made to the community, which will need to be honored.

The city council approved a use permit for a day care center to be developed in my old home, which stimulates the economy some by employing a few residents of Hammond Heights. It also offers some of the community children a place to hang out, and they are allowed to serve as teen aides for the licensed teachers. The kids want to help, and they are doing exactly what the Week of Work was all about: serving the community.

In the end, the folks of Hammond Heights looked forward to seeing those students coming and the students looked forward to going. They have made a connection by working and laughing together. They have learned through communication that cultural diversity can be embraced, and helping one another is not only the right thing to do, but it is rewarding on many different levels. Lasting friendships and valuable lessons have been achieved by that one little question, so innocently asked.

■ ■ ■

Barbara Seals recently graduated from East Central University and now runs a day care center in Hammond Heights.

References

Boyle-Baise, M. (2002). *Multicultural service learning: Educating teachers in diverse communities.* New York: Teachers College Press.

Coppernoll, C. (2005, April 24). Reclaiming a neighborhood. *Oklahoman,* p. 9A.

Erickson, J. A., & O'Connor, S. E. (2000). *Service-learning: Does it promote or reduce prejudice?* In C. R. O'Grady (Ed.), *Integrating service learning and multicultural education in colleges and universities* (pp. 59–70). Mahwah, NJ: Erlbaum.

Fertman, C. I. (1994). *Service learning for all students.* Bloomington, IN: Phi Delta Kappa Educational Foundation.

Freire, P. (1972). *Pedagogy of the oppressed.* New York: Penguin.

Freire, P. (1995). *Pedagogy of hope: Reliving pedagogy of the oppressed.* New York: Continuum.

Goodburn, A. (1999). *Racing (eracing) white privilege in teacher/research writing about race.* In K. Gilyard (Ed.), *Race, rhetoric, and composition* (pp. 67–88). Portsmouth, NH: Boynton/Cook.

Green, A. E. (2003). Difficult stories: Service-learning, race, class and whiteness. *College Composition and Communication, 55*(2), 276–301.

Hepburn, M. A., Niemi, R. G., & Chapman, C. (2000). Service-learning in college political science: Queries and commentary. *PS: Political Science and Politics, 33*(3), 617–622.

Hunter, S., & Brisbin, R. A., Jr. (2000). The impact of service learning on democratic and civic values. *PS: Political Science and Politics, 33*(3), 623–626.

Improvements get to heart of residents' needs. (2006, March 14). *Ada Evening News,* p. 4.

Langseth, M. (2000). *Maximizing impact, minimizing harm: Why service-learning must more fully integrate multicultural education.* In C. R. O'Grady (Ed.), *Integrating service learning and multicultural education in colleges and universities* (pp. 247–262). Mahwah, NJ: Erlbaum.

Marullo, S. (1998). Bringing home diversity: A service-learning approach to teaching race and ethnic relations. *Teaching Sociology, 26,* 259–275.

Novek, E. (2000, November). *Tourists in the land of service-learning: Helping middle-class students move from curiosity to commitment.* Paper presented at the annual meeting of the National Communication Association, Seattle, WA.

Plater, W. M. (2004). *Civic engagement, service-learning, and intentional leadership.* In M. Langseth & W. M. Plater (Eds.), *Public work and the academy: An academic administrator's guide to civic engagement and service-learning* (pp. 1–22). Bolton, MA: Anker.

Rappoport, A. L. (2001). Service learning and local government. *Service-Learning Network, 8*(3). Retrieved January 12, 2009, from www .crf-usa.org/service-learning-network/8_3-local-government.html.

Renes, S. (2006). *Service learning and political participation.* Paper presented at the annual meeting of the Oklahoma Political Science Association, Oklahoma City.

Robinson, T. (2000). Service learning as justice advocacy: Can political scientists do politics? *PS: Political Science and Politics, 33*(3), 605–612.

Rosenberger, C. (2000). Beyond empathy: Developing critical consciousness through service-learning. In C. R. O'Grady (Ed.), *Integrating service learning and multicultural education in colleges and universities* (pp. 23–42). Mahwah, NJ: Erlbaum.

Waters, R. (2005, March 27). Work begins in Hammond Heights. *Ada Evening News,* p. 1.

CHAPTER NINE

SERVICE-LEARNING IN AN URBAN PUBLIC SCHOOL DISTRICT

The Buffalo Experience

Joseph A. Gardella Jr., Heather M. Maciejewski, Mara B. Huber

At the formal ceremony to install John Simpson as president of the University of Buffalo (UB) in 2004, several former colleagues, friends, and family members made presentations about their experiences with him. One particularly stirring address came from Simpson's father, a businessman who acknowledged how out of place he felt in front of an academic audience. The senior Simpson told some funny stories about his son, but then offered a serious and direct challenge to the UB faculty and community. With a firm tone that set him apart from the other speakers, he lamented the current state of urban public education in

We gratefully acknowledge support for this work from the John R. Oishei Foundation, Buffalo, New York; the National Science Foundation Education and Human Resources for a Presidential Award for Excellence in Science, Mathematics and Engineering Mentoring; and strong support with research grants from the Chemistry Division, Analytical and Surface Chemistry program, the Vice President for Public Service and Urban Affairs at SUNY Buffalo, the William and Flora Hewlett Foundation, in support of the work reported in this chapter.

the United States and asked what a public university like UB would do to address this problem. His appeal was riveting, and his challenge reverberated among the audience, especially with his son.

From the outset, President Simpson's administration has been marked by top-level strategic planning focused on marshaling resources from all corners of the institution to improve public education in the Buffalo area. He viewed UB's urban location as giving the institution both an opportunity and a responsibility to address the many challenges facing public education, especially in the city's poor neighborhoods. He enlisted the help of colleges, schools, departments, and programs at UB to partner with the Buffalo Public School system (BPS) to start a comprehensive set of initiatives to help.

In December 2006, the UB-wide education initiative was announced, establishing a formal partnership between UB and BPS. The goal of the UB/BPS pre-K–16 partnership is to increase the percentage of BPS graduates who are ready to go to college and the percentage who actually enroll. A key goal of the partnership is to place UB students and faculty directly into urban schools in sustained service-learning and clinical partnerships. Mentoring of teachers and students and teacher professional development are central strategies to improve the performance of the public school students.

This chapter reviews the development and outcomes of the partnership, with a special emphasis on the relationships of the various participating individuals and groups. UB programs that focus on science, biomedicine, and engineering are used as case studies to illustrate the nature of the partnership.

BACKGROUND

Located in western New York, Buffalo is the state's second largest city. Currently there are 117 primary and secondary schools in Buffalo, serving approximately forty-eight thousand students. The Buffalo Public School system operates 73 schools (60 public and 13 charter schools), and the other 44 schools are private. The public schools serve an economically, culturally, and ethnically diverse population of approximately thirty-eight thousand students. According to recent information from the district, students identified their ethnic backgrounds as follows: 58 percent African American/black, 26 percent Caucasian, 13 percent Hispanic, 1.5 percent American Indian, and 1.5 percent Asian. Approximately fifty languages are spoken in the district, in part due to the U.S. Immigration and Naturalization Service efforts to resettle immigrant populations in the city. Data indicate that a large number of the district's students are living in poverty, with 77 percent of the student body eligible to receive free or reduced-price lunch. In addition, more than 7 percent of the district's students are identified as being Limited English Proficient, and 21 percent are classified as disabled by the Committee on Special Education.

Clearly BPS presents a huge and challenging opportunity for UB. President Simpson's father certainly issued his appeal in the appropriate city: the Buffalo schools could use help, and UB has the resources to help. Founded in 1846, UB is a research-intensive public university, and it is the largest and most comprehensive campus in the State University of New York system. The university offers more than three hundred undergraduate, graduate, and professional programs, all linked to a mission of research, education, and public service. More than twenty-six thousand students pursue their academic interests at UB each year. With its size and expertise, UB is an ideal institution to try to make a difference in the city's troubled public schools.

Under President Simpson's direction, UB has undertaken an intensive self-evaluation and review of its mission, aspirations, and goals, culminating in the report *UB 2020: A Plan for the Future*. Nine academic strategic strengths were identified as focus areas. One, entitled "civic engagement and public policy," includes efforts in K–16 education and outreach. To support the K–16 initiative at the top level, President Simpson's chief of staff convened a working group of faculty and staff to develop an institution-wide support program for K–16 education and outreach. The white paper that came out of this group states, "Most significantly positioned to participate meaningfully are the various departments within the College of Arts and Sciences (CAS) that address the core curriculum of the elementary and middle school" (Olsen, Granfield, & Gardella, 2007).

Elements of the Partnership

Building an effective partnership to improve Buffalo schools has been a complicated challenge. Several government partners are involved, along with many units of the university.

Government Partners: Roles and Responsibilities

The UB/BPS partnership involves all levels of the school district, from students and teachers, to principals and district administrators. Also involved are the City of Buffalo and New York State because of their funding and oversight responsibilities. Collaboration with both has been central to the development of the partnership. Finally, federal agencies, which provide funding for some partnership programs, have played a role in the partnerships too. As Table 9.1 details, each partnering organization has brought varied resources to bear on the task.

TABLE 9.1 Leadership and Participants in the UB/BPS Partnership

University Faculty	Students	Government Partners
Office of the President, vice president for external affairs, provost	Undergraduate: Honors students, science, engineering, humanities	School district: Buffalo Public Schools
Science, engineering, biomedical sciences	Biomedical sciences: Medicine, public health	State: Education Department
Humanities, education	Professional schools: Social work, law, education	Federal: U.S. Department of Education, National Science Foundation
Social work, law, clinicians, medical professionals		

The New York State Board of Regents and the New York State Education Department (SED) are also important to the success of the partnership. The regents and SED oversee all aspects of education in New York State, from K–12 education, higher education, and vocational education, to support programs for the disabled and for state libraries. The regents approve all education policy, interpret state and federal law, and recommend education funding levels annually to the governor and legislature. SED has influence over the structure of any collaboration between higher education and K–12 education. For an urban district, education performance is the measure of success. SED provides a series of evaluations and accountability measures for all schools in New York, with special focus on urban districts such as BPS.

State school funding is often tied to educational performance. First and foremost, in the current environment of the federal requirements of the No Child Left Behind Act, SED insists on a variety of student, school, and district assessments (American Association for the Advancement of Science, 1993; Bybee & Kennedy, 2005). These assessments are the basis of many SED actions at the school and district level, following the general philosophies of No Child Left Behind. For example, BPS, as of March 2007, has sixteen of seventy-three district schools categorized as Schools Under Registration Review. According to SED,

> the Registration Review Process is the primary method by
> which the State Board of Regents holds schools accountable
> for educational performance. Registration Review is intended
> to help school districts correct situations that impede quality
> education. Through Registration Review, low-performing schools
> are identified, and schools and districts are assisted to devise
> and implement strategies designed to produce measurable
> improvements in the academic performance of their students.

The Schools Under Registration Review designation is based on SED analysis of school "report cards," summarizing test results in English language arts, science, and mathematics at the fourth- and eighth-grade levels.

An important aspect of the UB/BPS collaboration has been the leadership of the chancellor of the board of regents, Robert

Bennett. Bennett was the former head of United Way of Buffalo and Erie County, and he has had a long relationship with UB, serving as an adjunct faculty member in the School of Social Work. This has meant that UB can communicate regularly and directly with the highest-ranking regent. Bennett has had an interest in urban districts, articulating significant challenges to these districts and setting expectations for improvements in learning. He has demanded better collaboration between social service agencies and urban districts. He has also been a tireless advocate of early childhood literacy and has set a goal to have all children reading at grade level by third grade.

Finally, federal funding has been critical to the partnership. The lead author (Joseph Gardella) was recognized with a 2005 Presidential Award for Excellence in Mentoring in Science, Engineering and Mathematics, administered by the Division of Human Resources at the National Science Foundation (NSF). The network of national winners of this award has given advice on the structure and operations of the UB/BPS partnership. For K–12 science education, NSF provides significant nationally peer-reviewed funding for universities and colleges to pursue projects in science, technology, engineering, and mathematics (STEM) fields. NSF also provides funding directly to school districts, science museums, and the media for public education activities in these fields. BPS has had a strong track record of NSF-funded activities for efforts to strengthen urban science education, with two Urban Systemic Initiatives through the Buffalo Museum of Science: Teacher Education at the Museum (TEAM and TEAM 2000).

Increased attention to the quality and impact of education and outreach activities is also central for all research grants in STEM fields. NSF has promulgated two review criteria for all grants: scientific merit and broader impacts. The latter has been a long-standing goal of large, multidisciplinary center grants in science and engineering, and it makes up a significant portion of educational funding from the NSF. This and other funding gives NSF national peer review a strong influence on content, pedagogy, and practice in all aspects of funded university efforts. Finally, there are substantial U.S. Department of Education funds for urban education. For example, Title 1 funding for improving performance in the lowest-performing schools represents a significant portion of the federal part of BPS's budget.

All of these initiatives and funding sources have separate and overlapping assessment requirements, and familiarity with the goals and responsibilities of the efforts is necessary for implementing successful service-learning in urban education.

UNIVERSITY PARTICIPANTS

Table 9.1 shows that UB faculty and students from a variety of disciplines participate in the UB/BPS partnership. An important aspect of this collaboration is the linking of undergraduate, graduate, and professional school students and faculty in service-learning activities. UB's professional schools, especially the Graduate School of Education and the Schools of Law and Social Work, have a long history of significant professional development and clinical activities. The School of Law has maintained the Special Education Law Clinic for nearly thirty years, assisting parents and staff in school districts across the region. The School of Law also provides legal assistance for BPS, with lawyers in education law supplementing the district's mandated support from the city's corporation counsel. Corporation counsel has not had lawyers specializing in education law, so the additional help gives the district access to expert advice without hiring outside law firms. The School of Social Work has had externally funded programs supporting students in BPS, with one particular focus being special support to lessen school violence. The Graduate School of Education at UB has strength in leadership training and a strong track record in teacher professional development in science and mathematics education. The former effort has been historically limited by the small number of faculty (only one or two), but it has a significant presence in collaboration with science and engineering faculty at UB.

Undergraduate service-learning efforts have been scattered across the institution, with no central office for coordination. External funding from the Hewlett Foundation from 2000 to 2004 (www.clir.buffalo.edu), directed by Gardella, financed a variety of programs to incorporate service-learning in the social sciences and humanities. A growing focus on service-learning in the honors program has allowed expanded efforts using freshman seminar courses and the honors colloquium as vehicles for recruiting highly talented undergraduates to the efforts. As noted in Table 9.1, students from a variety of undergraduate disciplines and majors have participated, with special emphasis on science and engineering students.

Finally, NSF leadership in identifying graduate K–12 science and engineering fellowships has brought STEM Ph.D. students into K–12 education and outreach efforts, including working within teacher professional development.

Putting in place a structure to take advantage of undergraduate service-learning activities with graduate and professional students, along with building sustained and districtwide initiatives, requires university leadership working with government partners, so that individual faculty and their students can spend time on the content and delivery of the projects.

UB/BPS INTERDISCIPLINARY SCIENCE AND ENGINEERING PARTNERSHIP

This section focuses on the program in the UB/BPS partnership that has received a great deal of the attention: the Interdisciplinary Science and Engineering Partnership. At its core, the partnership has four interrelated goals.

- *Teacher professional development* through collaboration between faculty and the STEM graduate fellows and teachers, using established interdisciplinary science and engineering research to develop curriculum materials and hands-on science and after-school support
- *Extended classroom and after-school staffing* coordinated and led by STEM graduate students with participation of other UB graduate and undergraduate students in service-learning groups to implement new curricula and hands-on science experiences
- *Developing mentoring relationships with students and parents* by faculty, STEM graduate students, and undergraduates
- *Faculty involvement in the classroom and in school exchanges and field trips* to facilities at UB and throughout the region

The UB/BPS program emphasizes the link between UB's interdisciplinary research strengths and BPS's teacher professional development. The major effort starts at the middle school level (grades 6 to 8) and works to move successes down to elementary school science and up to high school science. Research in science and engineering is increasingly focused on interdisciplinary approaches (Metzger & Zare, 1999; Rhoten & Parker, 2004) at a time when increased emphasis in state and national K–12 science curriculum standards is placed on interactions among science, technology, and society (New York State Education Department, 1996; National Research Council, 1996, 2000). Reform of science and technology curricula and pedagogy aligned with national and state learning standards in middle school offers great potential for three reasons. First, it has been well documented that while American elementary school students rank almost at the top internationally, American middle school students score at about the international average and high school students scored close to the bottom (Beaton et al., 1997a, 1997b; Martin et al., 2001). The declining trend in middle school students' science achievement is a national concern needing immediate attention. Second, middle school science curricula are based on integrated science and technology, and thus already take interdisciplinary approaches. Third, it is widely known that the loss of interest in science and technology occurs during the middle school years, particularly for girls (Kahle & Lakes, 1983; Osborne, Simon, & Collins, 2003). The vision to connect interdisciplinary science and engineering research with teacher professional development and curricular reform, while increasing the excitement and participation in science focused at the middle school level, is a means to address these challenges.

The success of the program in a majority-minority urban district such as Buffalo can also contribute to efforts to increase diversity in the STEM workforce, a pervasive and long-standing concern. There is a clear consensus that the participation of under-represented groups in STEM disciplines needs to be increased. However, despite numerous high-profile programs to address this concern, little progress has been made. Given the changing demographics in the nation's population, failure to increase STEM participation in workforce disciplines could result in a shortage of qualified workers at all levels of business and industry (Business Roundtable, 2006; Commission on the Advancement of Women and Minorities in Science, Engineering, and Technology Development, 2000; Council on Competitiveness, 2004; Lemonick, 2006; National Academy of Sciences, 2006; National Science Board, 2003, 2005; National Science and Technology Council, 2004; Owens, 2006; President's Council of Advisors on Science and Technology, 2004; Research and Policy Committee, 2003).

Students in the BPS are struggling to meet state learning standards. The most recent New York State school report card (April 2006) identifies BPS as a District in Need of Improvement for English Language Arts. In an effort to address academic difficulties, the district is implementing a three-year academic achievement plan that focuses on early literacy. In the sciences, approximately three thousand BPS students are assessed each year on state and district-level science curricula in grades 4 to 8, and approximately twenty-five hundred students are tested using the New York Living Environment and PS/Earth Science Regents Science Examinations. Typical of many urban public schools, recruitment and retention of qualified science and mathematics teachers is difficult. Twenty-three percent of BPS middle and high school science instructors are teaching at least one science class out of their science certification area. Furthermore, since the terrorist attacks of September 11, 2001, BPS has experienced declining state funding, with significant teacher layoffs from 2002 to 2004. These two critical issues, student performance and teacher professional development, are central to the activities of the partnership.

One strategy for addressing the student performance problem is supporting and rewarding mentoring techniques throughout the K–20 pipeline (Presidential Award for Excellence in Science, Mathematics, and Engineering Mentoring Working Group, 2006). Mentoring is a powerful activity that is especially effective in helping individuals reach their full potential in the sciences. Many successful engineers, researchers, and technical professionals point to the involvement of one mentor who made all the difference in encouraging them to persevere in their studies.

A comprehensive approach to mentoring is central to the vision of the UB/BPS partnership. The project not only promotes mentoring of middle and high school teachers and students, it also creates Professional Learning Communities (PLCs) (DuFour & Eaker, 1998; Fullan, 2001) that foster mentoring among all UB/ BPS partners (Presidential Award for Excellence in Science, Mathematics, and Engineering Mentoring Working Group, 2006). Thus, service-learning efforts at the graduate and undergraduate levels complement teacher professional development using interdisciplinary research efforts with faculty. Sustaining the long-term relationships is the key to successful mentoring at all levels, from students, to teachers, to parents.

Service-learning partnerships between universities and school districts in STEM fields are common (Ritter-Smith & Saltmarsh, 1998). Three examples serve to illustrate aspects of the program today. Cornell University, as part of a federal NSF Materials Science and Engineering Center (MRSEC) grant, has engaged STEM graduate students in service-learning outreach education to a rural area but not an urban area (deKoven & Trumbull, 2002). Similar to the UB/BPS effort, Auburn University faculty in education, collaborating with 4H and extension specialists, developed broad science participation programs focused on middle school science, but the program was limited to bringing students to campus for summer programs (Eick, Ewald, Kling, & Shaw, 2005). Faculty and students at the University of California at Davis collaborated in an extensive science-based service-learning program linking undergraduates in a variety of disciplines, but their interest was on the impact of the experience on the careers of the college students (Gutstein, Smith, & Manahan, 2006). All of these efforts have lessons for the Buffalo program, but none deals directly with the issue of helping urban public school students in in-class and out-of-class activities.

SERVICE-LEARNING STRATEGIES

The success of the UP/BPS Interdisciplinary Science and Engineering Partnership is due to recruiting motivated faculty and students, teaming them in programs with public school teachers, and regularly assessing outcomes. This section describes these processes for the partnership.

Recruitment of Students and Faculty

Building a service-learning program requires a focus area, content and curriculum, and college students willing to see that they will benefit from participating in the service activity. For UB students, the UB/BPS Interdisciplinary Science and Engineering Partnership offers an opportunity to serve high-need public school students. The UB participants in the partnership are recruited from both science and engineering undergraduate majors and from honors program students interested in education as a career. Science and engineering graduate students, in a manner similar to NSF's graduate teaching fellows in the K–12 education program (National Science Foundation, 2007), are recruited to help develop interdisciplinary classroom curriculum content, contribute directly in public school teacher professional development, and provide advising in regular classroom work. Science education and social science students often work in teams to provide expertise in pedagogy, assessment, and evaluation. A key aspect of the program is intensive and broad commitment from faculty. In each interdisciplinary science project, faculty participate in the K–12 education and outreach. This commitment can take many forms, from designing hands-on science projects to hosting demonstrations and field trips, to providing teacher professional development and in-class support.

Each semester, several small honors courses built around faculty interests offer service-learning opportunities in the UB/BPS partnership programs. These courses support service-learning in class staffing of the projects or helping with hands-on science experiment development. The majors of these students range from science and engineering to human services and health-related professions. Students write weekly reflection papers and have weekly reviews about their service-learning work. A final poster project is required.

Development of Teams Inside and Outside the Classroom

Teams of students and faculty help public school teachers. Generally a senior graduate fellow coordinates the school-based team. Duties include scheduling the service-learning undergraduate students and helping plan and administer specific in-class and out-of-class tasks, such as homework help and after-school programs. Efforts are made to recruit undergraduate students early in their careers so that they can give a multiyear commitment to the program. Many students come to see the service-learning commitment as a long-term collaboration that enriches their academic studies.

ASSESSMENT STRATEGIES

Both summative and formative analyses are currently underway. The formative evaluation is led by a science education faculty member at UB who is an expert in science assessment with a strong publication record. He is assisted by a doctoral student in science education. The student participates as an observer in all teacher activities during the summer research and in the teachers' classrooms. The student also interviews participating teachers regularly about their experiences in the program. The qualitative and quantitative data gathered through the student's observations, interviews, and surveys, are combined with ongoing summative quantitative teacher and student assessment data.

SCHOOL SELECTION AND PARENTAL INVOLVEMENT

Several district efforts influenced planning for the program. For example, BPS had begun a four-phase $1 billion school reconstruction program that allowed some input on how best to use the laboratory facilities in the refurbished schools. BPS was also developing magnet schools during this time. Finally, a number of smaller, limited-enrollment middle and high schools are now being considered that might influence the program in the future. Table 9.2 shows the six schools chosen for programs so far. These schools were all refitted with new laboratory facilities, except for Southside. The schools also represent a geographical distribution across the city, from districts in north, south, east, west, and central Buffalo.

Historically, parental support has been difficult to achieve in high-need urban districts like Buffalo. The UB/BPS project made substantial efforts to craft specific approaches to involve parents in the program and engage them in program leadership and design. Using Epstein's six levels of parent involvement as

TABLE 9.2 INITIAL FOCUS SCHOOLS IN UB/BPS PARTNERSHIP WITH DEMOGRAPHIC INFORMATION

School Name (Grades)	Enrollment	Percentage Poverty[a]/ Percentage Low Income[b]	Percentage African American	Percentage Hispanic	Percentage Native American	Percentage Special Education
Native American Magnet School 19 (K–8)	625	83/92	37	18	30	17
Seneca Math Science High School	145	NA	NA	NA	NA	NA
Drew Science Magnet School 59 (K–8)	631	71/85	75	2	1	36
Harriet Tubman School 31 (K–8)	515	85/93	94	2	0	34
North Park Academy School 66 (K–8)	355	68/80	80	5	1	25
Southside Elementary School	1200	73/90	23	7	1	22

[a]Defined by percentage receiving federally sponsored free or reduced-cost breakfast and lunch.
[b]Defined by federal family income levels.

a guide, the program leadership personnel meet regularly with parent groups at each school to try to involve them at all levels (Epstein, 1986, 1987, 2001, 2007; Epstein & Sanders, 2006). BPS has instituted the District Parent Coordinating Council, which meets monthly with representatives of each school's parent organization elected to represent the entire district. The council also provides leadership training during an annual retreat, setting goals for the district's efforts to involve parents.

Case Studies

This section describes two of the most interesting service-learning initiatives with BPS: the Native American Magnet School science project and the Seneca Math/Science Technology School project. Although quite different in many ways, both teamed UB faculty and students from the sciences and engineering with BPS teachers to deliver high-quality programs to middle and high school students.

School 19: The Native American Magnet School (K–8)

In 2004, UB/BPS initiated a pilot project in middle school science and interdisciplinary research with the Native American Magnet School in Buffalo, a school reconstructed in Phase I with a new science laboratory. One of the coauthors of this chapter, Heather Maciejewski, is the seventh- and eighth-grade science teacher in the school. She was chosen to participate in the program because of her experience with science education and her interest in parent involvement (the subject of her master's thesis). The demographics of the school offered a unique opportunity. As shown in Table 9.2, the school serves 625 students, with more than 80 percent living in poverty and over 200 being Native Americans. During the summer of 2005, Maciejewski began interdisciplinary research participation with the undergraduate biomedical materials and tissue engineering research program (www.ribse.buffalo.edu) and worked with several research teams pursuing tissue engineering and materials science.

Maciejewski participated in several experiments with UB teams dealing with membrane synthesis, controlled drug release, proteomics, imaging science, and stem cell engineering. She then completed four new curricular modules that were based on the interdisciplinary research approaches aligned with New York State learning standards (www.nylearns.org). In the fall of 2005 the chapter coauthors recruited twelve students to help implement the new curricula. The undergraduate students, along with the supervision of graduate students, helped staff the seventh- and eight-grade classes and work with hands-on components, demonstrations, and problem sessions. Faculty members from chemistry, physics, anatomy, and electrical engineering gave visiting lectures and participated in field trips for small groups of students. For example, after an extensive section on light microscopy, a faculty member accompanied a small group of students to the imaging laboratories in the UB Medical School to see the optical, confocal, fluorescence, and electron microscopy facilities.

As a follow-up to these class activities, a science after-school program was started during spring 2006. Fifty-five students (nearly 50 percent of the seventh- and eighth- grade classes) signed up for the fully voluntary program. The program has become the model for many of the curricular development programs and has continued for three semesters.

Finally, the UB/BPS team instituted a parent participation project focused on after-school events. The first event attracted ten parents who joined in a program that was focused on chemical separations and synthesis of hydrogel polymers (Slime). The use of the Slime experiment serves as a precursor to a unit being taught now, where various types of plants are being grown in different densities of slime/hydroponic materials to examine how the controlling nutrients influence growth. This week-long unit combines hands-on experiments developed out of the tissue engineering research.

In the fall of 2006, the program staffing was expanded using twenty honors students from a service-learning course taught by two of the authors, Gardella and Maciejewski. The service-learning students provided help in the classroom activities and the development of new after-school components. Several field trips to university laboratories and facilities were coordinated with curricular efforts. For example, the seventh- and eighth-grade students in the after-school program had worked on engineering protective packaging for an uncooked egg to see if it would remain unbroken after being dropped for a specified height. These students were later challenged to design stable structures, which were tested using the university's structural engineering facilities in the Midwest Center for Earthquake Engineering Research. This gave students the opportunity to use state-of-the-art facilities for their tests. Additional university field trip activities included relating light absorption to solar energy cells and the construction of cells for testing. Later, a larger parent event was held and attracted wide participation. The strategy was to have the students teach their parents. A series of ten science stations with hands-on experiments were developed, and the students were encouraged to show their parents what was fun and exciting about the experiments.

Based on these experiences, the current effort at School 19 is to broaden the involvement by extending the program to include two new science teachers and create a professional learning community program with fourth- and sixth-grade teachers. Furthermore, Maciejewski has developed an Advanced Placement course for the school, focusing on environmental and bioscience components. In addition, the after-school program has been formalized as a year-round part of the elementary and middle school.

SENECA MATH/SCIENCE TECHNOLOGY SCHOOL

The Seneca Math/Science Technology School opened in September 2006 with seventy-five students each in sixth and ninth grades. It will add two grades a year and eventually serve students in grades 6 through 12. The school is part of the College Board Schools program, which will create eighteen new, small, secondary schools in New York to serve low-income and minority students. The mission of College Board Schools is to give students, particularly those in urban environments, access to college and prepare them for success in college. The values of College Board Schools are clear and high expectations and an all-encompassing commitment to learning; meaningful relationships; challenging and engaging teaching, learning practices, and programs; and instructional and collaborative leadership. The Buffalo Seneca Math/Science Technology School is the first in the state to focus on science and technology, and it is the first College Board School in Buffalo. Learning communities are central to the College Board model. The Buffalo Seneca School focuses on creating innovation in middle school science and extending this to high school programs.

The program began in the fall 2006 with the recruitment of two teachers at the sixth- and ninth-grade levels, and the recruitment of a second set of service-learning students, led by graduate students in science. Late in the fall, fifteen engineering undergraduates joined in the efforts. Initial efforts were focused on in-class support for ninth-grade students, an after-school science program in the school that included extended hours (Saturdays were chosen), and plans for teacher professional development with research in the summer. The extended hours on Saturdays gave faculty from UB opportunities to develop new hands-on activities for large groups. As an example, solar cells based on advanced chemical absorption and DNA extraction and analysis with gel electrophoresis were developed with extensive faculty involvement, combining with hands-on experimental work with lecture and small group work. Alignment with ongoing curricular components was accomplished with weekly consultations with the teachers.

Summer 2007 saw expanded teacher professional development focused on topics in environmental science and engineering, including geographical information analysis, nanomaterials science, and engineering and bioinformatics, all interdisciplinary research and education strengths identified under the *UB 2020* report. The sixth- and ninth-grade science teacher will focus on nanomaterials chemistry in her two-year chemistry/Advanced Placement chemistry sequence.

RESULTS

Both case studies include extensive science and engineering faculty and student involvement in the classroom and in field trips. The sustained year-long collaborations have allowed the alignment of new curricular materials with state standards and learning goals. Teacher professional development is planned to take advantage of interdisciplinary research strengths. Extensive collaboration of service-learning students at the graduate and undergraduate levels is underway. Sustained year-long service-learning students develop mentoring relationships by working with public school students in a variety of roles, from tutoring and homework help, to regular staffing in the classroom, to after-school programs.

CONCLUSION

The development of service-learning-based partnerships between the UB and BPS for K–16 education and outreach involves detailed interactions with partners at many levels, from the federal and state government to students. A key lesson from the ongoing UB/BPS partnership is to educate university participants in the structure and operations of state education oversight of public education, especially as it relates to urban public school districts. Understanding the roles and responsibilities of state education regulators is critical to aligning novel efforts in university service-learning outreach with state and federal education and learning standards. Familiarity of faculty with state education structures and responsibilities is necessary for them to design successful service-learning opportunities.

Local government interactions center on the school district. In the UB/BPS partnership, it was critical that the BU president had a strong relationship with the BPS superintendent. This helped convince the faculty and students that the program is worthy and an appropriate institutional priority. The program also benefited from the superintendent's understanding of the central role of BU in regional science and engineering. At the school level, a key lesson is that it is important to choose partner schools with innovative and receptive teachers.

In short, partnering to build better public schools through service-learning requires an understanding of all of the players in public education, and it requires the cooperation of the public schools, from the top administrators to the classroom teachers. And it also helps to have a university president strongly committed to improving public schools.

Voices: The School Teacher

Stephanie Finn

"Hello, my name is Dave, and I am a faculty member in the University of Buffalo Chemistry Department. My service-learning students and I have been assigned to work with you and your students this year." This is the e-mail that greeted me at the beginning of the 2007 school year. I have to admit that I was concerned. As a middle school science teacher, I wondered whether a college professor would be able to relate to my students. How would he handle the wide range of student abilities and behaviors in a middle school classroom from the unmotivated "I hate science" student to the student always ready with the correct answer? Would he be able to adjust to teaching adolescents? The middle school atmosphere is so very different from that of a college. I was also anxious about how we would work together. What would he think about my curriculum? Would we see eye-to-eye on teaching matters?

My concerns and anxieties passed quickly after working with Dave and his service-learning students for a few weeks. We worked well together, and my students benefited tremendously from having their help. Dave and his students were excited about helping me, and they took the time to listen to me about the challenges of teaching science to middle school students. I benefited, too, by learning new ways to interest my students in science. Together Dave and I set goals at the beginning of the school year, including establishing two after-school science clubs, increasing science participation by students, introducing students to a variety of lab experience and concepts, and getting students thinking about science and its application to daily life. We did this through the after-school clubs, one of which focused on weather while the other planned our Science Olympiad. Students in both clubs became active participants in the clubs and in class, with weather club students especially becoming class leaders

One of the keys to the success of the service-learning project was that Dave and I communicated well. From the beginning, we agreed to speak up if we had concerns and to listen to each other's ideas. This carried over to his students. They were very open to our suggestions, and they too had many good ideas. With a foundation of good communication, it was easy to set goals and deliver quality education to my students.

There was good communication between the service-learning students and my students. It was immediately obvious that my middle school students looked up to the college students and paid attention to what they had to say. My students were used to having older adults as teachers, so it was a positive change to have college students as teachers. The college students served as excellent role models, showing my students that they could be "cool" and still be interested in learning. I was consistently impressed by the way Dave's students were able to joke around with my students but keep them focused on their lessons. At the end of the semester, his students told me how impressed they were in the abilities and eagerness to learn of my students, and I told them how impressed I was with their creativity and commitment to teach. I would welcome college students back into my classroom anytime.

■ ■ ■

Stephanie Finn teaches science to middle school students at the Seneca Math Science and Technology Preparatory School in Buffalo, New York.

References

American Association for the Advancement of Science. (1993). *Benchmarks for science literacy*. New York: Oxford University Press.

Beaton, A., Martin, M. O., Mullis, I., Gonzalez, P., Smith, T. A., & Kelly, D. L. (1997a). *Science achievement in the final year of secondary school: IEA's Third International Mathematics and Science Study*. Chestnut Hill, MA: TIMSS International Center.

Beaton, A., Martin, M. O., Mullis, I., Gonzalez, P., Smith, T. A., & Kelly, D. L. (1997b). *Science achievement in the middle school years: IEA's Third International Mathematics and Science Study.* Chestnut Hill, MA: TIMSS International Center.

Business Roundtable. (2006). *U.S. innovation and competitiveness: Addressing the talent gap.* Retrieved January 8, 2009, from www.tap2015 .com/resource/research_presentation.pdf.

Bybee, R. W., & Kennedy, D. (2005). Math and science achievement. *Science, 307*(5709), 481.

Commission on the Advancement of Women and Minorities in Science, Engineering and Technology Development. (2000). *Land of plenty: Diversity as America's competitive edge in science, engineering and technology.* Arlington, VA: National Science Foundation.

Council on Competitiveness. (2004). *Innovate America: Thriving in a world of challenge and change.* Retrieved January 12, 2009, from www .innovateamerica.org/files/InnovateAmerica_EXEC percent20 SUM_WITH percent20RECS.pdf.

deKoven, A., & Trumbull, D. J. (2002). Science graduate students doing science outreach: Participation effects and perceived barriers to participation. *Electronic Journal of Science Education, 7,* 88–110.

DuFour, R., & Eaker, R. (1998). *Professional learning communities at work: Best practices for enhancing student achievement.* Alexandria, VA: Association for Supervision and Curriculum Development.

Eick, C., Ewald, M. J., Kling, E., & Shaw, C. (2005). Reaching out to outreach. *Science Scope, 28*(7), 3–7.

Epstein, J. L. (1986). Parents' reactions to teacher practices of parent involvement. *Elementary School Journal, 86*(3), 277–294.

Epstein, J. L. (1987). Toward a theory of family-school connections: Teacher practices and parent involvement. *Education and Urban Society, 19*(2), 119–136.

Epstein, J. L. (2001). *School, family, and community partnerships: Preparing educators and improving schools.* Boulder, CO: Westview Press.

Epstein, J. L. (2007). Research meets policy and practice: How are school districts addressing NCLB requirements for parental involvement? In A. R. Sadovnik, J. A. O'Day, G. W. Bohrnstedt, & K. M. Borman (Eds.), *No Child Left Behind and the reduction of the achievement gap: Sociological perspectives on federal educational policy* (pp. 267–279). New York: Routledge.

Epstein, J. L., & Sanders, M. G. (2006). Prospects for change: Preparing educators for school, family, and community partnerships. *Peabody Journal of Education, 81*(2), 81–120.

Fullan, M. (2001). *The new meaning of educational change.* New York: Teachers College Press.

Gutstein, J., Smith, M., & Manahan, D. (2006). A service-learning model for science education outreach. *Journal of College Science Teaching, 36*(1), 22–26.

Kahle, J. B., & Lakes, M. K. (1983). The myth of equality in science classrooms. *Journal of Research in Science Teaching, 20*(2), 131–140.

Lemonick, M. (2006, February 13). Are we losing our edge? *Time,* 22–33.

Martin, M., Mullis, I., Gonzalez, E., O'Connor, K., Charostowsky, S., & Gregory, K. (2001). *Science benchmarking report: TIMSS, 1999—8th grade.* Chestnut Hill, MA: TIMSS International Center.

Metzger, N., & Zare, R. N. (1999). Interdisciplinary research: From belief to reality. *Science, 283*(5402), 642–643.

National Academy of Sciences. (2006). *Rising above the gathering storm: Energizing and employing America for a brighter economic future.* Washington, DC: National Academies Press.

National Research Council. (1996). *National Science Education Standards.* Washington, DC: National Academies Press.

National Research Council. (2000). *Inquiry and the National Science Education Standards.* Washington, DC: National Academies Press.

National Science Board. (2003). *The science and engineering workforce: Realizing America's potential.* Retrieved January 12, 2009, from www.nsf .gov/nsb/documents/2003/nsb0369/nsb0369.pdf.

National Science Board. (2005). *2020 vision.* Washington, DC: National Science Foundation.

National Science Foundation. (2007). *Graduate teaching fellows in K–12 education (GK–12).* Retrieved January 12, 2009, from www.nsf.gov/ pubs/2007/nsf07555/nsf07555.htm.

National Science and Technology Council. (2004). *Science for the 21st century.* Washington, DC: Author.

New York State Education Department. (1996). *Learning standards for mathematics, science, and technology.* Albany: State University of New York.

Olsen, N., Granfield, R., & Gardella, J. A., Jr. (2007). *Civic engagement and public policy.* Retrieved January 12, 2009, from www.buffalo.edu/ ub2020/strengths/civic.html.

Osborne, J., Simon, S., & Collins, S. (2003). Attitude towards science: A review of the literature and its implications. *International Journal of Science Education, 25*(9), 1049–1079.

Owens, M. (2006, February 6). Education mobilization. *Nation.* Retrieved January 12, 2009, from www.thenation.com/doc/20060206/owens.

Presidential Award for Excellence in Science, Mathematics, and Engineering Mentoring Working Group. (2006). *Mentoring for science, technology, engineering and mathematics workforce development and lifelong productivity: Success across the K through grey continuum.* Retrieved January 12, 2009, from www.unc.edu/opt-ed/events/mentoring_workshops/documents/PAESMEMwhitepaper.pdf.

President's Council of Advisors on Science and Technology. (2004). *Sustaining the nation's innovation ecosystems: Report on information technology manufacturing and competitiveness.* Retrieved January 12, 2009, from www.dodmantech.com/pubs/FINAL_PCAST_IT_Manuf_Report.pdf.

Research and Policy Committee, Committee for Economic Development. (2003). *Learning for the future: Changing the culture of math and science education to ensure a competitive workforce.* Retrieved January 12, 2009, from www.ced.org/docs/report/report_scientists.pdf.

Rhoten, D., & Parker, A. (2004). Education: Risks and rewards of an interdisciplinary research path. *Science, 306*(5704), 2046.

Ritter-Smith, K., & Saltmarsh, J. (Eds.). (1998). *When community enters the equation: Enhancing science, mathematics and engineering education through service-learning.* Providence, RI: Campus Compact.

CHAPTER TEN

STUDENTS AS POLICY RESEARCHERS FOR STATE LEGISLATURES

Anthony Gierzynski, Tom Rice

During the 2007 session of the Vermont State Legislature, many legislators relied on undergraduates from the University of Vermont to prepare policy research reports on a variety of issues. Similarly, many state legislators in Iowa turned to University of Iowa undergraduates to prepare policy reports for use during their 2007 session. In both instances, the students produced the reports as part of ongoing service-learning partnerships between the authors of this chapter and legislators in the two states.

The Vermont partnership, called the Vermont Legislative Research Shop (VLRS), has been operating since 1998, and the Iowa partnership, called the Iowa Policy Research Organization (IPRO), has been operating since 2006. The programs differ somewhat in design, but both provide nonpartisan policy research to state legislators and policy research skills to students. In this chapter, we review the history of these programs and how they are currently structured. We also provide practical advice for professors and state legislators who are interested in starting similar programs in their states.

GETTING STARTED

Historically, American state legislatures have been "citizen legislatures." Sessions have been short, pay has been paltry, and there has been little in the way of research staff. This began to change several decades ago, but the label "citizen legislature" is still an apt description of most state legislatures. In Vermont, for example, legislators meet annually for about fifteen weeks from January to April and earn $589 per week, with a $35 per diem. For policy research assistance, they must rely on the small staff of the legislative counsel's office, whose main function is to draft bills for legislators; individual legislators in Vermont have no state-provided staff. The story is much the same in Iowa. Legislators meet for about sixteen weeks and earn $21,380 per year, with an $85 per diem. They have limited access to a small partisan research staff and the nonpartisan Legislative Services Bureau.

The situation in Vermont and Iowa is the norm rather than the exception. The fact is that legislators in most states are part-time public servants with few resources at their disposal for policy research. This is the ideal environment for policy research partnerships like VLRS and IPRO to flourish.

VERMONT LEGISLATIVE RESEARCH SHOP

The idea of engaging University of Vermont students in policy research for the Vermont legislature originated in 1992 with a young state representative, Matt Dunne. Frustrated by the lack of research help available to legislators, he shared the idea with a student, who took it to one of us (Anthony Gierzynski). The idea appealed to Gierzynski immediately. He knew that Vermont legislators could use the help and also knew that many public-minded students at Vermont were looking for ways to make a difference outside the university. Moreover, he was personally interested in encouraging students to become involved in government, an interest that has also found outlets in his service as the internship director for his department and the faculty advisor for the Campus Democrats. So Gierzynski arranged to meet with Matt Dunne and the student in order to discuss how to set up such a project.

Their first approach was to propose a research institute that would provide the structure and resources necessary to implement the project. The proposal was ambitious, calling for a director and a research assistant, as well as space and office equipment, including computers. Students would do research under the supervision of the director, with additional guidance from faculty members who had expertise in the policy area being examined. Students would receive course credit for their work, and the best students would be offered research assistantships to help new students.

The proposal caught the eye of the university president, who arranged a number of meetings to consider the idea. As discussions continued, however, opposition to the project emerged. The director of the master's in public administration program was concerned that the project might jeopardize his relationships with state officials. In addition, a newly formed organization loosely affiliated with the university, the Snelling Center for Government, objected on the grounds that such an institute might encroach on its mission to provide nonpartisan leadership on issues facing the state. After several years of pushing for the institute, the proposal failed to attract funding, and Gierzynski took the idea in a different direction. Having recently received the protection of tenure, he decided to carry out the idea in the framework of a research class. In the spring of 1998, he set up the Vermont Legislative Research Shop course as an evening division offering at the junior and senior level. The VLRS was an immediate success, and it has been running ever since.

IOWA POLICY RESEARCH ORGANIZATION

The Iowa Policy Research Organization is modeled after VRLS. Tom Rice served with Gierzynski at Vermont in the mid-1990s, and he has followed the work of VRLS from its conception. In 2005 he decided to try to implement a similar program at the University of Iowa. He broached the idea with State Senator Jeff Danielson, whom he had had as an adult student in class several years earlier. Danielson was very supportive and agreed to help promote the project in the legislature. At about the same time, Rice took his idea to a two-week summer workshop on service-learning course development sponsored by the Center for Teaching at the University of Iowa. At the workshop, he was able to fine-tune plans for the course and get it ready for introduction. It was first offered in the spring 2006 and is now in its fourth year. The course has been well received by both students and legislators.

VLRS and IPRO Structure and Operation

The VLRS and IPRO service-learning courses are similar in many ways, but there are some significant differences in their structure and operation. These differences are highlighted in this section, along with a variety of tips for instituting similar programs on other campuses.

Course Configuration

One of the major differences between VLRS and IPRO is that the former is a three-hour spring semester course where students respond to the immediate needs of legislators in session, and the latter is a two-semester course where students take a one-hour training class spring semester in policy research and then a three-hour class in the fall semester to conduct research on issues that legislators expect to consider the following spring. Both models are effective, but the rhythms of the courses differ. The VLRS students are in an exciting deadline-driven environment where research requests must be turned around quickly, while the IPRO students have more time to develop their reports. The IPRO students also have the benefit of completing the one-hour policy research training course before they get their first requests from legislators.

The VLRS operates very much as a "shop," with work coming in and going out rapidly. Gierzynski has found that an evening class format works best. Bringing the students back to campus at night makes the research seem more like a job than course work, and it allows the class to meet for longer blocks of time. Most semesters, he has had the class meet for two two-hour sessions each week. These long sessions give him more time to help students as they are doing their work. This speeds up the research and report preparation, putting the policy information in the hands of legislators more quickly.

The IPRO students begin their experience with a one-hour training seminar in the spring. In this course, Rice covers basic material on policy research and then has each student prepare two research reports, one as a member of a team and one on his or her own. These reports often go through two or three drafts before they are considered complete. The fall course is held three days a week for fifty minutes. Students are expected to conduct most of their research outside class, with class time being dedicated to discussing the research findings and critiquing the reports.

THE STUDENTS

The VLRS students are mostly political science majors or minors, although those outside political science are encouraged to apply for the course. Students from other programs, such as business, environmental studies, English, psychology, and sociology, have participated in the course. These students have brought different perspectives and course work backgrounds to the research projects. The VLRS course is set up to require Gierzynski's permission for enrollment, and he uses that process to screen prospective students. Enrollment is limited to twelve students. Students are allowed to take the VLRS course twice since the policy questions addressed each semester are different. Such students provide valuable leadership and experience to their groups, resulting in better and timelier research.

Rice has teamed up with the university honors program to help attract top-performing students to the IPRO course. In October, an e-mail is sent to all honors students and all political science majors explaining the course and inviting them to apply. Applications are online and consist of basic information about year in school, grade point average, interests, and so on. These are returned to Rice, and he interviews selected students before making decisions about which students to admit to the course. Enrollment is capped at twelve students. Almost all of the students who get into the course are sophomores and juniors, although first-year students are eligible. Seniors cannot take the course because it starts in the spring of their final year and continues the following fall, after they have graduated. Over its first two years of operation, most of the IPRO students have been political science majors, but there have also been students from many other disciplines, including philosophy, business, and computer science. As with VLRS, Rice has found that it is useful to have students from different academic backgrounds because they bring different skills to the research process.

GETTING THE RESEARCH DONE

Learning in the VLRS and IPRO courses takes place primarily in the process of doing the research. Gierzynski does assign readings on state legislatures and the state of Vermont early in the semester to provide the students with the necessary background. Rice does much the same during the one-hour training class in the spring. It is, however, the process of doing the research that defines the courses. Conducting the research teaches students about the policy areas, improves their abilities to evaluate scientific and social science research, refines their information retrieval skills, and trains them in how to distill large amounts of information into coherent, well-written, and concise reports. This learning process starts slow, with the early reports going through many professor-evaluated drafts. But most students are quick learners, and by the end of the course, their work has improved substantially and needs much less editing.

At Vermont, the VLRS students work in teams of two or three. At the beginning of the semester Gierzynski has the students fill out a questionnaire regarding their skills (computer software, Internet, and computer database search skills) and their policy interests. Students are then assigned to teams according to stated policy interests and computer skills, with an effort to make sure that each group has at least one student with strong computer skills. The VLRS has undertaken a couple of projects in which the entire class has worked together. One example was when a legislator and the Vermont secretary of state expressed interest in assessing voters' views on the city of Burlington's first attempt to use instant runoff voting to elect their mayor. Gierzynski put the entire class to work to design and execute a citywide exit poll. In another example, the entire class was used to collect and enter campaign finance data in order to produce a report on a new set of state campaign contribution limits.

The IPRO students sometimes work on policy reports in teams of two or three and sometimes individually. Rice and Gierzynski experimented with teams of four or more, and both found that productivity generally dropped because students had difficulty coordinating research responsibilities and finding times to meet outside class. Nevertheless, large groups are sometimes necessary for projects large in scope. Assigning IPRO students individually to policy reports has worked very well when issues are not overly complex. For example, one legislator wanted a report on how other states tax their golf courses. This was a reasonably straightforward question that a single student handled quickly and competently. Another legislator wanted the class to research state cigarette tax rates, the impact of raising cigarette taxes on state revenues, and the impact of cigarette taxes on smoking rates. This was a much more involved study that was assigned to a team of students, each primarily responsible for a different section of the final report.

One point that needs special mention is that the VLRS and IPRO research reports attempt to be objective and nonpartisan. For some students, this is difficult to practice. Many students come to the class with strongly held political beliefs, and many are used to writing position papers in their classes, so the idea of separating their own opinions from their research and writing is new to them. Often students insert their own beliefs without realizing that they are doing so. One way to guard against this is to form research teams of students with different political leanings, thus creating environments where they police each other. Another challenge of conducting nonpartisan research is that legislators sometimes want reports with a partisan slant. Although they understand that VLRS and IPRO are nonpartisan, legislators occasionally try to steer the research in a certain direction. For example, one Iowa legislator wanted students to write a report on why Iowa needed to improve subsidies to wind power producers. Rice explained that the students would be pleased to write a report on what other states were doing on this issue and the costs and benefits of wind power generally, but they were not in the business of producing papers advocating policies or positions. Finally, it is necessary, and sometimes challenging, to make students understand that a nonpartisan report is not necessarily a report without firm conclusions. Often existing research on a topic is conclusive—global warming is a good example at the moment—and must be stated that way. So, if, for example, research findings consistently show that snowmobiles have a harmful effect on the environment, or that increases in the minimum wage have not been associated with job losses, or that mandatory sentencing has not worked as intended, the findings must be included in the report. Unfortunately, in our relativistic culture where every point is believed to have two equally valid sides, stating conclusive research findings leads some students to think that they are being biased.

THE POLICY REPORTS

Both the VLRS and IPRO research reports are modeled on the short policy papers of the National Conference of State Legislatures. The VLRS and IPRO reports are generally two to four pages and are well cited so that legislators know where to go for more information. Most legislators prefer short reports because they lack the time to wade through lengthy technical reports. The reports often include the same general types of information. They often summarize the actions that other states have taken in the particular policy area under study and report on the results of these policies. For example, a report on banning smoking in bars would include a list of bans already implemented in other locales and information on how those bans have affected the establishments, employees, and patrons. Reports also often include the latest research on the topic. For the report on banning smoking in bars, this might consist of research on the effects of second-hand smoke and the health care costs associated with it. Some reports include a review of the legal background or context, such as court rulings and federal statutes. A report on parental notification requirements for abortion, for example, would discuss the U.S. Supreme Court's position on the issue, as well as state judicial activity in the area.

Occasionally reports include primary data. For instance, following a severe spring ice storm that damaged trees throughout the state, a team of VLRS students contacted maple syrup producers to help determine what type of state assistance they needed. In another example, noted earlier, VLRS students designed and implemented an exit poll of voters in Vermont's largest city, Burlington, to provide legislators with an assessment of voters' opinions regarding the first use of an instant runoff voting method of choosing the city's mayor.

Perhaps the best way to get a sense of the policy reports is to visit the VLRS and IPRO Web sites and read a few of them (the VLRS site address is www.uvm.edu/~vlrs and the IPRO site is www.uiowa.edu/~ipro/index.html). Both sites include most of the reports from previous years so that legislators and others can refer to them if needed. The Web sites also include general information about VLRS and IPRO for legislators and prospective students. Web site maintenance is performed by the professors with substantial help from the students (in the IPRO program). In the case of IPRO, two students designed and created the current page in lieu of one of the practice research reports produced during the spring training seminar.

The Web sites are the major vehicle for report dissemination. When VLRS and IPRO students finish a report, it is immediately posted on the respective Web sites. In addition, the report is sent in hard copy and by e-mail to the legislators who requested that the report be done. In Vermont, a one-page mailing is sent to all legislators at the beginning of the legislative session and semester drawing their attention to the research posted on the VLRS Web site. In addition, legislators are sent the same announcement by e-mail. In Iowa, all legislators receive an e-mail approximately two weeks before the start of the session in January with a link to the IPRO Web site and a list of all of the reports completed during the fall semester.

Experience has shown that certain types of topics are better suited to the students' research skills than others. A team of IPRO students, for example, had a difficult time grappling with some thorny questions about the relationships between Native American tribal law and state civil and criminal laws. They also had difficulty comparing state programs to encourage entrepreneurial activity at state universities. State incentive programs often varied dramatically across different academic areas in the same state, and many of the programs were highly complex. Moreover, it was difficult to find the information.

The VLRS had difficulty with a request to look into the possible effects of offering a different legal structure for incorporating businesses, particularly a structure that would include incentives to make corporations more responsive to their shareholders. This work proved exceptionally challenging despite the fact that two of the students in the group that handled the request were business majors. The project required what proved to be a near-impossible understanding of highly complex laws governing corporations and the exploration of an issue about which there appeared to be almost no research.

There are no hard-and-fast rules for deciding that a topic is too difficult for the students, but we tend to look warily on topics that demand substantial legal analysis, require complicated cost-benefit analyses, and pose tax code questions. Our recommendation is that if you think a topic will be too difficult for your students, it is better to tell the legislator up front than to struggle with a report that may not be very good in the end.

SECURING RESEARCH TOPICS

Both VLRS and IRPO use a combination of personal contacts and marketing to solicit research topics. The mix has changed as the programs have become established. In Vermont, research requests are generated through flyers, e-mail, and personal contacts. Initially and for most of his tenure in the statehouse, Representative, and then Senator, Dunne, helped provide research topics—some his own, but most solicited from other lawmakers. Over time Gierzynski has developed his own connections with other legislators as a result of his work as internship director for his department and out of his role as advisor to the UVM College Democrats, where he worked to connect the students with the state party. Because Vermont is such a small state—one of Gierzynski's colleagues told him when he arrived that the state was like a neighborhood—it has been relatively easy to develop contacts with political officials at all levels of government. The procedure Gierzynski now follows to solicit research requests includes sending out an e-mail to all of the legislators prior to the start of the semester, as well as mailing a letter to each legislator (students are enlisted to stuff envelopes with these letters during the first class session). The e-mail and letter offer the services of VLRS, discuss what type of research VLRS is capable of, lists a number of past reports to show legislators examples of what is possible, and provide contact information and the VLRS Internet address. The number of research requests from legislators has varied over the years. Sometimes there have been enough requests to keep the students working throughout the semester. Other times, such as the year that the legislature was consumed with responding to a Vermont Supreme Court ruling requiring that the benefits of marriage be made available to same-sex couples, the requests from the legislators had to be supplemented with work that came from identifying research possibilities in bills introduced in the statehouse or senate (such reports would be sent to the bills' top sponsors). In recent years, Gierzynski has also had VLRS student teams update reports for legislators that had been written in previous semesters.

The IPRO program is just in its fourth year, so it is still gaining name recognition. State Senator Jeff Danielson played an important role in promoting IPRO in its first year. He arranged for the students to spend a day at the legislature in the spring and meet many of the leaders in both chambers. The students followed up their visit with thank-you letters and a general letter to all legislators explaining the program. Over the first summer, Rice contacted the legislators whom the students had met earlier and solicited research ideas. This generated eight or ten good ideas. A handful of other good ideas came as a result of the letter sent to all legislators. Finally, Rice invited several legislators to visit the class in the fall to talk with the students about the legislature and its policy research needs. These meetings generated several more ideas—enough to keep the students busy in that fall.

These same tactics are being implemented in subsequent years. It is worth mentioning that by the second year, many legislators were familiar with IPRO, and the students had more legislators to meet with when they visited the statehouse in the spring. Some of the members were so appreciative of the work that the previous class had done that they arranged for the new class to be recognized on the floor of the House. Thus, by year two, IPRO was already known by a substantial number of legislators, and the process of soliciting research projects was much easier.

Another addition to IPRO's solicitation effort has been the contacting of several bipartisan study groups that are set up by legislative leaders to examine issues in the fall that might be important in the next session. These groups are composed of legislators and have limited research assistance from the state Legislative Services Bureau. In past years, each of these groups has met two or three times during the fall and produced a report on the issue. The promise of help from IPRO has been welcomed by some of the groups, and they have made several requests for research.

SERVICE-LEARNING IN VLRS AND IPRO

Service-learning is commonly defined as an educational method that combines voluntary public service with reflective classroom instruction to enhance student learning and build stronger communities. The VLRS and IPRO courses lend themselves readily to this service-learning format, but there are some challenges. For one, the courses do not naturally encourage much contact between students and legislators. Most service-learning experiences involve substantial contact between students and service partners, with students often spending time under the direct supervision of the partners at the partners' workplace. This is clearly not the case with VLRS and PRO. The students in these courses have very little contact with legislators and do their policy research miles away from the statehouses. In the case of IPRO, the legislature is not even in session when the students are doing their work.

The lack of contact between students and legislators does reflect the reality of the policy research job. Typically, elected policymakers convey their research requests to professional researchers, and the researchers prepare and deliver their reports with little interaction with the policymakers. In this way, then, the students' experiences in VLRS and IPRO closely resemble the experiences of many policy researchers. That said, it certainly would be valuable for the students to have some direct contact with legislators. Such contact would allow them to learn about the challenges of legislating and about the role that research plays in the policymaking process. Fortunately, it has been possible to build in some contact points between students and legislators in the VLRS and IPRO courses.

For the VLRS, contact is almost exclusively using the Internet. If students have questions regarding a research request, Gierzynski encourages them to e-mail the legislator. In addition, legislators often send letters or e-mails thanking the students for their work. In the early years of the VLRS, Representative Dunne visited the class and discussed the need for their research help. On a number of occasions, Gierzynski has taken students to the statehouse and arranged for legislators to visit the class. One group of students even testified before a statehouse committee on their research. In another instance, students accompanied Gierzynski for his testimony regarding VLRS campaign finance research before a meeting of the House Government Operations Committee (legislators asked the students questions as well). Such visits add a rich context to the work that the students do in the class and heighten their motivation even more.

Contact with legislators in the IPRO class starts with a trip to the statehouse in the spring. This day-long visit includes many meetings with key leaders in both chambers and both political parties. These visits cover several topics, but the central focus of most meetings is to convey to students the important role that policy research plays in the policymaking process. The most recent trip to the capitol also included a visit to a committee hearing in which research on a pressing environmental problem was shared with legislators by a policy expert. This helped the students understand the role of research in the legislative process.

The fall semester is a good time for the IPRO students to have some direct contact with the legislators because the legislature is not in session. It is true that many of the legislators are busy with their regular jobs, but by planning far in advance, it has been possible to have four or five legislators visit the class over the course of the semester. Before each visit, Rice asks the legislators to come up with at least one policy research idea for the students (usually the legislator comes with many more). The legislators are also asked to talk about some aspect of the legislative process, from constituency contact and service to the role of partisanship in the legislative process. The specific topics for each visit are agreed to beforehand. These visits are important in giving students an understanding of the jobs of the people they are serving.

The IPRO students seldom have contact with legislators while they are actually researching and writing their policy reports. Questions do arise as the research is being conducted, but most of these can be answered by Rice. Occasionally, however, it is necessary to forward a question to specific legislators. In these cases, Rice approves the question, and the student or students working on the research e-mail the question to the relevant legislators.

Another challenge to making VLRS and IPRO effective service-learning courses is to build in helpful reflection exercises. For both courses, reflection includes encouraging students to think critically about the policy research process and what it means to be a good nonpartisan policy researcher. These happen almost naturally if students are asked to critique each other's work in class. Critiquing forces students to reflect on their work and defend their work. It also teaches them about accepting peer criticism and suggestions. When the critiquing sessions are supervised by the professor, he or she can encourage discussion and reflection around the points most useful to the students.

Reflection also takes place as the students go about revising their policy reports. It is then that they are forced to fully confront the suggestions offered by other students and the professor. They will need to consider whether and how the suggestions improve their report. This process, whether it takes place individually or with members of a research team, is an especially valuable reflective exercise.

Finally, toward the end of the semester, both Gierzynski and Rice review with their students what they have learned about conducting policy research and the policymaking process more generally. A group discussion on these topics is an excellent opportunity for students to reflect on what they have learned and how they have helped the process. Several lessons usually emerge. Among the most important is the difficulty of separating personal policy preferences from the task of preparing nonpartisan policy reports. Going into the class, most students assume that they can easily purge their personal beliefs from their research, but this is often not the case. Another valuable lesson is the challenge of finding information on many topics. Many students expect the information they need to be readily available on the Internet, but it seldom is. They often need to do extensive digging on the Internet, at the university library, and in other places. A third valuable lesson is that preparing succinct and useful policy reports is not easy. Students seem to think that they can complete a short policy report of a few pages in a couple of days or maybe a week at most. Often it takes several weeks and several drafts.

BEYOND VLRS AND IPRO: OTHER POLICY RESEARCH OPPORTUNITIES FOR STUDENTS

The success of VLRS and IPRO is due to the quality of the students. To be sure, Gierzynski and Rice have worked hard to promote their programs and to improve their students' research and writing skills, but the students who enter the programs, like good students everywhere, are already motivated and capable. These students are a reservoir of talent eager for the opportunity to make a difference in the real world. Conducting policy research for resource-strapped legislatures is an ideal way to get these students involved in projects that make a difference. With minimal supervision and training, they are able to produce first-rate research reports of value to lawmakers. If students can provide quality research to legislators, there is every reason to believe that they could do the same for other public officials.

Rice has already been exploring a sister program to IPRO that would team students with small cities and towns in Iowa that need research and technical assistance. Most small communities have even fewer resources than legislatures to respond to a growing number of needs. State associations of cities and towns often provide some general assistance, but when it comes to the unique needs of a particular community, these associations are often too strapped to help. The nature of the help that communities require is often quite different from the type of public policy research conducted by the students in VLRS and IPRO. At the local level, the needs frequently involve helping with a grant, assistance with understanding and complying with state and federal regulations, and collecting information on how other communities have addressed an issue or problem. Obviously students cannot substitute for professional consultants, but they do have the time and skills to help communities with relatively uncomplicated needs. They can also help educate local officials on issues and on whom to turn to for more expert advice.

In addition to cities and towns, many other government organizations could use student assistance, at least from time to time. County governments are a clear example, and there are many other local governmental units, such as school districts, water districts, emergency medical service organizations, and environmental districts. At the state level, administrative units, such as departments of transportation, natural resources, and education, can often use the type of general research assistance that good undergraduate students can provide. The point is that general VLRS and IPRO models of having students conduct research for state legislatures could be expanded to include almost any other state and local government agency and organization.

Voices: State Legislators in Vermont and Iowa

VERMONT

Matt Dunne

When I was first elected to the legislature in Vermont in 1992, I quickly identified three challenges in the legislature: (1) a lack of objective research capacity in our tiny legislative council, leading to an overdependency on lobbyists for policy decisions; (2) little collaboration between the legislature and the University of Vermont (UVM) in efforts to find policy solutions; and (3) low political civic engagement among young people in the state. The Vermont Legislative Research Shop (VLRS) at UVM has been surprisingly successful in addressing all three.

In a small state like Vermont, state legislatures have very small staffs. As a result, any policy information, even if it is simply a compilation of existing research from other states placed in the context of Vermont, can be incredibly powerful in shaping the direction of legislation. In addition, if this research is brief in format so that busy legislators can digest it, the research can have an even larger impact. VLRS has provided exactly this type of research for over a decade. In doing so, VLRS shows lawmakers the value of student research and, indirectly, the value of the university to the state. There is no doubt that VLRS has strengthened communication between the legislature and the university.

VLRS has also engaged students in the political process in a way that has probably kept them active. Research looking at the lack of interest in politics among young people, even among those who consider themselves committed to improving society, often concludes that young people do not think that politics is an effective or efficient way to achieve change. As a result, large numbers of young people put in hours volunteering for non-profit organizations, but they often do not bother to contact their elected officials to advocate for a policy change. And all too often, they do not even vote.

VLRS offers a way for young people to see how the policy process can be a lever for change. VLRS students quickly learn that their work is relevant to the legislative policy discussion and can change the outcome to a law. Once students see how a research project influences legislation, they often become hooked, looking for the next opportunity to make a difference through the policy and political process.

This innovative program engages students in the political arena in a noncontroversial, nonpartisan way. In this day and age, some colleges and universities seem to have deemphasized politics in an effort to avoid explosive protests or the perception of supporting one position or another. Although there is probably room to encourage more visceral political discourse, the VLRS model engages students in the political process by contributing to the political debate in a powerful way without having to challenge the status quo overtly. By doing so, it has the ability to generate politically engaged students committed to change through the normal political process.

■ ■ ■

Matt Dunne is a former Vermont state legislator.

Iowa

Jeff Danielson

The enemy of good government is bad information. Policymaking should be a rational process, and if policymakers have bad information, it is difficult for them to make the best decisions. The old adage, "garbage in, garbage out," applies nowhere better than in policymaking.

As a state legislator in Iowa, I am often frustrated by the lack of good information. Our Legislative Service Bureau provides valuable policy research assistance, as do the two party caucus staffs. Interest groups are also an important source of information. But beyond these groups, there is little in the way of research assistance to help us do our job. This is why I was immediately supportive of Professor Rice's idea to have students provide nonpartisan policy research to legislators on request. He and I worked together to sketch out the basic plan for the IPRO program, and I have played an active role in introducing the program to several fellow legislators.

From the perspective of legislators, the program has two important assets. First, it delivers high-quality research quickly. Legislators forward their research requests to Rice over the summer and early fall, and his students conduct the research in the fall. The research reports are available by the end of fall semester, well in advance of the start of the legislative session in January. Second, the program takes little of our time. We may be in contact with Rice and his students a few times as they are working on our research, but the job of supervising the research and editing the reports is all done by the students and Rice. Legislators are busy, so the fact that we can drop off our requests and receive first-rate research reports a few months later is a valuable service.

I am sure that there are plenty of talented students at every college and university who would be excited about participating in a program like IPRO. I am also sure that there are legislators in every state who would make good use of such a program. The challenge is finding professors to offer programs like IPRO. Legislators can play an active role in this process by suggesting such a program to contacts they have at colleges and universities in their state. If the contacts are senior administrators, ask them if they would take the idea to the faculty in political science, public policy, and public administration. A more aggressive approach would be to set up an appointment to meet with the department chair of political science, public policy, or public administration to talk about the idea. My guess is that the response will be warm.

■ ■ ■

Jeff Danielson is an Iowa state senator.

CHAPTER ELEVEN

LIVING THE THEORY
Local Politics and Service-Learning
David P. Redlawsk, Nora Wilson

At the University of Iowa, 2005–2006 was the Year of Public Engagement, where "during this year, the University community will be encouraged to intensify its efforts and sharpen its focus on engagement with the public and public issues at the local, state, national, and international levels" (University of Iowa, 2005). Putting aside the question of whether one year is enough to do "engagement" justice, Iowa's move was one in a series of efforts by American colleges and universities to better connect students, faculty, and staff to the community at large. This idea of engagement has spawned a mini industry as institutions of all types struggle with the question of what it means to be "engaged." While this is a very big question, this chapter focuses on a small, but critical, portion. We are interested in how political science can use civic engagement to enhance course work and reinforce not just involvement in a community, but involvement in the politics of a community. While not negating the importance of working in soup kitchens or cleaning up polluted streams, we suggest that these activities do not, by themselves, connect students to the *civic*—that is, the *political*—in their communities.

Concern for civic engagement is not really new, though perhaps the language of service-learning and civic engagement is,

---

An earlier version of this chapter was presented at the American Political Science Association's Third Annual Conference on Teaching and Learning, Washington, D.C., February 18–20, 2006.

at least for political science. Our discipline is, after all, the usual home of various internship programs, semesters in Washington and state capitals, and other hands-on projects such as campaign internships. If any department has been historically engaged, it is political science. Having said this, it is not obvious that political scientists have given much thought to how concepts from service-learning might directly inform the way we teach our courses. It is one thing to send students out to volunteer with campaigns; it is another to fully integrate the experience of campaign work with the material taught in class.

This chapter describes one such effort at the University of Iowa. The course, Local Politics, has been taught by the first author (David Redlawsk) since 1999, including units on the function and structure of local government, the role of citizens and interest groups, and the nature of local elections. The capstone of the course is a local government simulation called Camelot, which takes up the last three or four weeks of the course. Camelot is a published simulation, quite comprehensive in nature, and can be played by up to seventy-five players (Woodworth, Gump, & Forrester, 2006). Students were also assigned to observe the local city council election (the course is normally taught during the fall city elections) and to write an in-depth paper on one candidate's campaign. More recently, following Redlawsk's participation in a faculty Service Learning Institute at Iowa in summer 2005, the course was revised to incorporate a comprehensive civic engagement/service-learning section, which was implemented in fall semester 2005. The challenges and successes in implementing service-learning in this political science course form the basis for the rest of this chapter. We begin by considering some key elements of service-learning and then describe the design of the service-learning requirement, following which we examine the outcome of the experience from a student, faculty, and organization perspective. We close by drawing some broad conclusions about the value of such an exercise in political science.

THREE GOALS FOR SERVICE-LEARNING

There appear to be, in essence, three main goals in service-learning from the perspective of those who teach these courses. One is to partner with community organizations to determine and fulfill a need of the community. A second is to engage the student in the community immediately and increase that student's potential for future engagement. Finally, to be truly valuable, service-learning assignments must connect with and enhance the theories students are learning in the classroom at the same time they are completing projects in the community. While we found a version of these goals explicitly stated at the University of North Carolina at Chapel Hill (University of North Carolina, 2006), similar sentiments are found throughout the service-learning literature. Thus, the goals of service-learning are both to accomplish something of value in the community and to directly tie students' community experience to the content of the course. While this is accomplished by placing students in community organization settings, it seems necessary that these students produce something of value for their organizations, while working to connect their experience back to the classroom. This latter activity is usually carried out by a guided reflection exercise, where students consider the nature of their work and the connections it makes through the maintenance of a journal and in-class discussions.

The revisions made to the Local Politics class at Iowa were explicitly designed to accomplish these three goals. Students would become involved in campaigns or interest groups, discuss their real-world experiences in class at appropriate times that would coincide with appropriate readings, and maintain extensive journals, responding to prompts provided for them by the instructor. In the last part of this chapter, we consider the extent to which we managed to accomplish these goals.

SERVICE-LEARNING AND LOCAL POLITICS AT IOWA

One typical concern faculty have in implementing service-learning in the classroom is the potential significant increase in the instructor's own workload that it is likely to cause. Fortunately for our project at Iowa, a non-service-learning version of the Local Politics course had been offered in the May 2005 three-week session, and one of the students in that class developed a particular interest in learning more about service-learning. Since there were no local political campaigns going on at the time of this course, the student—this chapter's second author (Nora Wilson)—was especially interested in how the hands-on part of the course might work. We were able to structure an independent research tutorial that provided credit in exchange for developing a bibliography of work on service-learning and acting as the administrative support for the service-learning project portion of the fall 2005 version of the course. Without this administrative assistance, the course could not have been managed effectively. The student assistant did most of the work of maintaining contact with organizations, monitoring student work, and providing initial assessments of journals. The instructor maintained all grading authority and oversaw the work of the student assistant.

THE STRUCTURE OF THE CLASS

Local Politics is an upper-level elective course at Iowa, designed to give students a basic understanding of the forms and functions of local government. It is specifically not a "state and local politics" course and not an "urban politics" course. The course has several elements, designed to teach students how local government works, who gets involved in local politics and why, and some nuts and bolts about local election campaigns. This last is a particular interest of Redlawsk, who has himself run for local office, both winning and losing elections. The course attracts a substantial number of non–political science majors, especially journalism students, as well as a smattering of sociology and business students. The majority of the roughly forty students major in political science, however.

The service-learning project implemented in fall 2005 replaced a previous assignment to write a paper about a city council candidate's campaign for office. This new service-learning project accounted for 25 percent of the student's grade. Assessment of the service-learning work was to be based on actual completion of at least thirty-five hours of service during the course of the semester and the quality of a written reflection journal to be kept by students documenting their work hours, setting down their thoughts about their work, and responding to four specific guided reflection assignments spaced over the course of the project.

The projects available largely focused on the city council elections then ongoing in Iowa City. Six candidates were running for two open at-large seats (five of them participated with the class) and one candidate was running unopposed for a district seat (who also participated). City council elections are held in two stages in Iowa City, with a primary election in October to reduce the number of candidates to no more than two for each available seat, and a general election in November where voters pick from the remaining candidates. All candidates run on a nonpartisan ballot, and the local political parties do not actively involve themselves in the campaigns.

Given that there were to be more than forty students in the class, we were concerned that the local city council campaigns might be overwhelmed if every student chose to work on a campaign. City council campaigns are usually small affairs in Iowa City; it remains unusual for a candidate to raise and spend even ten thousand dollars on the race. Consequently, before the semester started, we determined that other placements would be necessary. Fortunately, two more campaigns were readily available. A group of local residents had successfully petitioned to place the question of "public power" on the November ballot. Voters were to be asked whether to potentially form a municipal electrical utility, thus removing the franchise from the private company that held it. The company, MidAmerican Energy, campaigned extensively against the measure, while the Citizens for Public Power worked in favor of passage. Both sides agreed to use any students who might be interested.

Finally, two other opportunities appeared. The president of the Iowa student government (UISG) planned a Get Out the Vote (GOTV) project, which was to focus on improving the abysmal voting rate of Iowa students in local elections. Second, a local public interest group had formed to petition the Federal Communications Commission (FCC) to open up hearings on the renewal of a local television license, asserting that the station was failing to operate in the public interest. Both groups became involved in the project, but while UISG was also election focused, the Iowans for Better Local TV (IBLTV) was the only placement opportunity that did not involve the local elections. In any case, the service-learning project was to end on election day in November. This was done to allow time to do the final local government simulation, Camelot, which continued to be the capstone of the course. To complete the required thirty-five hours by the ending date, students found it necessary to work in their organization about five hours a week.

GETTING STARTED

Before the semester started in late August, a short meeting was arranged with the candidates and the leaders of the organizations. This July meeting was to explain the project and ask if they would like to participate. It also gave them a chance to ask questions about the project. During this meeting, contact information was exchanged, and the best way for students to get in touch with each group was determined. Shortly after these meetings, approximately three weeks before the beginning of the semester, we decided to hold a job fair on the second day of class. To coordinate this, the candidates and leaders were either called or e-mailed an invitation. Each of the candidates and all other groups indicated they would attend. We arranged for everyone to have a table and allowed them to bring literature if they liked. Due to the size of the room and the large class size, we divided the class into two groups by alphabet. Each group of students was instructed to come at a different time, allotting about forty-five minutes for each group to meet the representatives of the campaigns and organizations.

The job fair gave the students some assistance in deciding on their service-learning project for the semester. They had an opportunity to meet the candidates and leaders personally to determine what kind of work they would do for them. To ensure that they did meet everyone, students were required to sign their name at each table, which most students actually did. While the job fair was a bit of a last-minute idea, it seemed quite successful; both students, and campaigns and organizations, were pleased to have the contact. In the end, one candidate did not come despite confirming: it is perhaps no surprise that no one initially signed up to work on his campaign. At the other extreme, one of the candidates brought a bowl of candy and treated the opportunity as a chance to meet potential voters, as well as volunteers. Her table was quite popular.

Students had been given placement forms that were to be filled out by the campaign or organization with which they were going to work. At the last minute, we decided to allow students to have their placement sheets signed at the fair itself, which turned out to cause some confusion when some candidates did not get the word that they could sign people up right then and there. The idea of the form was to create a formal way to guarantee that the organization and student had discussed their role and had the opportunity to exchange contact information. To avoid overwhelming any organization, we allowed only six available slots on each project. Once the placement sheets were turned in, the first six students were placed on a project. In the end approximately 10 percent of the class had to make a second choice when their first preference was full.

As students were placed with the organizations, we sent a confirmation e-mail to them. This included the group they would be working with and the contact information. A confirmation e-mail or call was also made to the organization so that they had a list of students who would be working with them.

JOURNALING AND GUIDED REFLECTIONS

Students were required to keep a reflection journal on their work. This served multiple purposes. First, it was their time log for their work. Second, it was a place to think about what they were doing. Third, it was the final "output" or "result" of the work students did, and as such, its content was a major piece contributing to the grade they received. The journal was required to be handwritten to avoid situations where students might be tempted to create a journal out of whole cloth the night before it was due to be turned in. While online course sites can provide time-stamped journaling possibilities, given all the other changes being made in the course, it did not seem an optimal time for the instructor to learn something new. In retrospect though, after trying to read forty-three handwritten journals, the instructor is considering encouraging online journaling in the future!

In addition to writing entries in their journals each time they did service, there were four guided reflections for the students to respond to in their journals. Before students did anything for their organization, we asked them to write about their current knowledge of local government. The other guided reflections were directly related to the service-learning project as it was in process and are in Exhibit 11.1. As much as possible, the reflections focused on an aspect of local politics that had been covered recently in course readings or lectures. In the final analysis, we required them to reflect on why their candidate or referendum had won or lost. Students were also asked to provide an overall evaluation of the service-learning project as the last entry in their journal.

EXHIBIT 11.1   LOCAL POLITICS: SERVICE-LEARNING REFLECTIONS

Reflection 1 (Due before any work began)

Answer the following in your journal. You may write more, of course, but at a minimum, please write at least two paragraphs in response to each question.

- What do you already know about the local political environment? Do you know who the key actors (people and organizations) are? If so, briefly describe them and explain what makes them important players. If not, imagine who they might be and why they would be important to the local political environment.
- At this point, what kind of campaign or organization would you like to join? Once you do sign on to work in a campaign or organization, what kind of work do you expect to be doing? What kind of work would you like to be doing and why?

Reflection 2 (Due about three weeks into the service-learning project)

Answer the following in your journal. You may write more, of course, but at a minimum, please write at least two paragraphs in response to each question.

- Is your time being used wisely? Why or why not?
- Why do you think that your work is or is not valuable to the organization?
- In what ways is your organization or campaign well organized, and in what ways is it disorganized?

Reflection 3 (Due the week after the Iowa City Primary Election, October 11)

Answer the following in your journal. You may write more, of course, but at a minimum, please write at least two paragraphs in response to each question.

• What happened in the Iowa City primary election? Why did the winners win and the losers lose? And why was turnout extremely low?
• To what extent do the activities of your campaign or organization reflect the ideas in Strachan's book (2003) on local campaigns? Are you using new style techniques? Old style? A mix of both? What are some of the approaches being used in your organizations?
• Have your original expectations changed based on your experiences thus far?

Reflection 4 (Due following the ending of the service-learning project)

Answer the following in your journal. You may write more, of course, but at a minimum, please write at least three substantive paragraphs in response to each question.

• How did your expectations and actual experiences relate to each other? What went the way you thought it would? What did not? Why do you suppose your expectations and reality were different, if in fact they were?
• In what ways did your experience connect to our readings and class discussions? Did you find campaigning to match the kinds of things we talked and read about? For those not in a campaign, was the process of organizing/activating an interest group or voting project what you would have expected from what we learned in class about the way local government works?
• Why did your organization win or lose? (for campaigns)
• What factors led to either the success or failure of the organization with which you worked? (for noncampaigns)
• How did your real-world experience compare to what happened during our Camelot simulation?

We also scheduled two in-class reflection days during the project. The discussions were to revolve around the guided reflections to which the students had responded. But there was a real problem with this idea because the students were mostly working for campaigns that were competing with each other. Thus, there was

a risk that confidential campaign information might be acciden-
tally disclosed in public. So to maintain campaign confidentiality,
the class was divided into discussion groups consisting of students
who were working on the same project. To vary the discussion, the
student government, referendum, and interest group members
were split apart and filtered in with candidates who had similar
philosophies. After the primary, we incorporated an all-class discussion about the results on a regularly scheduled reflection day.
The small group discussion time was shortened to allow approximately twenty minutes of class discussion.

WORKING WITH CAMPAIGNS AND ORGANIZATIONS

Political campaigns, especially local campaigns, are odd beasts.
In some cases, the primary contact was the candidate himself or
herself. In others, there was a campaign manager with whom the
students worked. In all cases, the campaigns were not large organizations, and the students made up a substantial portion of the
workforce available to the campaign.

At unsystematic times during the course of the project, we
checked in with the campaigns and organizations. This was initially
done within two weeks after assignment to be sure that the students
had been in contact with the organizations. If there was a problem
in communication, an e-mail was sent to the student to be certain
that he or she had received the phone call or e-mail from the organization. After that, other check-ins were carried out approximately
once a month. Our goal was to be sure that any problems that crept
up could be quickly dealt with, but at the same time we did not
want to be bothersome to the organization. Each of these check-ins
simply involved a phone call or e-mail to each organization. Finally,
at the end of the project, we contacted all the campaigns and organizations once more asking them for feedback on the project itself
and the role the students played in their organization.

THREE GOALS OF SERVICE-LEARNING

An initial assessment of the service-learning project suggests that
it was successful, at least in a general way. Although not all students had a well-structured experience and not all organizations

made effective use of the students available to them, even the students who found their projects particularly frustrating appeared in their journaling and in class discussions to be able to make connections between the classroom material and their real-world experience. Many students expressed either a written or verbal desire to participate in a local project again.

At the start of this chapter, we discussed three broad goals of service-learning, and now it is time to consider whether this project did indeed move us closer to any of the goals. If we believe that these goals are worth striving for—and we do—then we need to get some sense of how well we did. As a reminder, the first goal was to fulfill a need of the community or community organization. The second was to engage students now and increase their potential for future community engagement. Finally, we expressed a goal of enhancing the theories the students learn in the classroom through completing their projects in the community.

FULFILLING COMMUNITY NEEDS

In our follow-up discussions with the political candidates and other organizations where students were placed, there was general agreement that the involvement of the students was helpful to the organizations. Not only did the students add an element of excitement and an additional labor force, but several of the organizations found that these students offered innovative ideas. All the feedback that we received was positive during this follow-up, even as we asked specifically about problems or challenges. This is not to say that the process was without problems. There were obstacles that surfaced during the experience—many of which we will detail in the last section of this chapter—but from the standpoint of the organizations, the obvious result was that their needs were met.

There is another question at hand, however. There is no debate that having students work at a soup kitchen helps the community as a whole as well as the particular agency's clients, but what about political campaign work? We think it is clear that this work too is valuable to the community because of the impact that local government can have on its residents. The decisions that a city council makes directly affect everyone, whether they realize it or not and whether they like politicians or wish they would all go away. City councilors are often relied on by community members to help them when they are unable to get something they need. One of the local candidates who was already a city council member pointed out how his constituent work directly benefited members of the community, using as an example intervention in getting needed special services bus service for a disabled member of the community. Thus, while it may be in an indirect manner, the students' work in campaigns clearly has potential to be meaningful to the community.

CURRENT AND FUTURE ENGAGEMENT

While it is certainly too early to know whether students participating in this class will remain engaged in the Iowa City community or wherever they land after graduation, we did get some sense from reflection responses that for some, this experience was an eye-opener that might lead them to continue. Students wrote in ways that made clear most realized their actions would have a direct effect on the results of the election regardless of the manner in which they participated. Even students not working on a campaign—the UISG get-out-the-vote project and the IBLTV better television project—felt they had direct influence on events. It appears that the work done by the UISG to raise awareness of the election and get students out to vote had some success: student turnout was up significantly over the election two years before. And while the IBLTV project was not directly connected to the elections, students worked on a major public event that included attendance by two commissioners of the Federal Communications Commission and a crowd of about five hundred people to discuss the state of local television news coverage.

The after-effect for many students of seeing their work turn into results created at least an expressed interest in future involvement. This was especially the case for one student who worked on the UISG project. By seeing the results of her work in numbers—how many students were newly registered and how many students actually voted—she expressed that she was now encouraged to work in the campaigning process again. Students also became aware that they were not in it alone. Then there were the students who decided to continue with their project even after completing the thirty-five required hours. Finally, even students who were already active in their communities recognized the value in the project.

Connecting with the Academic

Whether adding the service-learning component to this class enhanced students' understanding of the material is difficult to assess. What we would like, of course, is some kind of controlled experiment, where one randomly selected group of students gets a version of the class with service-learning and another without. That is not available here or in very many other similar situations. However, while it is difficult to say whether grades were better in this class over a class without service-learning, it became obvious to the instructor that the projects helped the students bridge their work with class material that highlighted campaigning styles, the role of media in local politics, the structure of local government, and more. Thus, the students were able to see the reading in action. This was reflected by students in final assessments of the project.

So while we do not have the kind of evidence social scientists would like to say yes, definitely the service-learning component enhanced student learning of the class material, we are quite comfortable that it did exactly that for many students.

Now What About the Problems?

This is not to say that the project was without problems or that each goal was equally met for every student. Although the project as a whole ran fairly smoothly, there are changes that we would probably make the next time. Most of the major changes would be in initial selection of the groups, combined with smaller changes in the facilitation of the job fair, communication with the organizations, in-class reflections, and feedback on the project.

Problems with Some Organization Placements

The two major problems that were encountered were primarily caused by our decision to allow students to work on an unopposed incumbent's campaign and with the university student government (UISG) on their get-out-the-vote project. Although the incumbent had promised that she would be developing materials for her constituents, including guides to local issues, in the end all she did was participate in a few local candidate forums. Most of the students on this assignment expressed frustration and concern because of the lack of things to do. They were perhaps more concerned that there was not thirty-five hours of work to be had than actually bored, but in any case the experience was not what it should have been. In retrospect, given the focus on campaigns, it was wrong to assign students to a candidate without a campaign. In our defense, at the beginning of the semester, it was not yet clear the candidate would have no opposition, since the filing deadline was a couple of weeks after classes had begun. Regardless of their promises to keep the students busy, however, it is unlikely that they will have very much to do in an uncontested campaign. One student on this campaign decided halfway through the project to assist another candidate's efforts.

The UISG project had problems because of its structure. The project was student run and without any faculty or staff person overseeing the operation. The student in charge of the project had never run a campuswide voter registration and get-out-the vote campaign and was not even clear on the deadlines inherent in such a process, such as the need to get out the vote for the primary. He did not have a clear plan on how this was going to be done as campaigns normally would. There were no time lines, deadlines, or specific goals for the students. Initially the UISG leader intended to create mini-projects and place each student from the Local Politics class in charge of one of these projects. However, not all the students were prepared to lead; some would have preferred to be given small tasks to complete than design a plan of action on their own. There was also a major communication problem between the UISG leader and half of the students in the group, though it appears much of this problem came from the Local Politics students and not UISG. We suspect that a number of students who chose this project did so thinking that because it was student run, it would be easy to do, and thus less motivated students self-selected for this project. In any case, this small group of students failed to return e-mails and calls and did not show up for events to which they had committed.

Contrasting this effort with a candidate campaign, it seems in the end that the level of attachment to the project was much lower for UISG than it would be for any candidate seriously running for office. A candidate has a direct interest in involving the students because failing to do so could result in losing the election, but the student-run project did not offer the same motivation. If this project or a similar endeavor was repeated in the future, it would be advisable to receive a detailed proposal from the student group before agreeing to include it. The proposal should include a specific time line of events and the tasks that the students should complete. It may also be necessary to provide some oversight if there are no faculty or staff overseeing the operation.

FEELING THAT THINGS WERE NOT QUITE RIGHT

This experience was new for many students, so they did not have much of a base of knowledge to draw on in considering whether they were doing useful or effective work at times. Often the journals expressed some frustration about how the campaigns and organizations were run, even the most effective of them. Campaigns seemed particularly disorganized to our students, with many things done at the last minute. Disorganization seemed to be higher in these campaigns than in partisan, higher-stakes elections. It was necessary to assure students that this was normal, which we did repeatedly, even though some did not seem to always believe us.

THE JOB FAIR

The job fair was a major success overall, although there were isolated difficulties. Some students did not feel they had enough time to become well informed about which group they were choosing. In one case, a student signed up to work with IBLTV, which was challenging the license of a local TV station. She thought the IBLTV group seemed interesting, while not quite understanding what they were doing. After her first meeting with the group, she came to the instructor and begged to be allowed to change organizations. It turned out she was a journalism major, had recently interned for the TV station that was the target of the group, and felt that she could not in good conscience advocate against it. She was, of course, allowed to switch. The condensed time period for choosing their candidate or group likely had more to do with this than the fair itself.

Given that the idea of the job fair was a bit last minute, there was not much time available for planning. This left some confusion about the sign-up process for organizations and students. At the fair itself, the two authors went back and forth between themselves on when and how to collect the forms that would confirm a student placement. Since only six slots were available for students with each organization, this was more important than if an unlimited number of students could sign up to work with any given group. Because the class was broken down into two groups coming at different times, our initial thought to use first-come, first-served did not work well.

Some campaigns and organizations at the fair did not realize that they could sign students up on the spot. The result was that one of the organizations—working on the public power issue campaign—signed up only one student. Others expressed interest, but the organization representative told them they had to wait to sign up later; most then went to another organization. Interestingly, the campaign representing the other side of the issue ended up with only two students, so this may have not actually created a problem. We learned that it is imperative that the protocol be communicated clearly to everyone to avoid this confusion in the future. The decision to allow students to turn in their sign-up forms was made at the fair, so simply deciding this in advance would allow time to explain the structure.

RESOURCES AND OTHER COMMUNICATION PROBLEMS

Besides the problem of communication about the sign-up process, there were a few problems that surfaced during the project that could have been easily solved with clearer communication. Many candidates had students driving to put out yard signs and creating brochures for them. While these are common tasks for volunteers on a campaign, it may not be appropriate for students performing the task for a class. In some cases, students were not included in the decision-making processes of the campaign as we had hoped.

Mentioning potential issues like this to the campaigns, organizations, and students before the projects began would have been helpful in eliminating the problems. It is probably necessary for the professor or teaching assistant to do this, as the students themselves would more than likely be uncomfortable saying anything to either the organization or the professor (we did not hear about these problems until the end). Students might think that complaining about these issues might adversely affect their grade for the project. Had we known, we might have suggested that campaigns using student labor this way either offer to reimburse expenses or perhaps pair a student up with another volunteer who would drive while the student placed the signs. Letting groups and candidates know that expecting students to use their own monetary resources is not appropriate appears to be an easily overlooked but necessary communication. It is also important to fully describe their role to the students before beginning their projects.

We found that reiterating to the organizations that confidentiality would be protected was important. We wanted the students to be involved in the behind-the-scenes work of the campaign. Doing this would necessarily expose students to the insides of campaign strategy, something no campaign wants out in the open.

Scheduling Difficulties (on Everyone's Part)

One of our most significant problems turned out to be scheduling. Students have a variety of commitments that can all fall at very different times. It was challenging to get everyone working for any given organization together in the same place at the same time. Often at least one student would miss a weekly meeting for a group or would be absent from an event the campaign thought was important but the student thought was less critical than something on her personal schedule. There were two things that made this communication gap smaller. First, the organizations that used e-mail had a much easier time informing the students about activities that were happening each week. But given that these were local campaigns, several of the candidates were not e-mail users, and thus had a very hard time connecting with students who seem to be glued to their e-mail and nothing else.

Second, the couple of campaigns and organizations that had a volunteer coordinator on staff had far fewer problems connecting with students than those that did not. In spite of the obstacles, the experiences were overwhelmingly positive.

KNOWING ABOUT THE PROJECT BEFOREHAND

The class was not advertised as a service-learning course beforehand because course descriptions at Iowa are set a year in advance and because the instructor did not decide to ramp up to a full service-learning experience until two months before the start of the course Even so, the vast majority of students reflected a positive experience that they would repeat. We might not want to exclude students from this experience who, had they known ahead of time, would not have chosen to take the course. So it is a bit of a challenge to decide how much information to provide at registration. It may be useful, however, to include an example project in the description. Courses at Iowa fill up quickly, and changing schedules after registration can be difficult. In addition, the journals reflected that most students felt thirty-five hours was too large a requirement for the project. Of course, devoting a large amount of time to the work is necessary for students to understand what they are doing and why. Reducing the number of hours by very much would not give students enough time to make the project worthwhile.

REFLECTING ON THE EXPERIENCE

While in many ways this chapter represents our after-the-fact reflections on the project, students were required to reflect as they went along. This reflection process is key to the service-learning concept, enhancing the chances that the students will take something valuable away from the project. Overall, we found that the required written journals were an excellent way for students to reflect on their experiences. In general, we were very happy with the amount that they wrote and the thoughtfulness of the content. The journals were an excellent resource to consider improvements that could be made in the future, as well as how things were going throughout the project.

There was a lot of communication with other group members outside the class. This made the group discussions in class—which involved small group discussion organized around the existing groups—redundant. In addition, because so many of the students were working on campaigns that were directly competing with one another, it was difficult to structure these discussions because of the need to ensure confidentiality. This problem was very obvious in the first in-class discussion period. For the second, we intermixed the noncandidate groups—public power, UISG, and IBLTV—in the candidate groups, and this helped, but it still was too limiting.

One possible solution could be to always include groups like this so that there is a mix of experiences to talk about. Another would be to hold off all in-class discussion until after the election. (This was not an option here because of the need to move into the Camelot simulation immediately after election day.) Another idea would be to present students with a set of questions when they begin the in-class reflection to be turned in at the end of the class. This could extend their discussions beyond their initial written reactions.

The journals were collected for evaluation once during the semester and again at the end. After the first collection, the journals were read by both the student assistant and the professor. In addition to tallying the number of hours the student had completed thus far, detailed feedback was given on entries. The feedback may have instructed students to consider their experiences in more depth, asked pointed questions about their insights, or given them reassurance that things were going smoothly—for example:

> Sounds like the experience is going pretty well, with some of the usual challenges of any campaigns. (I hope he signs the book too!) Overall I think you're doing a good job of documenting your experience and commenting on it, which is what I am looking for in these journals. You've apparently put in about 7.5 hours so far, according to the journal—you'll need to do a lot more soon, unless the journal isn't covering everything you've done (it should be).

■ ■ ■

> You should be keeping a specific list of hours that you worked—the dates worked, and the hours (like 9/20, 4–6pm, 2 Hours). I know you're listing the total hours, but I'd like the dates and times as

well. Also, you should have included notes from your group's discussion about reflection #2 in the material you handed in. Good start though.

Would we do this again? From the instructor's point of view, this process was exhilarating and exhausting. Forty-three students is a lot to manage, and the whole project could not have been done without the support of the student assistant. But it is clear that in this Local Politics class at least, having the students do real work on local city council campaigns, referendum issues, and issue groups made it relatively easy to connect class material that highlighted campaigning styles, the role of media in local politics, the structure of local government, and more, with the actual experiences students were getting on the ground in politics. The students were able to see the reading in action.

Some service-learning purists may not agree that what we did was actually service-learning, and others may not agree that what the students did benefited the community in the ways that working at social service agencies might. But it would be hard to argue with the kinds of statements these students and others made. We may not be able to prove it scientifically, but we do believe that these students learned more about local politics than any other class Redlawsk has taught. And what more could any instructor ask?

Voices: A Service-Learning Teaching Assistant

Nora Wilson

As a college student myself, I have been an advocate of hands-on learning. Traditional educational experiences often frustrated me because I preferred an interactive learning environment rather than a lecture. That is why, in the summer of 2005, I approached Professor Redlawsk about any opportunities he might have had to work on something outside the classroom. The inquiry gave me the opportunity to help modify his Local Politics class into a service-learning course and to work as an undergraduate teaching assistant with the students in the course.

Professor Redlawsk and I were lucky that the fall of 2005 was a particularly active time in local Iowa City politics. There were six candidates running for two open at-large city council seats. In addition, there was a "public power" referendum on the ballot in November to determine whether to form a municipal electrical utility. Additionally, the president of the Iowa student government (UISG) planned a Get Out the Vote (GOTV) project to improve the voting rate of the student population. Finally, a local public interest group had formed to petition the Federal Communications Commission (FCC) to open up hearings on the renewal of a local television license, asserting that the station was failing to operate in the public interest. All the students worked with one of these organizations.

My initial role was to talk to representatives for each of the groups and see if they were interested in having students work with them. This required me to make the contacts and explain what we planned to do. All of the groups I approached were very interested—it was obvious that they looked forward to having workers for their cause. At that point, I worked with them to set up the job fair, and then once all the students had signed up for an organization, I sent out a complete list to each organization with student contact information. Throughout the semester, I served as the primary point of contact for the campaigns and organizations. This required me to check in with the groups to ensure that things were going smoothly. Overall there were few to no problems. At the very beginning of the semester, I helped remedy a few communication issues, but overall, the feedback I received from the organizations was very positive throughout.

I detail this because it was clear from the beginning of the project that in order to effectively place so many students in engaged opportunities, there would be a significant amount of administrative work, more than could readily be handled by the professor, who was also responsible for the content of the course. For both of us, it was even clearer by the end of the semester that implementing a project like this requires resources—especially time!

From the students' perspective, I was an additional contact if they were having difficulties with their engaged learning project. Initially I contacted students if we did not receive a sign-up form for a project. In a couple of rare cases, I had to reach out to students if their organization could not get successfully contact them. Finally, when I had a number of students working on the UISG GOTV contact me, I got directly involved with their project. I met with the UISG student leading the project to assess the activities they had for students and their communication methods. We also brainstormed about solutions to the problems they were encountering. Overall, my contact with the students was minimal, but I was the point of contact for them if they were having problems with their projects.

Before assisting Professor Redlawsk with this class, I had worked on seven political campaigns. The experiences are difficult to articulate in a way that gives others a sense of what goes on behind the scenes. It was exciting to anticipate the range of emotions that the students were likely to encounter. I fully expected their experiences to give them a better understanding of how local city council campaigns, referendums or interest organizations work and who participates in local politics.

The students' final journal entries gave an overwhelming sense that they had experienced what we set out to give them. There are some noteworthy highs and lows, but the majority of the students reflected that directly participating with the organizations made what they learned in class "come alive." Many of them said that without the service-learning project, they would not have made the same connections to the principles Professor Redlawsk taught in class.

There are specific examples that really show what the students received from their projects. First, a student on the UISG GOTV project reflected on her enthusiasm by the increase in voter turnout among the college-aged voters. There is nothing like winning an election, and as she talked about her feeling of accomplishment in reaching her numerical goals, it was clear that she experienced this euphoria. Other students gained an understanding of how important an organized campaign is. One group of students reflected on this. The candidate, as I recall, was inexperienced in local elections and gave the students very little leadership in what they were supposed to be doing. All the students in this group felt that there wasn't an overall campaign plan that they could ground their tasks in. Although it may not have been an extremely positive experience, their involvement helped them understand this important piece of local politics.

Finally, one student's reflection on an unfortunate event after election day had a lasting impact on me. The manager of the organization she worked for, after being defeated on election day, received a drunk driving ticket later that evening. Although it was an unpleasant event, she experienced a common feeling in politics: disappointment in your candidate. It is difficult to understand how the staffs of candidates feel when they are betrayed by a lie or action. She expressed feeling let down by the event, especially after dedicating so much of her time to the cause. These experiences, and the more common ones, made me satisfied that the service-learning project gave the students a holistic view of local politics.

For myself, I learned a great deal about managing projects like this and about the need to maintain connections between the service-learning partners throughout the course of a project. My role in facilitating communications turned out to be critical in the successful conclusion of the course.

■ ■ ■

Nora Wilson, a graduate of the University of Iowa, is a student at the University of Wisconsin Law School.

References

Longo, N. V., Drury, C., & Battistoni, R. M. (2005, September). *Democracy's practice grounds: Classrooms and campuses as platforms for democratic civic education.* Paper presented at the annual meeting of the American Political Science Association, Washington, DC.

Markus, G. B., Howard, J. P., & King, D. C. (1993). Integrating community service and classroom instruction enhances learning: Results from an experiment. *Educational Evaluation and Policy Analysis, 15,* 410–419.

Strachan, J. C. (2003). *High tech grass roots: The professionalization of local elections.* Lanham, MD: Rowman & Littlefield.

University of Iowa, Office of the President. (2005). *Case statement for the year of public engagement.* Retrieved January 12, 2009, from www.ype.uiowa.edu/about/index.html.

University of North Carolina. (2006). *APPLES service-learning program.* Retrieved January 12, 2009, from www.unc.edu/apples/about/index.html.

Woodworth, J. R., Gump, R. R., & Forrester, J. R. (2006). *Camelot: A role playing simulation for political decision making* (5th ed.). Belmont, CA: Wadsworth.

CHAPTER TWELVE

TRIANGULATED LEARNING

Integrating Text, Current Events, and Experience in State and Local Government

Fredric A. Waldstein

This chapter is based on my more than fifteen years of experience using elements of the service-learning pedagogy in the social sciences generally, and a course in state and local government in particular. Beginning in 1990, I started to explore the possibility of using experience-based learning opportunities to supplement classroom instruction. At an individual professional level, this has evolved over the years into a pedagogical approach that seeks to educate by triangulating learning. At an institutional level, fifteen years has seen the evolution of service-learning grow from its use in fewer than a handful of courses to a campuswide initiative with significant support from the senior administration. While the specific frame of reference is a course on state and local government, the triangulated learning methodology has relevance beyond this course or even social science courses in general.

The course in its current design addresses a single goal: to make learning about subnational government relevant enough to students that they will take an active interest in the subject matter and think about their impact on their lives beyond the limited confines of the semester and its conclusion, the final grade. It is about the challenge of seeking methods to increase the intrinsic value of their learning against the more extrinsic value of credentialing. This goal has led to the evolution of State and Local Government at Wartburg College in Iowa from a traditional classroom course relying on textbooks, research papers, the occasional guest speaker, and exams to what I define as *triangulated learning*, a term that describes the integration of three sources of information: traditional text-based learning, current events discussions, and experience-based learning. This chapter addresses some of the challenges and rewards I have encountered employing triangulated learning as a type of service-learning, and I hope it will allow readers to avoid some of the mistakes made and take advantage of the lessons learned.

The chapter is divided into four sections. The first makes the case for service-learning as a pedagogy worthy of greater attention by the higher education community of scholars. It also addresses a concern that has been expressed repeatedly over the years, especially by junior faculty members, who sometimes face resistance by colleagues who may convey skepticism about the value of integrating service-learning into the curriculum. The second section focuses on the concept of triangulated learning and its application to courses in State and Local Government. The third section is a user's guide for the development and implementation of a service-learning course based on the concept of triangulated learning. It focuses on the nuts-and-bolts matters that can make the difference in developing and implementing a course that maximizes the potential of service-learning to meet particular curricular goals. The fourth section reports on how service-learning has evolved over the years at Wartburg from a few courses taught by a handful of faculty members into a collegewide focus that includes the commitment of financial and human resources to facilitate various kinds of experiential learning including service-learning. In its most recent iteration, this institutional commitment has led to the creation of the Center for Community Engagement.

THE MEANING AND VALUE OF SERVICE-LEARNING

In this section, I define service-learning, review how it is different from traditional internships and field experiences, and discuss its value over other classroom methods.

MEANING

Service-learning is a type of experiential learning that seeks to integrate and connect student needs and community needs to the mutual benefit of each. The number of definitions for service-learning is large, but most align themselves more or less with how it is defined in federal law by the National and Community Service Act of 1990 (as amended through December 17, 1999, P.L. 106–170):

(23) Service-Learning

The term "service-learning" means a method—

(A) under which students or participants learn and develop through active participation in thoughtfully organized service that—
  (i) is conducted in and meets the needs of a community;
  (ii) is coordinated with an elementary school, secondary school, institution of higher education, or community service program, and with the community; and
  (iii) helps foster civic responsibility; and

(B) that—
  (i) is integrated into and enhances the academic curriculum of the students, or the educational components of the community service program in which the participants are enrolled; and
  (ii) provides structured time for the students or participants to reflect on the service experience [p. 10].

Various types of experiential learning opportunities exist at Wartburg College in addition to courses that aspire to the service-learning model. Two common opportunities are internships and field experiences. The distinctions among the three types may be ones of degree or of kind. Here the emphasis is on factors that may distinguish among them as one means to emphasize the characteristics of a service-learning experience. Internships tend to be focused on preparatory training for a career that is discipline related. This may range from a finance major interning at a bank to a biochemistry major interning at a research laboratory. In both instances, the purpose of the internship is to give the students an applied learning opportunity directly connected to their academic field that will enhance their opportunities for employment or graduate school within that field. Internships normally take place in the latter half of students' academic career after they have attained some level of professional proficiency or expertise.

Field placements are also generally oriented toward career goals. Students are placed in venues they are considering as potential career paths. The expectations for field placement students is they will observe, or job-shadow, in an applied setting. This may occur in a school classroom for students considering teaching as a career or in a judge's courtroom for a student considering a legal career. The students are not normally expected to bring the kind of expertise to the site placement that would allow them to add substantial value to the activity of the site. Field experiences may occur any time, but they tend to occur earlier in a student's academic career than an internship.

THE VALUE OF SERVICE-LEARNING

Recent developments in higher education place increasing value on active learning, whereby students are required to take initiative and responsibility for their learning beyond sitting in class, taking notes, and being tested for content (the American Association of Colleges and Universities and the *Chronicle of Higher Education* are two widely respected sources where this topic has been discussed at length). Growing interest in undergraduate research is but one example of this trend. Bringing out-of-the-classroom experiences into the academic endeavor is a pedagogical orientation with a long and rich tradition. This overview relies on the work of two prominent scholars as touchstones to help provide the context for using experiential education in general and service-learning in particular in courses pertaining to the study of state and local government.

The philosopher and psychologist John Dewey, a scholar at the forefront of educational reform in the early twentieth century, observed that intentional reflection on the value of experience in education traced its roots back at least to the writings of Montaigne, Bacon, and Locke. He believed that as civilized societies advanced, they needed a formalized structure of education for the young, but that this posed some inherent risks as the concepts and symbols of generalized education became increasingly abstract and less connected to life's experience. "As societies become more complex in structure and resources," he wrote, "the need of formal or intentional teaching and learning increases. As formal teaching and training grow in extent, there is the danger of creating an undesirable split between the experience gained in more direct associations and what is acquired in school" (Dewey, 1923, p. 11). Dewey believed that for formal education to retain its relevance, it had to connect experientially the learner to the greater society for which the learner was being prepared. Consequently, it is in the interest of professionals involved in formal education, the students who participate in it, and the greater society that supports it to be intentional about connecting experience with formal education.

Jean Piaget, a well-established and respected biologist, decided midcareer to refocus his attention on learning and education. He came to believe in the value of experience based on his interest and research in cognitive development. According to Piaget (1972), to maximize the value of learning and make it more meaningful requires the student to go beyond merely listening and to engage in self-discovery: "To understand is to discover, or reconstruct by rediscovery, and such conditions must be complied with if in the future individuals are to be formed who are capable of production and creativity and not simply repetition" (p. 20). The teacher is most useful as a guide who has confidence in the student's ability to learn on his or her own. This is not to denigrate the potential value of the lecture format, for example. It may very well be a necessary condition for some types of learning, but it may not be a sufficient condition to maximize learning.

The natural sciences have long understood the value of testing hypotheses through experimentation and reflecting on the implications of the experiment—a form of experiential learning. Both words share the same Latin root, *experiri*, meaning "to test, try." The natural and social sciences place a high premium on empiricism, which has its roots in the philosophical work of John Locke and David Hume, who held that the source of human knowledge is derived from the senses. If empiricism is at the core of the scientific method and if the social sciences aspire to be "scientific," as the name suggests, using experiential education seems both natural and congruent with this orientation.

Service-learning is a subset of experiential learning. It incorporates experience as a venue for learning and serving in a manner that is mutually beneficial to all parties involved in terms of meeting their respective goals and needs. The degree of reciprocity attained is one measure of its success. Service-learning is a goal to which State and Local Government at Wartburg aspires. Sometimes those aspirations are met, and sometimes they are not. The challenge is to create a learning environment that maximizes the potential for service-learning to be practiced.

DESCRIBING AND EMPLOYING TRIANGULATED LEARNING IN *STATE AND LOCAL GOVERNMENT*

Triangulated learning seeks to integrate knowledge and information primarily from three sources: text and other academic materials, current events from reputable news sources, and site placement learning experience to help the student understand better the intricacies of state and local government. How students make the connection is highly variable depending on their level of competence with respect to all three learning venues, but it must be made in a coherent manner that demonstrates their capacity to engage in critical inquiry by taking knowledge and information from one domain and transferring and applying it to another domain and conversing about it intelligently.

The first two parameters may be discussed fairly quickly, as they are widely applied in college and university classrooms throughout the country, and their value in the academy is largely assumed. It is not the purpose of this chapter to challenge or undermine that assumption, but rather to identify potential limitations and how those limitations might be mitigated using the other two approaches. Most textbooks on state and local government tend to be descriptive and not very theoretical. But with few exceptions, the description tends to be a general overview of institutional frameworks and processes that have relatively little to do with the particulars of a given locality. Both current events discussions and experiential learning projects, when appropriately overlaid with the text, can enrich its value by providing specific, concrete examples that can bring the material in the text to life.

Current events offer the opportunity to bring relevant news of the day to classroom discussion, but the media sources from which they are derived normally do not put them in a context most useful for an academic discussion. To account for this limitation, a worksheet template has been developed for students to complete prior to class. Items that the students are asked to address in the worksheet include: How does the current event relate to the topic? How does the news source inform your understanding of the topic as presented in the assigned reading? How does the assigned reading help you understand better the story covered in the news source you have identified? In what ways might this topic pertain to your site placement and experiential learning? It is relatively rare that multiple students identify the same news source and the same theme in the text. Consequently there is the potential for a discussion that is based on the individual "expertise" that each student brings independently to the discussion based on events he or she has self-identified as relevant to the general topic or theme.

The third side of the triangle, site placement, experience-based learning, creates a situation where each student is placed in an environment that gives him or her the opportunity to learn in-depth about a particular aspect of state or local government. Like the current events worksheet format, the site placement offers each student the opportunity to bring his or her own learning experiences to the conversation. The site placement experience provides each student with a particular perspective on state and local government that reflects the culture of the site where the student is placed. The students develop over the course of the term a sense of that culture, which they are able to bring to bear in the discussions pertaining to the other two sides of the learning triangle.

The experiential component of the triangle is a greater challenge to manage compared to the selection of a textbook and the design of a worksheet. The first management challenge involves communications. However the experiential learning experience is organized, the complexity of communication is increased at least threefold. With two individuals involved (the instructor and the student), there are only two lines of communication that need to function efficiently: communication from the instructor to the student and from the student to the instructor. Experienced teachers know that this relatively straightforward and simple communications network can be difficult enough to manage. When a community partner is brought into the communications network, this adds four more lines of communication that have to be managed: the two-way communication between the instructor and the community partner and the two-way communication between the student and the community partner. These last two lines can be especially problematic in terms of ensuring that the relationship meets the course goals.

The second management challenge (which is interdependent with the communications challenge) is logistical. Identifying and securing sites for placing students that provide an appropriate learning environment and an opportunity to add value to the organization with their presence is not a simple task. An appropriate learning environment is necessary if the experience is to be truly educational. Adding value to the organization is necessary if the participation of the community partner is to be sustainable over time measured in years. When both of these are present, the probability for service-learning to occur increases significantly.

If this learning triangle is constructed and implemented appropriately, then all sides of the triangle may complement one another and create a service-learning environment that brings at least three different dimensions to the educational enterprise. The text serves as a common point of reference for all. It provides a common language and context that is a necessary condition for fruitful intellectual dialogue. The worksheet allows each student the opportunity to identify a current event he or she finds interesting and how it relates to the common topic presented in the text. The experiential learning site placement allows the further development of expertise from the vantage point of a specific governmental organization. This is the essential design for the course. The challenge is to make the course operational in a manner that maximizes the learning outcomes intended in the rationale and design.

THE SERVICE-LEARNING MODEL IN *STATE AND LOCAL GOVERNMENT* AT WARTBURG COLLEGE

Wartburg College is located in Waverly, part of the Iowa Cedar Valley. A community of approximately ten thousand, Waverly has a robust municipal government and is the county seat of

Bremer County. Abutting Bremer County is Black Hawk County. Its county seat, Waterloo, with a population of more than sixty-eight thousand, is only fifteen miles from Waverly. Consequently, numerous local government organizations at both the municipal and county levels offer the potential for student placements.

Wartburg College is a small, private college in the liberal arts tradition with approximately eighteen hundred students. The students who enroll in State and Local Government span a range of academic majors and interests. As a 200-level course, it tends to attract first- and second-year students who are considering political science as a major or minor area of study. But students from business and finance, community sociology, and communication arts also routinely populate the course. It is not a group of students who aspire to careers in state and local government, although some come to that conclusion by the end of the term. In short, the student profile for the course is not one that would lend itself to a preprofessional field placement or internship format.

Matriculated students register for courses only once a year (in March) for the following academic year. (Students may add and drop classes after that, and new students register during the summer, but the general constellation of students for State and Local Government has remained relatively stable over the years after March registration.) In addition, I can go online and see an abbreviated profile of the students enrolled. This gives me the advantage of knowing well in advance what the likely composition of the class is going to be.

ADVANCE PREPARATION

The first decision to make is a determination of what organizations and agencies to include as potential site placements. During the first few years, I made an effort to restrict site placements to official government agencies. Although the large majority of site placements remain government agencies, other organizations have been included as site placements as well. There are two primary reasons for this, and both have to do with developing a more comprehensive picture of how different types of organizations serve the public, whether they are official government agencies or nongovernmental organizations that may or may not receive funding to fulfill public needs. One reason is that privatization of government services has affected local government. For example, Bremer County used to own and operate what was euphemistically called the "county poor farm" to serve an indigent population with little in the way of a social safety net. These same services are now provided by a variety of nongovernmental organizations that are partially funded by the county and state to pay for services that the county once provided. The second reason is that some organizations provide services that are perceived as highly desirable by local government, but due to certain regulations and other legal aspects, it is more convenient to have these services provided by a nongovernmental organization. The Waverly Area Development Group is an example of this type of organization. Part of its responsibility is to provide economic development assistance, and in this role, it works closely with city officials, both elected and professional staff.

The communication network begins to be constructed at least five or six weeks before the term in which the course is being taught. This communication is between the potential site supervisor and me as the instructor and between the student and me. The first effort is to contact individuals in state or local government positions who have served as site supervisors in the past. Experience has taught me never to assume that because an individual has agreed to serve as a site supervisor previously, he or she is in a position or cares to do so again. This information provides the base for determining how many, if any, new site placements may be needed. If new placements are needed, I recruit replacements with letters, personal visits, and telephone calls. This process is less demanding than it may appear on its face because of relationships I have built throughout eighteen years of teaching and civic engagement in the Cedar Valley.

Critical to a successful service-learning site placement is a clear understanding at the outset about what I expect from student placements. The best opportunities from the student's perspective are those that allow him or her to work with senior management and offer the opportunity for the student to develop an appreciation of how the work undertaken integrates into a broader perspective on the operations of state and local government. These may vary from a special project or activity of a more routine nature. The issue of reciprocity is also emphasized at the outset. The site placement candidates are encouraged to identify potential projects for students they think would be of value to their organizations, as well as provide students with a good learning opportunity.

Experience has taught me that student awareness of the course parameters prior to going into class is haphazard at best, catalogue copy notwithstanding. Consequently I send an e-mail to each student approximately three weeks before the course commences, reminding them about the structure of the course and the expectation that they will spend at least two hours a week throughout the bulk of the term with a state or local government organization where they will undertake some kind of project designed by the site placement supervisor. This also gives me the opportunity to offer the students a list of potential site placements and poll them to determine if there are particular types of state or local government organizations that they would like to experience. This invariably leads to the identification of individuals interested in law enforcement or parks and recreation management, to name two examples. Students are also encouraged to arrange their own site placements if they have contacts. However, students are forewarned that they are not guaranteed their first preference. A number of factors go into placements. This includes a breadth of placements that touch on different aspects of state and local government. Once students are assigned to a site, both the student and the supervisor are given a copy of the expectations students are to meet during the term, including a copy of the evaluation form the site supervisor will be asked to complete at the end of the term. In addition, the site supervisor is given a copy of the student self-assessment form each student will complete at the end of the term.

The purpose of this preterm communication is to establish a precedent for open channels of communication to encourage ongoing dialogue throughout the course of the term. There are two potentially negative consequences as a result of the preterm process. Some students, for a variety of reasons, drop the course prior to its start. It has also happened, although much less frequently, that a site supervisor has felt it necessary to back out of a commitment. In both instances, there is the risk of disappointment by the other party. This also discounts the value of the time and effort I put into the preterm work. But on balance, the potential risk is well worth the overall benefits that accrue to the quality of the course as a whole.

IMPLEMENTATION OF THE PEDAGOGY DURING THE TERM

The implementation of the pedagogy during the term in which the course is taught falls into three general stages that can be defined as orientation, implementation, and assessment and evaluation. These stages are linear but not discrete, as they bleed into each other in terms of both the process as a whole and the different rates at which students develop an understanding of the overall pedagogy. For example, one student may still be in the orientation stage, while another is in the implementation stage. Perhaps the most distinguishing characteristic of the three stages from a pedagogical perspective is the transference of teaching responsibility from instructor to students.

First Stage: Orientation

The first few class sessions tend to be rather chaotic and bifurcated as the students employ the three components (text, current events, and site placement) in a discrete rather than integrative fashion. Student anxiety can be rather high for those who have little experience with a multidimensional learning format. To counter this anxiety, I have found it useful to adopt a coaching approach in which I encourage the student to view me as an ally in the journey through the course. But like a good coach, I must encourage the reluctant students to accept responsibility for their own success in this kind of learning environment. It is up to the student to connect the dots that ultimately form the learning triangle. For the better students, this may take less than a week. For others, it may take up to three weeks. The length of time it takes is partially dependent on the degree to which students embrace the site placement opportunity and the degree of initiative they possess—two highly variable factors. Another factor is the availability of the site supervisor.

One of the most important aspects of the course is the initial meeting between the student and the site placement supervisor. It is the student's responsibility to make the initial contact and arrange a meeting. Students are asked to review the expectations of the site placement supervisor in terms of the project that will be undertaken, and they review with the site supervisors the evaluation form the supervisor will be asked to complete at the end of the term. The form also gives the student a concrete set of guidelines with respect to expectations regarding dress, attitude, and performance.

Second Stage: Implementation

The implementation stage takes up the bulk of the term. It is during this stage that the student develops a working relationship with the site supervisor and staff, engages in a project, and attends meetings, including a city council meeting and a board or commission meeting relevant to the site placement when that is appropriate. One challenge for me during this phase is to ensure that the student, while at the site placement, is engaged in learning that pertains to the goals of the course. Two mechanisms are used toward this end. One is the completion of weekly worksheets. The worksheet template explicitly asks the student if he or she is able to make some connection between the text, a current event, and the site placement. But the worksheet has its limitations in this regard. Its primary use is to generate a class discussion that allows students to develop a certain expertise and bring that to bear on whatever the topic for the day may be. Sometimes the topic and the site placement are too disparate to make a credible connection.

To compensate for the limitation of the worksheet, students are also required to submit journal entries. The entries are sent electronically at least once a week for the duration of the site placement. A review of these entries can give me a good sense of what the student is accomplishing and whether some type of intervention may be needed to ensure a maximum learning experience for the student.

Aside from the site placement work, this is also the stage where the textbook is used and I employ more traditional teaching techniques in the classroom: lecture, discussion, exams, and other familiar pedagogical devices. Little can be added regarding these devices that is not familiar to most instructors of State and Local Government or college instructors in general. Perhaps it is worth noting that student-generated worksheet discussions are used to construct items on exams. This is intended to demonstrate the degree to which I take seriously this aspect of the classroom experience, and it encourages students to do the same.

Another important aspect of the orientation process is to educate the students about how to learn while at their site placement. Toward this end, I provide a brief introduction to ethnography and ethnographic research. There are three reasons for exposing the students to an ethnographic approach. First, it gives them some tools about how to learn in a field setting: what to look for, how to follow up on observations, and how to analyze or interpret observations. Analysis and interpretation focus mostly on cautioning students to understand the limits of their expertise and not to jump to faulty conclusions as a result. The second reason is that it gives the students some context for how to use their environment to its best learning advantage. For example, working near the water-cooler in an open area with active human traffic may be much more productive than being isolated in a small office in terms of learning about the cultural norms of the site. Third, students who have options about the types of work they may be asked to perform can exercise the options that maximize the value of the site placement from an ethnographic perspective.

One of the site placement learning devices that the students are required to employ is keeping a journal. Part of the orientation stage is teaching the students how to use good journaling techniques as tools for reflection that can aid them in their ethnographic research and help them integrate the elements of the course. For this to be successful requires intentional work on my part to prevent receiving journals that simply record dates, times, and activities and not very different from a time sheet. Students are given literature about various benefits of journaling and what kind of journaling is appropriate to ensure intentional reflection pertinent to the purpose of the site placement within the context of the course.

The journaling process is one way to evaluate the student's capacity to understand successfully and use the triangulated learning process. Below are two journal entry excerpts (unedited) by the same student; the first follows the first site visit, the second follows the last.

In class, I learned much of the basic structure and responsibilities of a state government. I learned what decisions they have to make, how they make those, and how much of a direct impact they have on me. I learned that there are many ways these local branches coexist with the federal government, and how both work together to provide the best possible service to their constituents. Without the local governments as the backbone of our government, many of the great services that we take advantage of would be lost and our cities would be a much bigger mess. The reading simply managed to open my eyes as to all that these governments did.

My field experience with the Waverly City Council and their city administrator . . . simply astonished me. My duties eventually will consist of preparing the agenda for city council meetings as well as putting together and reviewing budget reports. As a part of my first day in the office, I looked over the agenda for last week's meeting. I was astonished as to the range of topics covered.

■ ■ ■

I helped to assemble the agenda for the study session next council meeting. The new budget has just been recently released, which has also put a buzz in the council. Of course, the copier that I helped research the first weeks was broken again, and the office was back to attempting to decide whether to buy a new one. Mostly though, I learned that there is a tremendous amount of responsibility invested in the city council. They have a huge budget, employ many people, and affect every single person in the city with whatever decision they made. I was amazed at how important all of the decisions they make are, and the experience has truly allowed me to appreciate how vital a good city council is to our city growing.

At the same time, I learned how to apply this to my home town, where I learned that Cedar Rapids is going through a budget crisis. They face the option of raising taxes drastically or making tough spending cuts. They have chosen the latter, and now must slash spending in all areas, angering a lot of people. This connected greatly with the fiscal chapters that we studied in class on

Wednesday, allowing me to understand how hard it is to simply take money from a program. Everyone feels that the money cut should be from the other program, not their own, which makes their job that much more difficult.

The level of analysis is more sophisticated in the second entry at several levels. The student makes connections between the site placement and the readings from the text and extrapolates from this learning to make inferences about policy decisions in his home town based on keeping up with current events there. There is strong evidence of triangulated learning in a service-learning environment.

Third Stage: Assessment and Evaluation

Just as it is important to prepare students for their site placements so they can begin their site placement experiences well, it is equally important for the students to conclude their site placements well. At least two weeks before the conclusion of the site placement work, students meet with the site placement supervisor to review the status of the project in light of the remaining time and to set priorities about what the site supervisor would like accomplished in that time. This process helps maintain mutual understanding among all participants with respect to expectations. Before I made this an intentional part of the program several years ago, one student simply stopped showing up. The student's site supervisor, who had developed a positive working relationship with the student, called me to ask if the student had an accident or had otherwise come into some kind of unfortunate situation. The student, for his part, thought the site supervisor was aware that his placement had come to an end because he had successfully completed the project during the time allotted. While this particular situation was ultimately resolved to the satisfaction of all parties, it became clear to me that a more intentional focus on how the site visit should be concluded was just as important as how it was initiated, and this has been an integral part of the course since.

The site placement process culminates with the site supervisor completing an evaluation of the student and his or her work. In this evaluation, the supervisor begins by estimating the number of hours the student was on site and describes the nature of the project the student undertook and its value to the organization. The supervisor then rates the student's performance on a ten-point Likert scale regarding seven items that pertain to professionalism, dress, attitude, performance, initiative, responsibility, and whether the supervisor would like to work with the student again. The evaluation ends with an open-ended item asking the site supervisor to make any additional comments he or she thinks are relevant to the student's performance and the experience in general. The survey is sent through the postal system with a stamped, return envelope. Completion rates by the site supervisor have been close to 100 percent over the years. The following is typical of the kinds of open-ended responses site supervisors provide: "[Student X] displayed a professional and friendly attitude during the entire experience. He represented both Wartburg and himself in an extremely positive manner. I enjoyed getting to know [student X] and wish him success in whatever profession he chooses." Site supervisors tend to offer more reassurance than concrete information helpful in the evaluation process. Nevertheless, such reassurance has its own value.

Students complete a self-evaluation at the conclusion of their site placement that replicates in part the evaluation form completed by the site supervisors (for example, on the nature of the project undertaken and the amount of time spent on the project). If there are discrepancies in the descriptive data provided by the site supervisor and the student, further discussions ensue, although this happens very rarely, and in only a few instances over the years has reconciliation of the differences proved to be problematic. Because everyone knows what the expectations are and what evaluations will look like going into the project, there is relatively little opportunity for misunderstanding in this regard.

Much of the student self-assessment is open-ended and seeks to determine the quality of placement and supervision. Self-assessment items include (1) aspects of the project with which the student was most satisfied and least satisfied; (2) reflections about what the student would do differently given what he or she knows at the end of the term if given the opportunity to start over; (3) reflections on what the site placement experience contributed to the student's understanding about state and local government;

(4) assessments of what the student learned about state and local government by undertaking the project; (5) what the student thought he or she learned that would not have been learned without the site placement experience; and (6) anything else the student wants to add about the experience. Below is a representative example of one student's self-assessment as it pertains to questions 5 and 6.

> 5. What do you think you learned about state and local government that you would not have learned had you not undertaken an active learning project?

> Obviously basically all the things in the prior question that I talked about are the things I would not have learned had I not had the active learning project. This is due to the fact that I would not have been directly working with all these issues. In addition to all the different aspects of state and local government already listed, I would not have had the opportunity to work with the people I met and to continue to improve my people skills and in this situation in the area of local government. Without the active learning I would have been limited to what I read in the books. While it was good information I find that my project did a great job of reinforcing many of the things we learned in class and our books. As a result I was able to get a much stronger grip on many of the topics we covered this semester in class.

> 6. Is there anything else you would like to add? (optional)

> The things I covered on this evaluation are not everything I have learned while at my internship. For a much more in-depth look at all the aspects see my journals and semester end project.

It is worth noting that the amount of student learning that takes place is sometimes not recognized by the site supervisor, and there have been times when the site supervisor has been almost apologetic that the student did not get more out of the experience. For example, the site supervisor of the student quoted directly above wrote the following:

> [Student Y] is an extremely likable, intelligent young man. He was willing to do any job requested with very minimal supervision. The work we do is fairly routine but [student Y] never acted

bored. He also helped organize our health insurance packets for employees.

The discussion the Election Deputy and I had with him about "same day [voter] registration" eased our concerns. [The nature of these concerns was never stated.]

Thank you for the opportunity of working with [student Y].

Students are also asked to rank their educational experience on a fifty-point scale. The self-evaluation is graded according to the quality of the responses measured in the student's capacity to demonstrate the skills of critical inquiry in terms of making connections between the placement experiences and the course content and taking a level of responsibility and ownership in the learning experience. This exercise is treated much like a take-home final.

The final three weeks of the term are devoted to the preparation and presentation of student-led seminars in the field of expertise they have cultivated over the course of the term. Part of the preparation includes identifying a suitable reading assigned to the class, which is intended to provide all participants some background information that permits an interactive discussion. In recent years, the typical session begins with a PowerPoint presentation that describes the site placement experience and the project undertaken, how it relates to the material discussed in class over the course of the term, and a set of discussion questions. Students are expected to have enough material to engage the other students for at least thirty minutes, but normally sessions last forty-five minutes or longer. This experience reveals as few other methods of assessment can what the students learned and how engaged they were in the site placement. The interactive and spontaneous nature of the seminar format allows student presenters to demonstrate how much they know (or do not know). Each presentation is peer-reviewed using a ten-point Likert scale to assess preparation, clarity, coherence, discussion questions, and overall effectiveness. Students are also asked to identify the strongest and weakest parts of the presentation. These data are aggregated and shared with the presenter. The content of these student-led seminars serves as the basis for the final examination of the term.

Moving to Active Learners

The three stages of the course are designed to move the student ever increasingly to the role of active learner with shared teaching responsibilities. The assessment and evaluation tools are designed to aid in this process. Initially I placed less weight on the experiential learning and peer evaluation portions of the course for two reasons. First, there was uncertainty about what tools should be used to evaluate the site placement and how they would be used by site placement supervisors and students. Second, there was a sense that self-assessment and peer evaluation might result in grade inflation that could distort the final results beyond the norms acceptable to me. Confidence in the tools and their use has increased over the years as both site supervisors and students have used them responsibly and effectively (it is not uncommon that site supervisors rate students higher than the students rate themselves in their self-assessment). Similarly, self-assessment and peer evaluation have produced results well within parameters the instructor finds appropriate.

MOVING TO AN INSTITUTIONAL EMPHASIS ON SERVICE-LEARNING

From my perspective, the triangulated learning model has created a positive environment for service-learning to occur within the framework of the State and Local Government course at Wartburg College. But beyond this, there has been a larger institutional commitment to this pedagogy by the college as a whole. Testimony to this is the Voices piece at the end of the chapter by the president of Wartburg, which takes an institutional perspective on the evolution of service-learning on campus. Here the perspective is that of a faculty member.

In 2004, Wartburg College recognized the expanded interest of faculty in developing experiential learning courses including service-learning courses. While the college and certain members of the faculty have long advocated the expansion of this pedagogy throughout the curriculum, its growing use has brought additional challenges. First, many faculty members who experimented with service-learning saw and appreciated its advantages, but simply did not think they could afford the additional time and effort that setting up a quality service-learning course required. Also, instructors who had been employing service-learning witnessed increasing "competition" for site placements, a potential source of disruption. In addition, there was increasing confusion in the community as different instructors from the college approached potential partners with different agendas according to their disciplinary or course-level needs.

To address this concern, the college administration took a proactive approach with support from the Eli Lilly Foundation to create the Center for Community Engagement (CCE). Currently the CCE has a full-time staff of four individuals: a community partners coordinator, a school partners coordinator, an internship coordinator, and a service trips coordinator. Most relevant for purposes of this chapter is the position of the community partners coordinator, although this model applies more or less to all staff members of the CCE. Once it was the responsibility of the individual instructor to set up site placements; that responsibility has started to shift to the community partners coordinator. In its first year, the transition has worked quite well and has indeed shifted some of the logistical burden of setting up site placements away from the instructor. It is anticipated that as the community partners coordinator gains greater familiarity with the community (this is only his second year at Wartburg) this opportunity for one-stop shopping for faculty will add considerable value to experiential learning courses by reducing the workload side of the equation for faculty members with respect to logistics.

There are also potential costs associated with the creation of an office like the CCE beyond the obvious resource issues. First, the challenge to the instructor of remaining informed about the learning that is taking place on site and the relationship between the site supervisor and the student may be even more problematic with the reduced level of contact between instructor and site supervisor. Second, the CCE is staffed by academic staff personnel, and these kinds of positions often experience relatively high turnover. Key to the development of a strong pool of potential site placements is the development of relationships between a representative of the college and the site supervisors. Staff turnover presents challenges to maintaining the kinds of relationships that are necessary for maintaining a strong, sustainable pool of potential site placements. On balance, the creation of the CCE has been met with approval by the faculty, but it is not a panacea. It requires an intentional approach on the part of the college or university to ensure that its structure and staffing are appropriate for both the institution and the larger community in which it resides.

CONCLUSION

At the start of the chapter, I indicated that service-learning is a pedagogy to which the instructor aspires. While the instructor can guarantee an experiential learning opportunity, he or she cannot guarantee a service-learning experience. This is the case because even if the course is implemented as an integrated learning experience, it involves collaboration among three individuals: the instructor, the student, and the site supervisor. As is true with any other collaboration, the capacity to turn aspiration into reality is dependent on the effort and understanding that all collaborating partners are willing to put into it. Consequently, it is possible in any given class to have some students for whom the course meets the service-learning threshold and some for whom it does not by virtue of a number of variables, including student initiative, interest, and intellectual capacity. Simultaneously, the degree of understanding and skill that the site supervisors bring to the table is equally important. They have to understand the sense of reciprocity that service-learning entails and provide the opportunity for students to engage in meaningful activities that add value to the organization if service-learning is to occur. My experience is that the more often state and local government professionals participate as site placement supervisors, the better they understand the purpose of service-learning and the better able they are to provide a site placement experience that meets its pedagogical objectives. Finally, the instructor must be open and flexible to the unexpected and be willing to serve as a broker and mediator to ensure that everyone is benefiting from the experience.

There are no guarantees that the triangulated educational experience will be successful for every student. It requires the genuine commitment of all three partners: the instructor, the student, and the site placement supervisor. It means more work for the instructor than simply preparing lectures and otherwise engaging the more traditional learning models. But it can also be much more interesting and rewarding for all parties. For the students, it provides a learning experience that encourages them to take greater ownership of their education and challenges them to think about different contexts for learning and what that might imply about applying the skills of critical inquiry throughout their lives. For site supervisors, it provides the opportunity to play a mentoring role to college students, an opportunity that may be underappreciated by instructors in the academy who work with talented college students on a daily basis. There have been several instances where site supervisors and students have remained in contact years after the student has completed the course. For the instructor, it creates a dynamic and exciting learning environment with new challenges and opportunities. It also creates closer relations between higher education and other significant institutions in the community that can help foster a more positive community atmosphere of collaboration.

Skeptics frequently ask what evidence the practitioner has that service-learning is effective. By this, they normally seek to ascertain whether quantitative empirical evidence exists supporting the view that the pedagogy improves learning. Others and I have addressed this topic at length elsewhere and need not repeat it here. Suffice it to say for purposes of this chapter that I am confident that triangulated learning has produced a more sophisticated understanding of the course content through an integrated learning process consistent with the higher-order learning outcomes suggested by the work of Dewey and Piaget. Student performance on exams, the quality of writing, feedback in course evaluations, and other means confirm my professional judgment that this pedagogy provides a learning experience that transcends the traditional classroom model.

Parenthetically, it is worth noting a heuristic device that is widely cited (more than 700,000 results from a Google search, including scholarly references) as providing evidence that active learning techniques consistent with the theoretical perspectives of Dewey, Piaget, and many others lead to increased retention of what has been taught. This device, the learning pyramid of retention, is attributed to research associated with the National Training Laboratories in Bethel, Maine. According to this source, the rates of student retention of knowledge increase dramatically as the degree of interactivity on the part of the learner increases. For example, the rate of retention for "lecture" (identified as the least active form of learning) is reported to be 5 percent, while the rate of retention for "teaching others" (identified as the most active form of learning) is reported to be 90 percent. Intuitively appealing as the learning pyramid may be, the research data supporting these percentages seem nowhere to be found. I bring this to readers' attention because it is equally, if not more, important that faculty members and scholars who employ active learning techniques including service-learning retain the same level of rigor in assessing the evidence mounted for its value that they employ for other types of research. To do otherwise is both a disservice to respect for the pedagogy and to the methodological standards of the social sciences.

Voices: Partners in Service-Learning

THE WAVERLY LIGHT AND POWER AND WARTBURG COLLEGE PARTNERSHIP

Glenn Cannon

Waverly Light and Power values the relationship with Wartburg College and the students who partner with us daily. When we were first approached by Wartburg on the idea of having students involved in our operation, I looked at it as time we would spend teaching them about what we do. Instead, we learn a great deal from the students, and they are an immense help in giving us fresh ideas and perspectives. In a large sense, the students keep us young. The students come to work in our building to be exposed to many different occupations and experiences. They are able to work around their college classes and outside activities. Waverly Light and Power gains a valuable person with fresh training and new ideas to help our experienced staff perform many tasks. In fact, much of the work we produce could not be accomplished without the help of the students. In our financial area, a host of students over the years have helped design, implement, and update numerous reports for us. A few of these include our performance indicators (comparing our operations to that of others in our industry), outage records (tracking our annual electrical disturbances and the causes), and financial models (which help us forecast our future financial performance and are the basis for when we need to issue bonds and change rates and our energy efficiency records)—comparing our customer take rate on various program offerings and the effectiveness of each. We have also had students who worked on special projects like a summary history of our pioneering the development of soybean-based transformer oil. One of our Wartburg students went on to work for the accounting firm of Virchow Krause and Company and initially worked on utility auditing. A side benefit that we had never considered was the diversity that we gain from having new students work with us. We have had students from Nepal, Rwanda, Colombia, and the Republic of Georgia. We also had a young woman from Ukraine who ended up with a C.P.A. and is working for a major insurance company in Des Moines. Two of our Wartburg students married each other.

We will continue to seek the partnership of the college and its students. The students routinely visit us after they have graduated and share how their experiences helped them gain an understanding of the real world and how to prepare for it. It is in all respects a win-win situation.

■ ■ ■

Glenn Cannon is general manager of Waverly Light and Power.

Service-Learning as an Institutional Priority at Wartburg College

Jack R. Ohle

The power and authority of college and university presidents and chancellors is often exaggerated and misunderstood. But given the privilege of our perspective, we do have the opportunity to see the big picture of the workings of the institutions we serve. Following is one example of how this unique perspective permitted the identification of a need and the means used to mobilize the Wartburg campus community to help address that need.

When I became president of Wartburg College, one of the first tasks I set for myself was to see what elements of the college aligned most closely with its mission: "Wartburg College is dedicated to challenging and nurturing students for lives of leadership and service as a spirited expression of their faith and learning." My inventory led me to identify a few curricular offerings that embodied what I understood as elements of service-learning. Beyond the curriculum, I discovered in the Office of Student Life a cocurricular Volunteer Action Center (VAC), which served as a clearinghouse for matching community needs with student interests. Student Life also had responsibility for facilitating the organization of service trips, which occurred during our fall and winter term breaks. Both initiatives had been created as a result of the work of the director of Wartburg's Institute for Leadership Education (ILE) by securing outside funding to help satisfy the needs of students involved in leadership education. But the primary responsibilities of the ILE are academic, and its focus is helping students meet the requirements for the Leadership Certificate Program, an academic minor in the college curriculum.

These were aspects of the college that spoke to its mission of "leadership and service" in a direct and compelling manner, but it seemed from my vantage point as president and as a result of conversation with various faculty and staff that these experiential activities were rather fragmented. Each had its own constituency of loyal advocates, but they focused on their individual needs, which at times led them to compete with one another, sometimes inadvertently, for resources and other forms of support. As a result, Wartburg was not maximizing the value these enterprises could add to the vibrancy of the college community as they might if there were a greater sense of collaboration and cohesion among them.

The opportunity to address this challenge came when Wartburg College was invited to apply for a grant from the Lilly Endowment. To take full advantage of this opportunity required giving voice to the entire campus community in setting the agenda for how the grant might enhance Wartburg's mission. The final result was a campuswide initiative called "Discovering and Claiming Our Callings." One of the many contributions of this program has been to bring greater recognition of the value of collaboration and coordination among curricular (such as service-learning courses) and cocurricular (such as service trips) activities pertaining to leadership and service. This has helped to elevate to a higher level of consciousness the centrality of these activities to the mission of the college.

Meeting this threshold required both symbolic and substantive change. The campus community needed a concrete image that spoke of the college's commitment to the mission, especially as it pertains to leadership and service. But it also had to produce results that confirmed the commitment of resources to such an enterprise. To accomplish this effectively, the decision was made, after a year-long study of how best to integrate existing programs, to create a new entity on the campus, the Center for Community Engagement (CCE), and associate it closely with the ILE. The rationale for this decision was that many of the support services under the direction of the CCE were created to benefit students working toward their leadership certificate. The creation of the CCE and its close association with the ILE was the end product of the effort to merge symbolic and substantive change.

The symbolism has been apparent to the campus community and beyond. The CCE and the ILE are colocated in a prominent public space on campus and staffed with significant resources. In addition, with its own director, the CCE brings under one administrative structure the Volunteer Action Center, academic internships, service trips, and support for service-learning courses. Changes in administrative structure alone do not necessarily mean greater effectiveness, but preliminary response to the creation of the CCE has been positive by faculty members, students, and community members alike. We will continue to monitor all three constituencies to ensure that this trend continues. To date, the collaboration between the CCE and ILE has had a dramatic impact in increasing student involvement in both curricular and cocurricular activities, which fall under their respective leadership portfolios. Record numbers of service trips and leadership students speak to the value of the new organizational structure. This is the direct result of the close professional relationship between the two directors and their ability to take advantage of the resources the other offers, to the mutual advantage of both.

Each institution of higher education has its own mission and unique set of circumstances, and it is not the purpose of these reflections to offer a universal template formula for success. Rather, its purpose is simply to note that it behooves all of us in positions of leadership to take advantage of our unique perspectives to continually review what is already happening on our campuses that effectively enhances our respective missions at the microlevel and do what we can to elevate them to a macro or institutional level. Such a strategy has the advantage of building bridges among various constituencies of the campus community because it acknowledges and rewards those among the faculty and staff most committed to the institutional mission. In this particular instance, it has had the further advantage of building bridges out into the broader community in which the college resides and serves. This has the potential to create a sum-plus environment to which all chief administrators should aspire.

■ ■ ■

Jack R. Ohle is president of Wartburg College.

References

Dewey, J. (1923). *Democracy and education: An introduction to the philosophy of education.* New York: Macmillan.

Piaget, J. (1972). *To understand is to invent.* New York: Viking Press.

CHAPTER THIRTEEN

SERVICE-LEARNING IN THE ENGINEERING SCIENCES

William Oakes

Service-learning offers many opportunities for students to learn skills that are difficult or almost impossible to learn in traditional classes (Eyler & Giles, 1999). The pedagogy also provides opportunities for students and faculty to have an enormous impact on local, regional, or even global communities while participating in this highly effective learning environment. While many disciplines have adopted service-learning in significant ways, the technical fields of engineering, computing, technology, and other sciences have been much slower to adopt the pedagogy. Many faculty members in these fields struggle to see how to connect a meaningful service experience with their course work. Some are even scared off by those of us in the service-learning community who become very passionate about the impact of the service experience on students. We can fall into a trap of talking much more about the service and the transformational experience it can be rather than the academic learning gains of the pedagogy. What some colleagues hear is that this experience is better suited for general education classes than for their own core classes.

I acknowledge the foresight and dedication of Leah Jamieson and Edward Coyle for their founding of the EPICS Program and their work to bring it to the current state of development. I also acknowledge Pam Brown, Carla Zoltowski, and our dedicated staff who have made the Purdue EPICS Program what it is today.

The reality is that service-learning can have a profound impact on the learning of fundamental engineering and computing concepts and aligns very well with ongoing efforts to reform our fields within higher education. The ABET (the accrediting agency for engineering programs) accreditation standards include a broad set of outcomes for engineering graduates that go beyond just strong technical skills. They include attributes such as being able to function on multidisciplinary teams, strong communication skills, an understanding of contemporary societal issues, and an ability to apply ethics. Service-learning is well positioned to meet these while strengthening technical skills.

A more recent effort is the National Academy of Sciences' publications *The Engineer of 2020* (2004) and the follow-on *Educating the Engineer of 2020* (2005). These publications add to the list of desired attributes of graduates to include leadership, practical ingenuity, high ethical standards, agility, and professionalism, among others. A third report, *Rising Above the Gathering Storm* (2006), addresses the global competitiveness of the United States. Service-learning is a tool that can be used to adapt the curricula to meet these calls for reform. It offers a solution to the challenge of how to integrate experiences into our curricula without adding many new courses. Rather than creating new courses, leadership, ingenuity, and the other attributes of the twenty-first-century engineer can be taught using service-learning approaches.

Moreover, within the engineering, technology, and computing education community, the integration of research findings on learning into our design of courses has become an important area of concern. The work of cognitive scientists and educational researchers is finding its way into our curriculum reform efforts as they tell us about differences in learning styles. For example, service-learning work can connect to students who learn better hands-on. As Bransford, Brown, and Cocking (1999) tell us, "Learners of all ages are more motivated when they can see the usefulness of what they are learning and when they can use that information to do something that has an impact on others—*especially in their local community* [emphasis added]" (p. 49).

A final dimension of how service-learning fits into current issues in our fields is the continued underrepresentation of women and minorities in engineering, technology, and computing.

Beyond the moral and ethical implications of unequal access, sufficient cause in themselves for concern, underrepresentation is a critical and compelling issue for society in general. Several reports show that demand will outpace the available pool of qualified professionals in the technical fields if trends are not reversed. Approaches that encourage women to stay in engineering include (1) framing engineering in its social context; (2) stressing general educational goals, including communication, in engineering education; (3) employing cooperative, interdisciplinary approaches; (4) and undertaking problems with a "holistic, global scope," all of which are consistent with the pedagogy of service-learning (Noddings, 1992; Rosser, 1990). Matyas and Malcolm (1991), Oakes, Gamoran, and Page (1992), and Hawkins (2005) all suggest that many similar factors are relevant for attracting and retaining minorities. Service-learning has a potential to have an impact on the overall interest in our fields and to be a powerful tool in diversity.

With all of the benefits and the profound impact the experience can have on students and faculty participants, we are left with the question of why service-learning has not been adopted on a larger scale. Although we will not attempt to answer this fully, we provide examples of a successful model with the hope that more faculty will adopt the pedagogy using the example of the Engineering Projects in Community Service (EPICS) Program at Purdue University. EPICS is a series of design courses that have been linked together to create long-term partnerships with local community organizations, schools, and governmental agencies. In particular, in this chapter, the focus is on some of the governmental partners we have worked with in EPICS over the years.

EPICS OVERVIEW

The EPICS Program was started at Purdue in 1994 by Professors Leah Jamieson and Edward Coyle (Coyle, Jamieson, & Sommers, 1997) as a way to improve the design education of engineering undergraduates while simultaneously addressing compelling needs in the local community. Since its founding, it has grown into its own academic program and, while remaining engineering centered, become very multidisciplinary. Under the program, undergraduates earn academic credit for their contributions to long-term, team-based design projects that deliver innovative, technology-based solutions to problems identified by nonprofit organizations in the community. The curricular structure and support of the EPICS Program enables designs of significant benefit to the community to be created. The EPICS model has these key features (Coyle, Jamieson, & Oakes, 2005):

- *Community partners.* Each EPICS team has a project partner: a nonprofit organization, educational institution, or governmental agency in the local community. The team and the project partner work closely together to identify and solve the project partner's technology-based needs. The result is the delivery and support of systems that are used to improve the services to the community.
- *Large, vertically integrated teams.* Each EPICS team consists of eight to twenty undergraduate students, enabling multiple projects to be developed for each partner and for projects of significant scale and potential impact on the community to be undertaken. The teams are vertically integrated, with first-year students, sophomores, juniors, and seniors. In general, the juniors and seniors provide technical and organizational leadership and mentoring for the sophomores and first-year students, although we have seen several younger students rise to leadership levels very quickly.
- *Long-term student participation.* A student can participate in an EPICS team for more than one semester and even an entire college career. Students can elect to take EPICS any time in their undergraduate program starting with their first semester as part of one of the first-year learning communities. While most students take EPICS for multiple semesters, a few students take EPICS for all four years. Combined with the large team size, the continuity of a core membership provides a mechanism to allow projects to pass from one semester to another and thus not be restricted to single-semester projects. This continuity also provides each student with the time and mentoring opportunities required to learn and practice different roles on the team, from trainee to design engineer to team leader.

- *Variable credit hours.* An EPICS student can earn one or two credits per semester. As most of the classes that EPICS can substitute for in the traditional curricula are three credits, students have to take EPICS for at least two semesters to get the same number of credits. This intentionally provides a longer-duration and lower-intensity design experience. A by-product is that it provides motivation for the students to repeat the course, which creates the continuity that is so valuable to our community partners.
- *Multidisciplinary teams.* The service-learning context provides a rich learning experience where students from many disciplines can participate and are valued. The large team size enables students from disciplines across engineering and around the university to participate in an EPICS team. The disciplinary composition of an EPICS team can be tuned to a project's needs. In the 2006–2007 academic year, thirty different majors were represented in EPICS.
- *Start-to-finish design experience.* EPICS provides a start-to-finish design experience for students. Projects begin with problem identification done by the students and the project partner. The project develops through the design process and culminates with a delivered project that is used in the local community. The long-term structure allows EPICS to provide support for fielded projects, an additional value to the community partners. Our lab has many projects that are returned for routine maintenance and upgrades. The student teams balance service and redesign efforts with the development of new products. This balance is an excellent example of a real-world learning environment and added value to the community in the service we provide.

SELECTING PROJECTS

When the EPICS Program started in 1994, there was a question whether there were service-learning projects to be done in the local community. Professors Jamieson and Coyle contacted many different service agencies by making a presentation about the envisioned program and its goals to the directors of all local United Way agencies (Coyle et al., 1997). This single presentation led to many discussions with individual agencies and a long list of potential projects. As the program has evolved and word has spread about our program, we are in the position where more potential partners approach us each year than we can accommodate. The long-term nature of our partnerships means that most of the partnerships continue, and we look for new partnerships only to develop the program and meet strategic needs in the underserved community or to engage strategic university partnerships such as a new department.

The selection of new community partners is based on four key criteria:

- *Project partner commitment.* This element has become an increasing priority in the selection as the program has matured. The reciprocal relationship with our partners is a crucial element of the program. The commitment of one or more individuals in the partner organizations to work as partners, meet the community needs, and educate the students is a necessary element of the partnerships.
- *Significance.* Since not all projects can be undertaken, partners whose projects should provide the greatest benefit to an underserved community are selected.
- *Appropriate design opportunities.* The community needs must present design opportunities that are challenging to, but within the capabilities of, the undergraduates in engineering, computing, and the other disciplines that EPICS attracts.
- *Expected duration.* Projects that will span several semesters offer the greatest opportunity to provide extensive design experience on the academic side and address problems of potentially high impact on the community side. It has proven valuable to have a mix of short- (one semester to one year) and long-term (multiyear) projects, especially when new partnerships start. The short-term projects build confidence and help establish the relationship between the student team and the community partner.

The number of partners with EPICS has continued to expand and evolve. The 2007 portfolio has thirty partnerships within the four broad areas of human services, access and abilities, education, and the environment. Among those we have worked with are a series of government agencies. With some agencies, we have done specific projects, as summarized in Table 13.1. We have also

TABLE 13.1 SELECTED EPICS PROJECTS WITH GOVERNMENT PARTNERS

Project Name (Partner)	Mission	Technologies	Disciplines	Impact
Education and Outreach (Imagination Station)	The team designs interactive and fun exhibits for a children's museum (Imagination Station). Projects include a Mars rover exhibit, a sensor network, a wind tunnel, a magnetic power drag racer, a water cycle exhibit, and an eight-foot-tall dinosaur-shaped kiosk.	Electronics, mechanics, electricity and magnetism, computers, human-computer interfaces, fluid mechanics, electromechanical devices, mechanical design and fabrication, microcontrollers, optics, power electronics, elementary education, child development	Aeronautics and astronautics engineering, child development, computer engineering, computer science, education, electrical engineering, industrial engineering, liberal arts, mechanical engineering, technology, visual design	Improved science and engineering educational resources for the community
C-SPAN (C-SPAN Archives)	To provide a publicly accessible video database containing local government and community agency meetings. The mission of the database will be modeled after that currently implemented by C-SPAN, such that all videos will be completely unedited. The team is working on developing tools and methods to acquire, edit, stream, and analyze video content	Image processing, history, political science	Computer engineering, science or technology, history, political science, communication, journalism	Improving access to public affairs programming

Chemical Sensing Initiative (Drug Enforcement Agency, Tippecanoe County Sheriff, other local law enforcement agencies)	Working with local law enforcement, specifically the DEA and Tippecanoe County Sheriff's department, this team will be leading projects based on the use of sensors for law enforcement. Specific focus is the inhibiting of drug-making laboratories by using sensors and sensor networks such as chemical detectors. Cybercrime prevention through computer engineering will be investigated, such as database and search algorithm development.	Sensors, sensor networks, chemical analysis, computer engineering, computer technology	Agriculture, chemical engineering, civil engineering, computer science, computer and information technology, electrical and computer engineering, interdisciplinary engineering, industrial engineering, liberal arts, mechanical engineering, pharmacy, prelaw, sociology/criminal justice, pharmacy	Improving law enforcement ability to detect drug-making laboratories
Assistive Technology (Greater Lafayette Area Special Services)	The team began in spring 2004. It formed from the previous Wabash Center teams (Wabash Center–Electrical and Computer Engineering Focus and Wabash Center–Mechanical Engineering Focus) when the Children's Clinic	Electronics, computer controls, software development, electromechanical systems, motors, structures, actuators	Audiology, child development and family studies, education, computer engineering, computer and information technology, electrical engineering, liberal arts, mechanical engineering, mechanical engineering technology, nursing	Expanded capabilities and control of their environment for children with disabilities

(Continued)

TABLE 13.1 (continued)

Project Name (Partner)	Mission	Technologies	Disciplines	Impact
	closed. Mission is to develop hardware, electromechanical, and software solutions that enable students ages three to twenty-one with disabilities to function more independently and enjoy a better quality of life. This includes projects aimed to accomplish daily living tasks, assist with communication, or help participate in educational or recreational activities.			
Judicial Database Systems (Tippecanoe County Probation Department)	Design, build, and support sophisticated database-driven business software for Tippecanoe and Jasper County Probation Departments to track clients. The future of JDS is expanding as additional counties and agencies have expressed interest in the system and as we launch new features such as the Web-based client interface.	JAVA, ATPSwing, Web services, SOAP, Unix, SQL Server, SSL, JAVA Enterprise Server, Eclipse, CVS	Computer science, computer and information technology, electrical and computer engineering, management, sociology and criminal justice	Improved and more accurate system for tracking client information and delivery of services

forged an ongoing relationship with the Indiana Department of Corrections. (A complete list of EPICS projects is available at www.purdue.edu/epics.)

Development of the EPICS Program

EPICS at Purdue University has grown to become its own academic program under the dean of engineering. Support comes from the provost for its multidisciplinary educational role. Over four hundred students participate in an academic year from about thirty departments. These students are distributed on thirty teams, with about ninety projects in process at any one time, ranging from data management for human services to mitigation of agricultural pollution and from designing learning centers for local museums to developing custom play environments for children with disabilities. The success at Purdue motivated the creation of programs at other universities. In 2007 there were eighteen universities with EPICS programs within the United States and Puerto Rico, as well as the first international program at the University of Auckland, New Zealand.

The opportunity to affect the pipeline of those entering college motivated the creation of a high school program modeled after the university program. In the first year of the national pilot, over 650 students from five states participated. The high school program is showing a great deal of promise to use service-learning to introduce careers in engineering, computing, technology, and science.

Curricular Structure

The EPICS course is split into two components: a laboratory/team meeting and a parallel lecture/workshop learning experience. Once a week, each team—which works with one specific partner—meets for a two-hour laboratory time. Teams involve eight to twenty undergraduates who themselves may be working on multiple projects in project teams. The overall team meets each week to update the project's status and take care of administrative issues. We have found it important to instill a sense of the larger group on the team to help them see that they are all partnering with the same community organization or agency.

Each team is supervised by one or two advisors. We intentionally call them advisors and not instructors, as their role is to work alongside the students and advise when appropriate. The advisors are partners in the service-learning process. Most are faculty; however, we have had great results including staff and community advisors. There are many qualified staff, such as information technology professionals, who can add value to the student experience and are interested in both the education and the service we are providing. Local professionals from industry have also added a great deal to our program. These professionals come in once a week to advise the teams with the support of their companies. This mix of faculty from multiple university departments, staff, and local industry creates a diverse advising pool and expertise for the students to draw from.

In addition to the laboratory time, a second component is a parallel set of lectures and workshops provided once a week. For students in the first semester of EPICS, there is a required series of lectures to integrate them into the program and teach our models of design, project management, teaming, and communication (Lima & Oakes, 2006). Students in their second semester and beyond are given choices of lectures and workshops on topics including design, projects management, leadership, ethics, social responsibility, communication, and public policy, among others. Students taking two credits attend ten lectures and workshops, while those taking one credit only attend five per semester.

The long-term nature of the program has required some innovation in the lecture and workshop series. Students may be involved in the program for several semesters and do not want to hear the same lectures over and over. This has been addressed by rotating the lecture topics on a cycle of two to three years and by creating specialized workshops called skill sessions. Example skill session topics include learning to operate a mill or lathe, developing effective surveys, conducting patent searches, and tutorials on multimedia software and in-depth reflection activities.

Student Team Roles

We have found it important to designate specific roles on the teams. Students volunteer, are elected, or in some cases are selected to the roles by the instructor. These roles include:

- *Team leader.* The overall team has a team leader or two coleaders. This person is responsible for running each lab meeting, setting the agenda, holding the teams accountable to their time lines, and ensuring deadlines are met during the semester.
- *Project leader.* Each project team has a leader or coleaders who are responsible for the integrity and progress of the individual project. They manage the work of the project and hold the team members accountable for their time lines during the semester. They are responsible for ensuring that the team follows the EPICS design process and requirements, including the criteria for delivery.
- *Financial officer.* Each team is required to develop a budget for their materials, supplies, and services. The financial officer works with all of the project teams to track expenses and process budget modifications when needed. This process allows us to manage our program budget for our teams to ensure we can cover the expenses. When large expenses are needed, we work with the teams and the community partner to identify sources of funding. These funds are provided by corporate partners that sponsor our teams—another example of their contributions to our efforts.
- *Personnel officer.* We refer to the personnel officers as EPICS Students Advisory Council (ESAC) members. These students have primary responsibility to develop a staffing plan and lead the recruitment and selection of students for the team for the next semester. Each semester, a portion of the team plans to return to the course, and new students are added. We have developed a Web-based system for students to indicate their preference for projects and to allow teams to review this information as we make appropriate placements.
- *Manager of intellectual property.* This officer is responsible for learning about patents and the process to search for patents to ensure the team is not infringing on existing patents. The

officer also looks for opportunities for developing new intellectual property. Purdue has developed a special relationship with community partners to share the intellectual property developed by the teams. Our products are always given freely to our community partners, but when the teams examine how more people and communities could benefit from the products, a commercial solution is sometimes the most effective. The discussion of options for dissemination of the results of the team's work is a rich opportunity for reflection and discussion.

- *Liaison.* We have learned that the community partners do not want twenty students e-mailing them, so we assign one individual to manage the communications with the community partner. This person has responsibility as the prime communicator and works to engage as many of the team in effective communication as appropriate for the project and the partner.

BROADER PARTNERSHIPS: DEPARTMENT OF CORRECTIONS

We have found that building partnerships has been a key to the success of the EPICS Program. In the conceptual model, government institutions are presented as one of the partnerships. We included examples where government was a recipient of services; however, there are other opportunities for multifaceted partnerships where they offer assistance while addressing issues in the local communities. One of our partnerships has been with the Indiana Department of Corrections vocational programs that benefit both of us.

Many of the projects require a casing, table, or support structure to house the electronics and mechanics that are designed and built by the undergraduates. Early in the program, students built the entire project. We produced very good-quality student work, but many people could tell that they were student built. The vocational training programs include classes in wood and metal working that offer the advanced skills that our undergraduates do not have nor would it be appropriate to give course credit for them to gain these skills in our courses. We are interested in our students learning design of the systems, not in their becoming carpenters, for example.

Now we have our students do the designs and ship the drawings to the prison for construction. Under the supervision of the prison staff, our students present and discuss their designs. The staff and students in the prison often add to the designs and then produce the work, which is delivered to our campus labs to be integrated with the remaining electronics and mechanics and fully assembled, tested, and delivered to the community.

This relationship has had many benefits for all participants and is an excellent example of the conceptual model presented in Chapter One. First, the quality of the service we provide for the community has dramatically increased. The work now has a truly professional look, and we often add features or capabilities. One example is a laser harp project that was built to demonstrate lasers for an elementary school classroom. This harp has a series of lasers that act as the strings. When a child breaks a laser beam, a tone sounds. Different lasers have different tones, which allow students to play tunes just as they would on a real harp. The original student design was a rectangular support with the lasers running from one side to the other. When it was presented to the prison, they asked why it did not look like a real harp. The answer was that the students did not think they could make that complicated a shape. The prison staff and students modified the design to look like a harp, and the result was a four-foot-high laser harp that is actively used at a local elementary school. In another project for a local science museum, a computer kiosk was made to look like a dinosaur.

The vocational training programs have benefited from the inclusion of challenging and interesting projects. The partnership began with a relationship with the Indiana Women's Prison where the women were reported to be very engaged when they knew the projects were going to local schools and museums for children. The staff has repeatedly reported their appreciation for compelling projects and the value it brings to their program.

The EPICS program has benefited by the considerable increase in our capabilities. The complementary skills of the students in the vocational training programs also allow us to focus the student work on the design and integration of the systems.

A final benefit from the perspective of the correctional department is the interaction of our students with the offenders.

Since the goal of the training programs is to equip the offenders with skills they can use after they are released, it has given us the opportunity to address through reflections our students' views of former offenders. Many of our graduates move into management positions in corporations, and we are planting seeds for them to consider how they would look at someone with a prison record and trying to make a second chance for him or herself.

CHALLENGES FACING MULTIDISCIPLINARY TEAMS

Even with the compelling context of service-learning, many obstacles remain to creating a truly multidisciplinary learning environment. These include language that fails to allow the inclusion of all members. Each discipline has its own jargon, which may not be understood by all members of the team. Assumptions are made by students and faculty about what other students from varying disciplines can and cannot do. We have tried to address these barriers through our introductory materials and the first classes. Each team goes through detailed introductions that include sharing why they are taking the class and what they want to get out of the experience. In the second week of the semester, the teams go through a teaming reflection and develop a set of team values and expectations for each other. These are referenced again later in the semester during peer assessments, reflections, and midsemester grading, and they have helped set common language and expectations (Zoltowski, Oakes, & Jamieson, 2005).

Another way that we have tried to encourage and foster multidisciplinary teams in the service-learning program is to provide leadership from different disciplines. In the fall 2006 semester, the program had faculty from eleven disciplines, as well as staff from the university and local industry with a variety of backgrounds. In addition, the program had teaching assistants from seven disciplines. This diversity provides a voice for the disciplines within the program, ensuring that their specific needs are met, and provides a wide range of support for students who are encouraged to reach out to advisors for other teams for help where appropriate.

Service-learning often places faculty or industry advisors in a situation where they cannot answer the students' questions. For the faculty, this is a significant change in paradigm and perhaps discomforting. We have found it interesting that industry advisors are comfortable with this. They do not look for their manager to answer all of their questions and are comfortable referring the students to others in the program for specific assistance. With such a diverse set of students and problems we are addressing, it would be virtually impossible to align each team with all the expertise it needed for a semester.

Another challenge has been establishing course outcomes that are appropriate across such a wide array of disciplines. We have tried to encourage and support the multidisciplinary composition of the program by developing a set of common learning objectives appropriate for students from all disciplines. The outcomes of the course align with those used in engineering accreditation (ABET) but are written using language that is not engineering specific. For example, we changed the phrase *technical knowledge*, perceived as pertaining only to the engineering or technology students, to *disciplinary knowledge*. Furthermore, using the phrase *nontechnical* to describe all other disciplines and expertise devalues the knowledge and expertise of those disciplines and has been eliminated. With this in mind, our course outcomes are stated in this way (Zoltowski et al., 2005):

- Disciplinary knowledge: Ability to apply material from their discipline to the design of community-based projects
- Design process: An understanding of design as a start-to-finish process
- Lifelong learning: An ability to identify and acquire new knowledge as a part of the problem-solving/design process
- Customer awareness: An awareness of the customer
- Teamwork: An ability to function on multidisciplinary teams and an appreciation for the contributions from individuals from multiple disciplines

- Communication: An ability to communicate effectively with widely varying backgrounds
- Ethics: An awareness of professional ethics and responsibility
- Social context: An appreciation of the role that their discipline can play in social contexts

ASSESSMENT

The key to assessment has been the generation of artifacts that can be graded. Our course is a design course, and as such academic assessment is based on the demonstration of mastery of design and design learning. Students keep notebooks where they record their activities and thinking and demonstrate their work. In other fields, this might be called a journal or portfolio, but in engineering it is called a design notebook. The one addition to the traditional design notebook is that the students add guided reflection questions to their work. Each student completes a series of additional reflections captured on our course management software. Other artifacts include design documentation that is a synthesis of their work and is intended to be left as a reference by future semesters. Each team participates in one poster session and two formal presentations during each semester, which are also evaluated. In addition, students evaluate each other through a peer assessment system.

Many students find it confusing that there is no formula for our course. Most classes have a point system, but we have intentionally steered away from a formula. When faculty members have tried to put a formula into place, we have seen the students optimize to the formula, and we want them instead to focus on meeting community needs. An example of the negative results was one colleague who weighted delivery of a project very highly in a formula. What happened was that the team always selected projects that could be done in less than a semester to ensure delivery and maximum points rather that looking at the most appropriate approach to the needs.

Each student develops two sets of goals at the beginning of the semester. The first is a team set of semester goals developed by the team as a whole, and they result in a time line. Next, each student develops his or her own set of individual goals, including contributions to the team project and individual learning and development goals. The team's advisor approves the goals as appropriate or suggests changes. Once these are agreed to, the student has a set of criteria that will be used for evaluation during that semester. Each student creates a summary of accomplishments every four weeks and a summary of how goals are being met. We evaluate these accomplishments relative to goals much like a performance appraisal is done in industry. We assemble and grade all of the artifacts that the students have created twice during the semester. The first is at the midsemester and is called a "dry-run" grading. When the dry-run grading is done, students are given grades as if the semester were to end at that point and provided comments on how to improve their performance. Students are encouraged to talk with their advisor if they feel their grade and comments do not reflect their accomplishments and documentation. This has helped students and faculty calibrate their expectations with each other. The process is repeated at the end of the semester for final grading.

Additional assessments are done on the community partnerships. We conduct a survey for the partners each semester for them to provide feedback to the advisor on the team's performance. Annually we survey the partners on their experience with the EPICS Program. Including assessments of our partners has been valuable to the program and also builds confidence with our partners. Our results have been overwhelmingly positive over the years of the program.

CONCLUSION

Service-learning aligns well with the current calls for reform within engineering, computing, and technology education. It offers the opportunity to create truly multidisciplinary teams of students and faculty and has the potential to diversify our student populations. The EPICS Program approaches long-term partnerships using the model presented in this book. Working together, we are having a profound impact on our community, faculty, and students.

A final piece of advice to those who are new to the field is to start small and build successes. Start with a partner and project that you feel good about, and do not worry if it has all of the attributes of a perfect service-learning project. We and others in the field have found that getting started provides experiences to equip us to advance and improve each time we teach. We, like the students, continue to learn and grow. Done right, it has the potential to be one of the most rewarding and exciting experiences of your career.

Voices: Long-Term Relationships

Tim Frye

The enormously successful partnership between Imagination Station and EPICS has spanned more than a decade. It has significantly enhanced the Station's ability to develop professional quality, interactive educational exhibits. These technically sophisticated exhibits are prohibitively expensive to create and maintain. Without this collaboration, our small nonprofit museum would not be able to provide our visitors with such a rich, multisensory learning experience.

The long-term relationship with EPICS has actually become more valuable over time. Station personnel, the students, and their faculty advisors have learned a great deal about the complex nature of developing engaging, educational exhibits designed primarily for children. It has cultivated a cooperative environment where user-centered design is paramount. As a result, the quality of the projects has improved over the years.

The first generation of exhibits developed during the first years of the partnership would be what I would characterize as academically oriented student projects. Although they were functional, they lacked many of the attributes of professionally developed displays. It was only after the projects were deployed and the users identified deficiencies that the students begin to assess how the projects could be improved. What followed was a second generation of replacements that reached the level of professional museum quality exhibits. We have reached the point now where the first-generation projects reach this level. The students have learned from our partnership and the previous work.

The teams look at the work of previous teams, and we partici- pate in detailed discussions about the characteristics that go into the professional-level exhibits. A best practice is to work explicitly with the students on what professional-level expectations are and what you expect from them. Students can think in terms of tradi- tional classes, where they want to know how hard they have to work to get the grade they want. In service-learning, we want the students focused on the work and doing it excellently, not just good enough for a grade. We have found that setting the expectations that they are part of our important partnership and we expect professional- ism in that partnership to work very well. As members of our team, we expect them to act and produce professionally, and they do. We talk explicitly about the high caliber of work that has gone before and the high expectations we have for them. They really respond to this, and the grades seem to work out for the students too.

We have learned to be very explicit in communicating our expectations to the students. Student schedules are much more flexible than standard working hours, and they can forget about that. Our facility has specific hours we are open, and we discuss when that is and how they can reach us. Each EPICS team is required to designate a student as project partner liaison. This student is the point person for communications between the partner and the team. The EPICS team meets with our staff at the start of the semester and provides us with a formal update on their progress every four weeks thereafter. Informal and indi- vidual communication and contact happens regularly during the semester, but the structure helps us keep up to date. Frequent communication with the team is key to ensuring that projects meet specifications when delivered.

In addition to the communication, EPICS asks the students to lay out a plan for the semester, and we discuss that at the begin- ning of the semester. This is very helpful and allows us to set appropriate expectations with the students and the faculty. The monthly updates provide a mechanism to keep us apprised on progress and alert us to changes.

The final suggestion is to enlighten team members on the importance of designing for end users early in the process. During the initial meeting, the team tours the facility, and we discuss the Station's mission and the unique characteristics of our patrons. This provides them a broad spectrum foundation for their projects. In addition, we encourage them to interact with the children at the Station throughout the design and development stages. College students sometimes forget what it was like to be a child, and we encourage them to come and observe and interact with the children to get a better idea of what they need to do for their projects. Generally the more they are engaged, the more effective they become. In fact, the experience is so positive for the EPICS student that some continue to observe user behavior even after the exhibit has been delivered. Our experience has been that using the children as focus groups and beta testers often results in much better exhibits.

Support from EPICS does not end when an exhibit is delivered to the station. The agreement with EPICS specifies that once projects are placed at the museum, they are to be serviced by students from the EPICS teams for an extended period of time. These projects are in daily use by the museum patrons, many of them children. So as you might expect, the exhibits require regular maintenance and repair. The students provide consulting and diagnostic service to keep the projects up and running. Because many of the EPICS students have training in engineering, their technical abilities are far beyond that of the Imagination Station staff. This readily available expertise has allowed the Station to expand our instructional efforts into many diverse areas. I would encourage faculty who are thinking about service-learning projects to consider providing support for the partnership over a long time.

Our relationship with EPICS has been a partnership, and I would encourage any faculty engaging in service-learning to think about partnerships, not just projects. We have learned a great deal from our initial projects that we felt very good about, but we have moved to a much higher level over the years as we have learned about each other. The long-term partnership has allowed us to understand the students and faculty and has given great value to our organization. We have learned a great deal about how to work together, and we know that EPICS will be with us next year and the year after. Our partnership has allowed us to rely on them as part of our mission, and that has added a great deal to our organization.

■ ■ ■

Tim Frye is a member of the board of directors at Imagination Station in Lafayette, Indiana.

References

Bransford, J. D., Brown, A. L., & Cocking, R. R. (Eds.). (1999). *How people learn: Brain, mind, experience, and school.* Washington, DC: National Academies Press.

Coyle, E. J., Jamieson, L. H., & Oakes, W. C. (2005). EPICS: Engineering projects in community service. *International Journal of Engineering Education, 21*(1), 139–150.

Coyle, E. J., Jamieson, L. H., & Sommers, L. S. (1997). EPICS: A model for integrating service-learning into the engineering curriculum. *Michigan Journal of Community Service Learning, 4,* 81–89.

Eyler, J., & Giles, D. E., Jr. (1999). *Where's the learning in service-learning?* San Francisco: Jossey-Bass.

Hawkins, C. (2005). *Listening to the voice of African-American graduate students in chemistry.* Unpublished master's thesis, Purdue University, Indiana.

Lima, M., & Oakes, W. C. (2006). *Service-learning: Engineering your community.* Okemos, MI: Great Lakes Press.

Matyas, M. L., & Malcolm, S. (1991). *Investing in human potential: Science and engineering at the crossroads.* Washington, DC: American Association for the Advancement of Science.

National Academy of Sciences. (2004). *The engineer of 2020: Visions of engineering in the new century.* Washington, DC: National Academies Press.

National Academy of Sciences. (2005). *Educating the engineer of 2020: Adapting engineering education to the new century.* Washington, DC: National Academies Press.

National Academy of Sciences. (2006). *Rising above the gathering storm: Energizing and employing America for a brighter economic future.* Washington, DC: National Academies Press.

Noddings, N. (1992). *Gender and curriculum.* In P. W. Jackson (Ed.), *Handbook of research on curriculum* (pp. 659–684). New York: Macmillan.

Oakes, J., Gamoran, A., & Page, R. N. (1992). Curriculum differentia-
tion: Opportunities, outcomes, and meanings. In P. W. Jackson
(Ed.), *Handbook of research on curriculum* (pp. 570–608). New York:
Macmillan.

Rosser, S. V. (1990). *Female-friendly science*. Elmsford, NY: Pergamon
Press.

Zoltowski, C., Oakes, W. C., & Jamieson, L. (2005). Equipping multidisciplinary student teams to manage multi-semester design
projects. In *Proceedings of the 2005 American Society for Engineering
Education Annual Conference and Exposition*. Washington, DC: American Society for Engineering Education.

CHAPTER FOURTEEN

RECIPROCITY
Creating a Model for Campus–Community Partnerships

Marsha K. Turner, Rosa Ramos Morgan

The development and implementation of a campus-community partnership that includes governmental, institutional, and community partners, as well as service-learning participants, requires the dynamic cooperation of many different organizations. Creating a self-sustaining campus-community partnership focused on community revitalization requires creativity, planning, and mutually beneficial collaboration, with active support and contributions from all involved parties. Successful community revitalization itself benefits from active participation on the part of state and local governments, nonprofit organizations, faith-based groups, institutions of higher education, K–12 school systems, business owners, and community residents. The hallmark of a successful program is that all parties work as a team, engage in this holistic approach, and are proactive in regard to the associated structured activities.

In this chapter, we describe the use of this holistic approach to neighborhood revitalization in the context of a campus-community partnership, the Community Neighborhood Renaissance Partnership (CNRP) Project, conducted in collaboration with the Apalachee Ridge Estates (ARE) neighborhood located in Tallahassee, Florida. This partnership of the community, the City of Tallahassee, and Florida State University (FSU) has benefited from a strong sense of reciprocity among the participants, which has allowed the project to achieve its goals and become

self-sustaining. By reciprocity, we mean the mutually beneficial interactions that allow all participants to provide their own
experience and expertise and to benefit from others. Campus-
community partnerships as envisioned in service-learning must
truly be reciprocal—all parties must benefit—or the project is
unlikely to continue as a self-sustaining entity.

Implementing the CNRP campus-community partnership
involved bringing community members and universities together
by building a communication infrastructure that made clear
for service-learning projects the benefits of working together in
order to fulfill shared goals of neighborhood revitalization. With
a focus on mutually beneficial action-oriented strategies, reciprocity became fundamental to the implementation and success
of the basic and essential campus-community partnership, community revitalization driven by local government, and university-
based service-learning programs and projects.

THE SERVICE-LEARNING PROGRAM AT FLORIDA STATE UNIVERSITY

The FSU Service Learning Program mission statement reads:

> In coordination with faculty, students, and community partners,
> as well as administrators and staff, it is the mission of the FSU
> Service Learning Program to support the integration of experi-
> ential learning (service-learning) in the academic curriculum by
> working very closely with faculty and to foster partnerships with
> community-based agencies in order to:
>
> • Enhance student learning and development;
> • Encourage student civic responsibility;
> • Foster community-based scholarship teaching, service, and
>   research;
> • Provide for student leadership development; and
> • Address community-identified needs, problems and social issues
>   [Florida State University, n.d.].

To accomplish the goals of this mission, it is critical that
faculty, students, and community partners be actively and

cooperatively involved in all aspects of service-learning. While the specific indicators of success might differ from partnership to partnership and service-learning project to service-learning project, one foundational principle remains static: parties become involved in campus-community partnerships and associated service-learning activities when it is beneficial for them to do so. The goal of service-learning is to create win-win partnerships: a fusion of the needs and efforts of all partners in which everyone participating has their needs met.

To establish and maintain this win-win sense of reciprocity at FSU, the staff members at the Service Learning Program, currently made up of a director, program assistant, and three student assistants, work with faculty and community organizations to develop partnerships with community-based organizations that lead to placement opportunities for students in close collaboration with faculty members teaching service-learning classes. In order to ensure that the learning objectives established for students in a specific service-learning class connect to their activities at their placement sites, written student position or project descriptions are collaboratively developed by each site supervisor and the respective faculty member. The service-learning students are able to choose "what they want to do and where" from a variety of placement options at many different agencies. This ensures that community-based agencies receive students who are interested in the goals and objectives of the agencies. This system, benefiting faculty, students, and community-based agencies, serves an even greater purpose: a vital social or community issue is addressed—which is a win-win situation for everyone.

This philosophy has guided service-learning efforts at FSU and has contributed to the rapid growth of service-learning on campus. In 2001, there were 10 documented service-learning classes. By the end of the 2002–2003 academic year, there were 156 service-learning classes, representing 12 academic departments. The number of service-learning partnerships grew at an incredible rate as well. In 2000, only a handful of community partnerships existed; by 2003, there were fifty-six. By 2007, there were at least five hundred service-learning classes representing thirty-nine academic departments with more than four hundred functioning partnerships.

This growth in programs could not have taken place without the development of a strong information infrastructure. The infrastructure is based on a variety of information technologies that support office functions, documentation, and communication with campus and community partners. We have found that the development of computerized communication, information, evaluation, and assessment systems is critical to managing the tremendous volume of information from the many constituents, partners, and partnerships. This has allowed the service-learning program to be more productive and make service-learning activities more visible on the FSU campus and within the community.

THE COMMUNITY NEIGHBORHOOD RENAISSANCE PARTNERSHIP

During his tenure at the Florida Department of Community Affairs, former Tallahassee mayor and Leon County commissioner Steve Meisburg authored *Rebuilding Our Neighborhoods—A How To Manual for Holistic Neighborhood Revitalization* (1998). This manual was in response to a request to assess the effectiveness of urban revitalization initiatives. The system described in the manual and embodied by the CNRP was structured around the need for a holistic, collaborative, community-driven approach to community revitalization. Understanding that neighborhood revitalization is very different and much more valuable than neighborhood redevelopment, he did not use the traditional redevelopment strategy.

Over the past generation, billions of dollars of public redevelopment funds have been spent nationally on infrastructure projects such as street improvements, parks and recreation facilities, housing improvements, human services, and police services. Unfortunately, these neighborhood redevelopment efforts have often fallen short of their goals for three key reasons: they tended to address problems one at a time, there was little or no coordination in service delivery between participating governments and institutions, and community ownership of these efforts was often limited or entirely absent. In addition, redevelopment regularly split neighborhoods with expansions of federal highways,

destroying traditional neighborhoods and demolishing housing
and small downtown enclaves of commerce and community.

Meisburg stressed that when a neighborhood group, such
as a neighborhood or homeowners' association, is able to make
decisions about what the residents feel is best for their area, in
conjunction with governmental entities and other community
partners, the results are often positive. He put this into practice
in 2007 when he created a network that joined top-level administrators from city and county governmental bodies with executives
from the private sector. He challenged them to work together on
a comprehensive approach to neighborhood revitalization. Furthermore, he gained the participation of Tallahassee's two universities, Florida State University and Florida A&M University, as
well as Tallahassee Community College. The presidents of these
institutions of higher education pledged their support and the
participation of faculty and students in this new type of community engagement: neighborhood revitalization.

In addition, a group of churches, collectively called the Covenant Partners, were asked to use their experience in conducting many small projects within their own congregations in order
to help with the project. Covenant Partners includes ten local
churches: five churches with predominantly African American
congregations and five with a higher number of white parishio-
ners. These ten were paired together to contribute time, expertise,
and resources to the development of neighborhood revitalization
projects.

In late 2000, under the leadership and guidance of Meisburg,
the Community Neighborhood Renaissance Partnership (CNRP)
was formed in the State of Florida as a nonprofit and federally
recognized 501(c)3 tax-exempt organization. Since its inception, the CNRP has been administered by Community Assets, an
organization located in Tallahassee that provides organizational
development, training, and capacity-building services to nonprofits and local governments throughout the southeastern United
States. The second author of this chapter, Rosa Morgan, is the
director of Community Assets and has served as the director
of the CNRP. The mission of the CNRP is to form partnerships
between neighborhoods and the broader community in order

to rebuild distressed communities one neighborhood at a time using an approach that is:

- *Neighborhood driven*—the residents themselves decide what problems the neighborhood needs to address, strategies to employ, and on which priorities to act. They build on the assets and strengths already present in the neighborhood.
- *Holistic*—multiple deficiencies and assets are addressed simultaneously (housing, crime, health care, employment, education, recreation, culture, transportation, and others).
- *Collaborative*—truly cooperative and well-coordinated support efforts prosper among multiple government agencies and institutions. These efforts are based on honest and ongoing communication, as well as concern for the well-being of the targeted neighborhoods.
- *Empowerment/capacity building*—a partnership strategy that encourages outside investment while enhancing the internal capacity for action of the neighborhood residents and organizations.

The CNRP board includes representatives from the City of Tallahassee; Leon County; Leon County School Board; Leon County School District and Schools; Florida State University; Florida A&M University; Tallahassee Community College; the United Way of the Big Bend; Bank of America; Capital City Bank; AmSouth Bank; Apalachee Ridge Estates Neighborhood Association; Providence Neighborhood Association; and the Covenant Partners. While each of the organizations on the CNRP Board contributes ten thousand dollars annually to fund program administration, it is the neighborhood residents who ultimately determine what issues and concerns are important to the neighborhood in this collaborative venture. The CNRP combines the financial contributions from participating partners with the expertise and energy of faculty, students, and administrators from area universities; employees from local government; other public and private sector leaders; and residents themselves. Apalachee Ridge Estates was the first neighborhood in Florida to undergo revitalization under the guidance and assistance of CNRP.

THE PROJECT IN THE APALACHEE RIDGE ESTATES NEIGHBORHOOD

The Apalachee Ridge Estates neighborhood is located on Tallahassee's south side, an area of lower socioeconomic neighborhoods. It includes approximately three hundred single-family homes, of which 60 percent are owner occupied by low-income residents. This was not the most poverty-stricken neighborhood in Tallahassee, but it was experiencing unemployment, substandard housing, decreasing home ownership, and rising crime rates. It also had a failing elementary school—an issue that urgently mobilized the neighborhood leaders. The challenge for the CNRP was to engage with a neighborhood sliding into decline. The hope was that this area that had once been vibrant could be reestablished as a stable, sustainable neighborhood.

In keeping with the CNRP mission, residents were given a definitive voice as to how their community transformation would occur. To do this, a new kind of planning document that addressed the wants, needs, and dreams of the residents had to be created. All community stakeholders, including elected officials and the residents themselves, would be held accountable to accomplish the goals and strategies included in the revitalization plan. The challenge was to create a process to develop the plan that included everyone. Four major components made up the planning process: (1) assessment phase, (2) neighborhood plan development phase, (3) implementation/monitoring phase, and (4) evaluation phase. Throughout this process, the needs and desires of the community were the priority. The FSU Service Learning Program involvement included faculty and students from a wide range of colleges and programs; to date more than a thousand students have been part of service-learning projects in the neighborhood, supported by fifty-seven faculty.

To get the process started, the Apalachee Ridge Estates neighborhood appointed a steering committee that was composed primarily of home owners and renters in the neighborhood but also included landlords, business owners, representatives of adjacent neighborhoods, students, church leaders, school administrators and teachers, and representatives from neighborhood-based, nonprofit organizations. The inclusiveness of the steering committee gave credibility to the process and allowed many opinions and ideas to be voiced. The key to the success of the steering committee model was not only its comprehensive composition, but the fact that the committee was empowered to make its own decisions and prioritize the neighborhood needs. The members of the steering committee worked with representatives from local government and individuals from CNRP to develop a neighborhood renaissance plan that addressed issues pertinent to their neighborhood. Another vital factor was that a specially trained and objective facilitator from the Florida Conflict Resolution Consortium housed at Florida State University facilitated each of the meetings for the steering committee. This guidance ensured that all committee members were heard and no one monopolized the conversations to push his or her own agenda. The neighborhood planning team chart in Figure 14.1 provides a graphic representation of all team entities and their relationships.

Planning and action teams were also established. Similar to the steering committee, these teams were composed of neighborhood residents and appropriate community stakeholders. Again, discussions and deliberations were facilitated by individuals from the Florida Conflict Resolution Consortium. Creating increased empowerment and a sense of control over their own environment, neighborhood residents used and developed their leadership skills by chairing the planning and action teams. These teams were divided according to three major neighborhood interests: (1) housing, infrastructure, and economic development; (2) education and community involvement; and (3) community-based services and social issues such as health care and crime. In collaboration with the steering committee, these needs were discussed in depth over eight months; thus, specific goals, objectives, and strategies for each interest area were formed.

In order to prepare a plan for the revitalization of the Apalachee Ridge Estates neighborhood that would identify the most pressing issues and then assign those issues their specific strategies for success, three steps were taken: (1) a consensus-seeking workshop was organized in order to prioritize the issues and interests of the neighborhood; (2) the planning and action teams refined their recommendations based on input from the workshop; then (3) city staff drafted a revitalization plan that was distributed throughout the neighborhood for further input.

FIGURE 14.1   APALACHEE RIDGE ESTATES PLANNING TEAM

Neighborhood

| Neighborhood Association |

| Board of Directors |

| Neighborhood Steering Committee |

| Neighborhood Block Captains |

| Council of Neighborhood Associations |

Community Partners

| Community Neighborhood Renaissance Partnership |

| Institutional Partners |

| Faith-Based Organizations (Covenant Partners) |

| Program Administration |

Neighborhood Planning Team and Action Teams

Governmental Entities

City of Tallahassee	Leon County	Leon County School Board	Potential State Partners
City Commission	County Commission	Leonard Wesson Elementary School	Department of Community Affairs
Planning Commission	Planning Commission	Fairview Middle School	Other State Agencies
Tallahassee-Leon County Planning Department	All Other County Departments (As Appropriate)	Rickards High School	
Department of Neighborhood and Community Services		Parent-Teacher Organizations of These Schools	
All Other City Departments (As Appropriate)			

On the completion of this process, all information gathered was compiled into a final implementation plan by members of the steering committee and the board of the Apalachee Ridge Estates Neighborhood Association (ARENA). This final, synthesized plan specified the most important issues; established goals and objectives; identified strategies; outlined the desired outcomes; assigned entities that would be responsible for the execution of specific goals and objectives; and established a time line matrix for the completion of each goal. At this time, specific commitments were sought from the CNRP, the city, the county, and others, including FSU, to assist in the implementation of this plan.

Quarterly meetings were held by the ARENA to monitor the progress of the implementation plan. During these meetings, neighborhood residents learned how local governments work, how to work with them successfully, and with whom to work in local governments in order to make things happen in their community. This knowledge empowered the residents to take even more active and confident leadership roles for their neighborhood revitalization. When any task fell behind schedule, the residents immediately knew the responsible entity, how to contact them, and how to advocate for successful accomplishment of the task. Residents also assigned themselves tasks for completion and followed through with these tasks.

One of the best examples of the synergy found in this partnership was the establishment of the Apalachee Ridge Technology and Learning Center, located in the middle of the neighborhood. An abandoned residential home in poor repair was purchased by the City of Tallahassee. Through collaborative efforts involving the neighborhood residents and ARENA, CNRP, the City of Tallahassee, Leon County Schools, and many corporate partners, it was renovated into the Apalachee Ridge Technology and Learning Center. The center has computers for public use, and every year, many hours of mentoring and tutoring services are provided to the neighborhood residents, especially the children, by FSU, Florida A&M University, and Tallahassee Community College students.

Participation by FSU in the Project in the Apalachee Ridge Estates Neighborhood

It was clear from the beginning that the CNRP Project in the Apalachee Ridge Estates neighborhood was an extraordinary opportunity for the Florida State University community. Linking the service-learning network of FSU with a strong community revitalization infrastructure developed by CNRP, and executed by the neighborhood, could provide a "real-world" environment in which true reciprocity—one of the foundational principles of theories of service-learning—could be planned, experienced, and reflected on by all participants. It also became clear that the ideas of reciprocity would need to come into play in order to maintain ongoing relationships. Thus, the partnership that was formed between the FSU Service Learning Program, acting as the campus coordinating partner, and the CNRP project in the neighborhood has served as a base for describing and testing the roles of reciprocity in service-learning.

The key ingredient to developing self-sustaining partnerships among faculty and their students with this initiative was to do everything possible to ensure mutually beneficial participation. For interaction and activities to be reciprocal and provide a sense of satisfaction, all individuals and organizations in the project had to be actively involved at several different levels. The reciprocity model itself was used as a tool to prompt and document the activities and interactions associated with collaborative program planning, management, implementation, and evaluation. Its current incarnation reflects the efforts that led to the success of the program and outlines how this success was achieved.

It can be said that efficiency is associated with doing "things" right while effectiveness is measured by doing the right "things." Both were certainly goals in this partnership, but what has sustained the success of the partnership is the focus on understanding the accomplishment of the right "things." In the reciprocity model (Figure 14.2) this translates to recruiting or obtaining the right (1) resources and inputs; implementing the right (2) program activities; providing the right (3) outputs; accomplishing the right (4) outcomes; and achieving the right (5) impacts. These are the roles of reciprocity in providing mutual benefit for participants in a campus-community partnership, especially one that involves service-learning.

The reciprocity model was used to help the partners accomplish the following:

- Clarify the foundational theory of reciprocity
- Document the five major elements or roles of reciprocity

FIGURE 14.2 THE RECIPROCITY MODEL AS USED IN THE CRNP PROJECT

Holistic Approach	Communication	Collaboration	Community-Focused	

ROLE 1 Resources and Inputs	ROLE 2 Program Activities	ROLE 3 Outputs	ROLE 4 Outcomes	ROLE 5 Impacts
• Community constituents—participation, monetary contributions, sponsorships • Neighborhoods and associations • Higher education institutions • Professors • Students • City and county governments and staff • School district and schools (staff and students) • Community-based and nonprofit organizations—CNRP, United Way, and others—staff • Private sector organizations—banks, for example—staff • Covenant partners—staff and members	• Community needs • Information management • Advocacy and policy • Leadership and empowerment • Planning/infrastructure • Promotion and awareness • Collaboration • Resource development • Service-learning • Training and development • Reflection • Evaluation and community-based research • Recognition and celebration	• Products of the program activities—information transfer and participation • Services and projects including meetings, presentations, assessments, recruitment, and training delivered by the resource and input entities	• Specific community need addressed • Short- and long-term changes in recipients over a six- to ten-year period • Awareness • Knowledge • Skills • Abilities • Attitudes or opinions • Behaviors • Decisions • Policymaking • Social advocacy and action	• Fundamental changes in social, economic, civic, and environmental conditions associated with participating entities of the campus-community partnership • Holistic approach and program activities at local government institutions and community entities institutionalized • Personal, trusting relationships among leaders of government institutions and community organizations • Innovation based on past experiences

- Identify the major actors, activities (including service-learning), and interactions within each of the roles of reciprocity
- Demonstrate how reciprocity is associated with the program resources, program activities or actions, outputs, outcomes, and impact
- Integrate reciprocity with program planning, implementation, and evaluation within the context of a campus-community partnership

These five supporting roles of reciprocity must be both very intentional and very flexible—intentional in the sense that campus-community partners need a lot of encouragement, facilitation, logistical assistance, and infrastructure. However, all of this, ideally, must be accomplished in a nonrestraining manner that promotes freedom, creativity, and synergy. This philosophy served as the guiding principle in the development of the interdisciplinary service-learning partnership involving FSU students, faculty, and staff in collaboration with the CNRP and Apalachee Ridge Estates residents.

In jump-starting the partnership efforts on the part of FSU with the CNRP Project in the ARE neighborhood, a great deal of time and effort were put into communicating with CNRP representatives and neighborhood residents and with deans, chairs, and faculty members at FSU in order for all participants to develop an understanding of the reciprocal value of the partnership. As it turned out, mutual enthusiastic agreement was quickly established, and CNRP, the neighborhood leaders, and FSU began to collaboratively plan and develop the structure that would channel the expertise, time, and energy of faculty members and students into service-learning classes, activities, and special projects. This pulling of resources on a structured, systematic basis assisted the CNRP and Apalachee Ridge Estates residents in achieving the goals and strategies as expressed in the neighborhood plan.

Over time, a jointly supported infrastructure has been created that maintains strong commitments to individual projects and the campus-community partnership as a whole, and provides the space, encouragement, and friendly accountability necessary for all constituents to fill and fulfill their roles of reciprocity. This infrastructure, as represented in the reciprocity model, supports the desired activities and interactions associated with the five roles of reciprocity. Six years later, this campus-community partnership continues to represent, and benefit from, reciprocity.

A wide range of partners signed on with this project at the beginning and remain intricately involved in the neighborhood:

- *Community agencies and staff.* These include the Apalachee Ridge Estates neighborhood and the neighborhood association, United Way of the Big Bend, Covenant Partners (a coalition of religious organizations), AmSouth Bank, Bank of America, and Capital City Bank.
- *Government institutions and staff.* City of Tallahassee (offices and departments), Tallahassee City Commission, Leon County (offices and departments), and Leon County Commission.
- *Educational institutions and staff.* Florida State University (colleges/departments and service-learning program), Florida A&M University, Tallahassee Community College, and Leon County School Board and Schools.
- *Faculty members.* Faculty members from seven colleges and departments at FSU have participated in this partnership over time. The range of disciplines represented gives some sense of the variety of service-learning projects that have been mounted in the area. Overall, fifty-seven faculty members have participated in the CNRP at Apalachee Ridge Estates, representing education, medicine, nursing, social work, human sciences, urban and regional planning, and information studies.
- *Students.* From each of these colleges and departments, students have become directly involved in a wide range of activities. Overall more than a thousand students have participated to date. Example of projects include:

    - Education—mentoring, tutoring, visiting and interacting with local schools, coordinating career fairs at neighborhood schools
    - Medicine—health surveys, presentations, education, demonstrations, and screenings; coordinating health fairs at neighborhood schools
    - Nursing—health surveys, presentations, education, demonstrations, screenings, and flu shots

- Social work—advising and counseling; tutoring and mentoring
- Human sciences—physical education, recreational, and fitness activities; nutrition presentation and cooking demonstrations
- Urban and regional planning—neighborhood surveys, planning for sidewalks and roads, working with departments of city and county government
- Information studies—computer hardware, networks, and software—setup, diagnostics, troubleshooting, help desk; Internet research; Web-based system design and development; tutoring and mentoring

These short summaries of student involvement do not give the full extent of student participation. Given the limits of space, we will focus on just the service-learning activities, but this is only the tip of the iceberg of partner activity in the CNRP program.

SERVICE-LEARNING IN THE CNRP PROJECT

The FSU Service Learning Program hosts a monthly meeting of an interdisciplinary service learning council, made up of faculty, students, staff, and other government and community representatives from the partnership. The meeting is used to plan service-learning classes, activities, events, and projects. The result has been an exciting range of projects carried out by students, overseen by faculty, and connected to the full range of community partners. Projects have included:

- Health presentations, flu shots, blood pressure screenings, and other projects such as the "Healthy Soul Food Cook-Out," "Apalachee Ridge on Wheels: A Day of Safety and Fun," two community-wide health fairs, "Healthy Breakfasts Make Better Grades" (food preparation and tasting), "Walking to Fitness," "Diabetic Education and Internet Use," and "Careers in Medicine and Nursing" (at the local middle and high schools) provided by the medical and nursing students.
- Tutoring and mentoring at the Apalachee Ridge Estates Technology and Learning Center provided by the education students.

- Information technology, Web design, networking assistance, and summer technology youth programs at the Apalachee Ridge Estates Technology and Learning Center, including the Digital Media Camp held in summer 2006. The Digital Media Camp provided training in videography, music production, Web site design and construction, and field trips to the FSU Film School and the WFSU radio station. These service-learning activities were provided by the information studies students.
- Development of walking routes and programs for neighborhood residents provided by the human sciences students.
- Parenting workshops provided by the social work students.
- Fun days and block parties, pre- and postsurvey of neighborhood, and workshops on:
  - Leadership development for neighborhood association members
  - Neighborhood and traffic safety
  - Home ownership versus renting
  - Quality of life
  - Flooding
  - Crime
  - Safety

Many service-learning projects have been ongoing for years, establishing trust, interdependency, and sustainability among faculty, students, community-based partners, and residents.

Almost all of the constituent groups of the CNRP have over the course of the years supervised and provided placement sites to service-learning students. These same groups have met with faculty and students on many different occasions to plan and implement specific projects or events. For example, in April 2006, neighborhood youth planned and implemented a "Day of Youth Service" as a way for them to reciprocate for the mentoring and tutoring services received from the FSU service-learning students at the Technology and Learning Center over the years. These young people helped to paint and install a mural inside the center, planted a vegetable garden, and conducted a yard cleanup in the neighborhood. The day ended with the youth from the neighborhood and the FSU service-learning students enjoying a cookout together.

Government institutions have, of course, been significant players in the service-learning activities of the partnership. The City of Tallahassee, Leon County, and the Tallahassee-Leon County Planning Department worked with faculty and students to develop ongoing projects associated with neighborhood infrastructure and planning, residential and street flooding, recycling, energy, and transportation. The city planner established several service-learning positions each year in the Tallahassee-Leon County Planning Department for urban planning students. These students were able to gain experience in researching neighborhood topics, preparing white papers on the topics, and assisting in presentations to the City of Tallahassee and Leon County Commissions. In addition, staff members from the FSU Service Learning Program attended monthly meetings with the deputy city manager and key departmental directors to discuss needs and progress of the CNRP at Apalachee Ridge Estates neighborhood.

Service-learning has been an integral part of the overall project in Tallahassee, but by no means the only part. The scope of this work has been quite large, perhaps as large as any such project anywhere. The key to making it all work has been the sense of reciprocity developed within the project and by and among the partners.

Reciprocity has been and is the heart of this campus-community partnership. Each of the participating entities came to the table as equals, each with needs and resources. True reciprocity cannot remain a theory. Actualized reciprocity is made up of mutually beneficial successes obtained through active, collaborative participation on the part of all partnering individuals and entities: tangible resources, activities, outputs, outcomes, and impacts as represented in the reciprocity model that has guided the work of CNRP and the FSU Service Learning Program.

Voices: Community Revitalization with a Collaborative Partnership

Steve Meisburg

Recognizing that very little had been done to address the problems facing the residents of distressed neighborhoods in the community I began researching the issue of neighborhood revitalization and attending national conferences that dealt with the topic. It became clear to me that these neighborhoods were often being overlooked by local governments and elected officials.

It is true that the neighborhood residents must be a driving force in the revitalization of their community. However, it is also true that without a full partnership with local government under the leadership of at least one elected official, and with the cooperation of key staff members in local government, community or neighborhood revitalization cannot occur or be sustained.

Poor family structures, dysfunctional school environments, school dropout rates, juvenile crime occurrences, drug abuse, and poverty in general are signs of a community or neighborhood in trouble. We tend to look at the signs one at a time depending on what is getting the most press.

However, these problems are complex and interdependent. Addressing them takes time and a long-term commitment. It takes a holistic, strategic plan supported by full and equal partnerships, implemented over years, among local government institutions and other community organizations. Those of us in local government are not good at this. This fact is very ironic in that city and county governments have a great deal at stake in trying to prevent the decay of neighborhoods. After all, neighborhoods make up these geographical areas that we refer to as city and county.

There had been few successful partnerships between the city of Tallahassee and the Leon County governments. When you add the universities and the school system to the picture, it gets even more challenging. For example, the city and the school system historically become partners only when sharing facility space. In order to achieve success, participating institutions and individuals have to leave their institutional baggage and boundaries at the door. This is practically impossible unless an elected official is leading the charge.

I recognize that elected officials are notorious for short-term visions, short-term memories, and short time frames in which to act. All of these aspects make true community revitalization within the context of a community partnership very difficult to achieve.

So the question remains: Is neighborhood revitalization even possible? I believe we have come as close as humanly possible with the comprehensive process employed by the Community Neighborhood Renaissance Partnership in the Apalachee Ridge Estates Neighborhood.

As a county commissioner involved with this project, I had to step outside the traditional role of voting on policy. I had to try to affect practice to change policy. My first objective was to establish a trusting relationship with a county commissioner. If I could not do that, this idea was not going to go anywhere. When I called this individual to see if we could have lunch, he said he didn't have time. Luckily, he called me back in a few days and said that he just realized that if we couldn't talk, then something was really wrong. A forty-five minute lunch turned into a three-hour meeting.

We talked about our youth: mine in Mississippi and his in Tallahassee. We learned a lot about each other. We began to build trust. We ended up saying that we believed we could work together on this partnership project. The county had to be involved, and he could make that happen because most of the neighborhoods in need, including Apalachee Ridge Estates, were, for the most part, in his district. He trusted that I could bring the city commission and critical city staff members along. In fact, what I had to do, one partner at a time, was to build trust and develop a relationship. This was true for our partners in the neighborhood, school system, universities, school system, United Way, banks, churches, and so on. This took over six months and included many meetings and phone calls. But, as they say, the rest is history.

It is my hope that this holistic approach to community revitalization will catch the eye of other local governments. We have implemented this approach in two neighborhoods in Tallahassee with great success. However, it is difficult because local governments are caught up in their own mechanics and lose the necessary political leadership and personal contacts.

Every city, or county for that matter, is unique, and carries its own history and tensions. How educational institutions, government agencies, and other local organizations have or have not worked together to get things done in the past is important. If they will buy in to the idea that working together in a community-based partnership for neighborhood revitalization can and will be mutually beneficial or reciprocal in the accomplishment of this goal, then it all becomes possible.

■ ■ ■

Steve Meisburg is former mayor of the City of Tallahassee, Florida, and former commissioner of Leon County, Florida.

References
Florida State University. (n.d.). *Service learning.* Retrieved January 13, 2009, from http://thecenter.fsu.edu/service_learning.html.

Meisburg, S. (1998). *Rebuilding our neighborhoods: A "how to" manual for holistic neighborhood revitalization.* Tallahassee: Florida Department of Community Affairs.

SERVICE-LEARNING WITH GOVERNMENT PARTNERS
A Summary of Additional Examples

Charlotte Ridge

The projects highlighted in this book are excellent examples of service-learning with government partners, but they are far from the only examples. More are summarized briefly in this appendix. There are a lot of good ideas in these summaries, and for readers who want to learn more about them, contact information has been provided. The service-learning courses in these examples are organized into four categories based on their government partners: public schools, environmental agencies, community planning and improvement agencies, and policy research and legal agencies.

SERVICE-LEARNING WITH PUBLIC SCHOOLS

Rhythmic Aerobic Training at Indiana University–Purdue University Indianapolis (IUPUI) engages exercise science and fitness studies students in Indianapolis public schools. The IUPUI students work as personal trainers in the school's fitness centers with public school students, staff, and community members. The IUPUI students are responsible for teaching proper exercise safety, exercise technique, and healthy lifestyle behaviors to the participants.

The program is also open to physical education students interested in gaining high school classroom experience. *Contact:* NiCole Keith and Jennifer Anderson, Department of Physical Education, Indiana University–Purdue University Indianapolis, nkeith@iupui.edu.

■ ■ ■

LEAP to the U is a partnership between students at the University of Utah and local high school students, many of whom are potential first-generation college students. The goal is to encourage high school students to see the university as a place where they can succeed. The university students host the high school students three times during the school year: once in a tour of the university and the other times in various activities such as bowling. The high school students host a joint service project, a Scholarship Day, and a final banquet. *Contact:* Carolan Ownby, LEAP Program, University of Utah, c.ownby@leap.utah.edu.

■ ■ ■

In fall 2006 and 2007, students in music theory at Fresno State engaged with Teilman Education Center, a Fresno County Court and Community School. The university students observed classes, met with Teilman teachers, devised lesson plans, delivered music lessons, and hosted Teilman students at the university. Results of questionnaires on the service-learning class were presented at the 2007 Western Regional Compact's Continuums of Service Conference. Research is being conducted to determine which interaction strategies are most effective at decreasing behavioral referrals, suspension, and detention incidents. A video on the service-learning project is available at www.benjaminboone.net/educational.shtml. Click on "Changing Lives Through Music." *Contact:* Benjamin Boone, Department of Music, California State University Fresno, bboone@csufresno.edu.

■ ■ ■

In this course, at-risk students from an alternative high school are collaborating with Concordia University students enrolled in

Adolescent Psychology to create public service announcements centered on youth issues. The high school students are gaining exposure to higher education, being given an opportunity to express their ideas on an important youth issue, and in a mentoring partnership that encourages their academic growth. Concordia students are conducting literature reviews on their public service announcement topic and will share the research process with their high school partners. This research will be used as the students collaborate to develop an effective public service announcement on the important youth issues, as by the high school students. *Contact:* Professor Kris Bransford, Department of Social and Behavioral Sciences, Concordia University–St. Paul, bransford@csp.edu.

■ ■ ■

The service-learning component of this Arizona State University (ASU) course addresses the needs of K–8 children. The ASU students spend two days a week for one semester matched with public school children from kindergarten to eighth grade as academic tutors/mentors. One-on-one and in small groups, the ASU students make learning fun and interactive to increase academic achievement, self-esteem, positive attitudes toward literacy, and college-going practices. The university students also participate in a learning component consisting of assignments and reflections regarding their service experience and social justice issues affecting that community. *Contact:* Deborah Ball, Academic Community Engagement Services, University College, Arizona State University, http://uc.asu.edu/servicelearning.

■ ■ ■

Every semester for the past decade, students in Community Psychology and Community Mental Health and Atypical Development in Childhood and Adolescence at Rutgers University have taken a one-credit service-learning internship. They are placed one half-day per week for a semester in the federally funded Middlesex County (New Jersey) Head Start Centers, where they serve as assistants to teachers and provide special help to three and four year olds experiencing learning or behavior problems.

In addition to this assistance, all students do a good-by project in which they leave something behind to improve the classroom learning climate. Some examples include a book about each of the Head Start students and their strengths and a photo tree with pictures of all the students in the class with their names. *Contact:* Maurice J. Elias, Department of Psychology, Rutgers University, RutgersMJE@AOL.COM.

■ ■ ■

Students in French: Culture and Community at Rutgers University teach beginning French language twice a week to children at various grade levels at Lord Stirling Community School in New Brunswick, New Jersey. The students also run an after-school French club at the school during which they teach children from ages six to ten various aspects of French and Francophone culture by engaging them in art, music, dance, literature, history, geography, science, and cooking lessons. *Contact:* Mary Shaw, French Department, Rutgers University, maryshaw@rci.rutgers.edu.

Environmental Projects

The Indiana University–Purdue University Indianapolis (IUPUI) Center for Earth and Environmental Science (CEES) coordinates and facilitates the Environmental Service Learning Program for campus. The goal of the program is to engage students in urban water quality education and environmental stewardship activities to promote behavioral change and greater environmental awareness. Service-learning workdays are part of community-based research programs conducted at research sites throughout central Indiana in conjunction with over ten community partners, including government and nonprofit agencies and corporations. CEES staff coordinate program logistics and community partner relationships while also leading up to ten project workdays each semester with participation from approximately ten instructors and three hundred students. The workdays provide students with opportunities to apply course material to contemporary environmental problems while contributing to improved environmental quality. *Contact:* Center for Earth and Environmental Science,

Lenore P. Tedesco and Kara A. Salazar, Education Outreach Coordinator, Indiana University–Purdue University Indianapolis, cees@iupui.eduwww.cees.iupui.edu.

■ ■ ■

Students in Environmental Mathematics at the College of the Holy Cross partner with local nonprofit and government agencies in Worcester, Massachusetts to work on environmental projects. The projects often include extensive quantitative analysis that the agencies could not afford on their own. Partner projects have included student analyses of water quality data collected for several years from the Blackstone River. Other examples are student analysis of visitation data for a local ecology museum and an examination of how trash is distributed in different neighborhoods. *Contact:* Catherine A. Roberts, Department of Math and Computer Science, College of the Holy Cross, croberts@holycross.edu.

■ ■ ■

University of Oregon students in the Environmental Leadership Program have engaged in service-learning in many classes. Four of these are described below.

• Students in the Forest Team worked in collaboration with the H. J. Andrews Experimental Forest and the U.S. Forest Service to design an interpretive trail brochure and supplemental lesson plans for the Lookout Creek trail in the Willamette National Forest. In addition, they created an online virtual tour of the Lookout Creek trail, including photographs and interviews with key scientists at H. J. Andrews. These materials serve to educate the public about old-growth forest structure and management practices.
• The Marine Team of students served as environmental educators and interpreters in the rocky intertidal ecosystem at Sunset Bay and Cape Arago State Parks. They led field trips for K–12 students from regional public schools and provided interpretation services at Simpson's Reef, a popular tourist destination where four marine mammal species can easily be observed. To further their knowledge of local marine

ecosystems, they attended classes at the Oregon Institute of Marine Biology during their term of service.

- The Wetlands Educational Team worked in collaboration with the Willamette Resources and Educational Network (WREN) and the Bureau of Land Management. During one winter term, six undergraduate team members created lesson plans that focused on various wetland themes. During the spring term, they presented these programs at a public event as part of WREN's annual celebration of American Wetlands Month. The team also facilitated outreach programs in schools, field trip activities for students visiting the wetlands, and interpretive roving at the wetlands.

- In collaboration with the Middle Fork Ranger District of the Willamette National Forest, the X-Stream Team students helped the U.S. Forest Service build outreach and education programs. Using a stream simulator, the team developed lesson plans to teach stream ecology to grades K–12 in local schools. The stream simulator, acting as a watershed model, can be manipulated by students to demonstrate processes such as stream bank erosion and ideal organism habitat. Through the workshops, participants learn ways in which they can minimize their ecological footprint on stream ecosystems. *Contact:* Kathryn A. Lynch, Environmental Leadership Program, University of Oregon, klynch@uoregon.edu.

■ ■ ■

Since its inception in 2005, the Restoration Stewardship Team has worked with the Long Tom, McKenzie, and Middle Fork Willamette Watershed Councils and the Mohawk Watershed Partnership to monitor riparian restoration sites throughout the Willamette basin. During one winter term, the team monitored over 350 native trees and shrubs and completed a yearly progress report for six restoration sites. During spring term, the team continued monitoring while also working on a GIS mapping project and extended data analysis. The team completed a plant identification book and facilitated a one-credit field studies class designed to help students get hands-on experience doing watershed restoration work. *Contact:* Steve Mital, Environmental Leadership Program, University of Oregon, smital@uoregon.edu.

Students in Introduction to GIS at Wesleyan University partner with local government agencies and nonprofit organizations to apply their newly acquired GIS skills to solve environmental, conservation, and land use problems. Examples of past projects include an open space assessment for a town planning office and an investigation of a proposed wetland buffer expansion and build-out analysis for area conservation commissions. In these projects, students have generated new GIS data, synthesized these data with existing data, and completed a spatial analysis. Results were presented to partners as public presentations, written reports, and digital data collections. *Contact:* Phillip G. Resor, Department of Earth and Environmental Sciences, Wesleyan University, presor@wesleyan.edu.

COMMUNITY PLANNING AND IMPROVEMENT

Starting in fall 2005 and continuing to the present, students in city and regional planning at Ohio State University have partnered with Harrison County, Mississippi, to prepare long-range rebuilding plans for rural communities following Hurricane Katrina. The students held town hall meetings, met with local officials, and appointed steering committees. The student-prepared community plans were adopted by the county as the official plans for each community. The plans have won a variety of state and national awards. *Contact:* Jennifer Evans-Cowley, City and Regional Planning, The Ohio State University, cowley.11@osu.edu.

■ ■ ■

During 2007–2008, students in several courses at California State Polytechnic University in Pomona developed and implemented a public art inventory for the City of Pomona Cultural Arts Commission. Students in research design for planning developed the inventory template and beginning documentation of public art sites in Pomona. Students in ethnicity and the arts did additional archival and field research to enrich the information available on selected entries, while students in ancient world expanded the survey to include documentation of historic cemetery sites. Students in Diversity, education, and the arts developed standards-based lesson plans based on the material collected for use in

K–8 classrooms. Campus participation was coordinated by the Center for Community Service-Learning in cooperation with the City of Pomona Cultural Arts Commission and the Pomona Public Library. The City of Pomona has signed a service-learning agreement with Cal Poly Pomona, which has paved the way for students to participate in programs with multiple city agencies. *Contact:* Sandra Mizumoto Posey, Center for Community Service-Learning, California State Polytechnic University, Pomona, sposey@csupomona.edu.

■ ■ ■

Students in a landscape design class at Clemson University partnered with the city and county government of greater Clemson, South Carolina, to design and install a streetscape. This attractive road corridor included plantings with seasonal interest and pedestrian trails to encourage active recreation and provide alternative transportation corridors promoting healthy living. Low-maintenance, drought-tolerant, wildlife value plants were selected. Students prepared and presented designs, interpretive signage, and reports. A student was the lead author on a published refereed journal article documenting the project. *Contact:* Mary Haque, Department of Horticulture, Clemson University, mhaque@clemson.edu.

■ ■ ■

Two sections of Technical Writing at Clemson University partnered with the City of Clemson in 2006 to create a series of documents about services provided by the city. The deliverables included a Web site and five brochures: information for new residents, a downtown parking map, a downtown business directory, a walking tour of old Calhoun, and a dining guide. The projects helped students develop a variety of skills, including research, communication, document design, project management, collaborative learning, and critical thinking. *Contact:* Xiaoli Li, Rhetorics, Communication and Information Design, Clemson University, Clemson SC 29634, xiaoli@clemson.edu.

■ ■ ■

Students in teledramatic arts at California State University at Monterey Bay worked with the Watershed Institute at the school and the City of Salinas to create a film entitled *Carr Lake: Cultivating Community*. The students worked as a classroom media collective, investigating local histories, and interviewing community members to create this fundraising and community-building tool, which the city uses to enhance awareness of the Carr Lake Project. *Contact:* Enid Baxter Blader, Teledramatic Arts and Technology, California State University Monterey Bay, http://enidbaxterblader.com.

■ ■ ■

Students enrolled in community health nursing at Loyola University have partnered with city and county officials as well as state and federal legislators in addressing numerous community health issues. For example, several years ago, students participated in a lead task force that resulted in legislation and community interventions aimed at lead abatement and lead poisoning prevention. Students have also been working for the past three years with the same group of community leaders in developing interventions targeted at reducing childhood obesity. Students have been invited to begin work on an asthma initiative. *Contact:* Pamela Andresen, Niehoff School of Nursing, Loyola University Chicago, pandres@luc.edu.

POLICY RESEARCH AND LEGAL ISSUES

The Bentley College Consumer Action Line (BCAL), now in its fifteenth year under a grant and the auspices of the Massachusetts Attorney General's Office, provides students with a hands-on service-learning experience in which they mediate consumer complaints against area businesses. It is the only student-run, service-learning consumer complaint mediation program in the state. Since its inception, BCAL students have successfully resolved 75 percent of the cases handled, resulting in refunds to consumers exceeding $600,000. Students in The Legal Environment of Business and other related courses earn one credit for researching and writing a ten- to fifteen-page paper on a consumer-related topic. They are also required to keep and turn in a journal of their experiences and cases. *Contact:* Stephen Lichtenstein, Law, Taxation, and Financial Planning, Bentley College, SLICHTENSTEI@bentley.edu.

■ ■ ■

At Macalester College, students in Legislative Politics serve as interns with the Minnesota legislature. While in the legislature, students are exposed to the structures, politics, and policymaking of the legislature. In class, students read broadly from political science literature to understand how legislatures operate. Time is spent reflecting on how their experiences in the Minnesota legislature compare to what they have learned from the readings. *Contact:* Julie Dolan, Department of Political Science, Macalester College, dolan@macalester.edu.

■ ■ ■

The Practicum in Policy Evaluation and Applied Research provides Oberlin College students with the opportunity to do research for local nonprofit organizations or government agencies. Students are divided into teams, and each team develops a research design and writes a letter of understanding that is negotiated with, and signed by, the community partner. During the course, students receive skill-building sessions from a professional public speaking trainer, a grant writer, and a political and technical consultant. The final product is presented in a formal consultancy report provided to the community partner. *Contact:* Eve Sandberg, Politics Department, Oberlin College, eve.sandberg@ oberlin.edu.

■ ■ ■

Master's-level students in organizational behavior at George Washington University work with clients in nongovernmental organizations, businesses, or government agencies as part of a service-learning experience. When President Clinton signed the welfare reform bill, there was concern in the District of Columbia government that there would not be enough places in day care centers for the children of women who would have to find jobs. Students called day care centers in the city and found that there was adequate capacity to absorb the additional children. Another group of students created a directory of services to assist elderly people in maintaining an independent lifestyle. The directory was created for the Office on Aging of the Washington, D.C., Department of Human Resources. *Contact:* Stuart Umpleby, School of Business, The George Washington University, umpleby@gwu.edu.

■ ■ ■

Students in Issues and Human Services at George Washington University work with a variety of government partners in the metropolitan Washington area each semester. Several students have worked with the Corporation for National and Community Service. A few examples of their responsibilities included research on the baby boomers and civic engagement and research on volunteer motivation, recruitment, and retention. *Contact:* Honey W. Nashman, Department of Sociology, George Washington University, hnashman@gwu.edu.

■ ■ ■

Community groups and government agencies submit proposals for students at Wesleyan University in Middletown, Connecticut, to do research as part of a community research seminar. A faculty board selects four proposals. During the spring semester, students learn sociological research methods as they work on the projects. Results are presented in a written document and at a public forum. Examples of projects include an exploration of school readiness in Middletown for the School Readiness Council, a census of affordable housing in Middletown for the Department of Planning, Conversation, and Development, and a study of recycling set-out rates in single family units in Middletown for the Department of Public Works. *Contact:* Rob Rosenthal, Department of Sociology, Wesleyan University, rrosenthal@wesleyan.edu.

■ ■ ■

Wesleyan University students serve as research assistants at a local community health center while enrolled in The Health of Communities. They work in teams with preceptors from the health center on research projects designed to evaluate or improve current practices and treatment in areas such as health care for the homeless, assessment of the needs of children living in shelters, and reduction of the risk of obesity in school-aged children. The projects introduce students to many research skills, including questionnaire design, interviewing, and the analysis and reporting of data. *Contact:* Peggy Carey Best, Sociology Department, Wesleyan University, pcarybest@wesleyan.edu.

■ ■ ■

Proposal writing is critical to almost any effort that requires raising funds. As part of an Earth and Environmental Sciences class at Wesleyan University, community groups submit requests for research and writing assistance. A faculty committee selects a proposal for students to develop. The students learn how to read a request for proposal and write competitive proposals. Working closely with their community partner, the students complete the proposals and submit them for funding. *Contact:* Suzanne O'Connell, Earth and Environmental Sciences, Wesleyan University, soconnell@wesleyan.edu.

APPENDIX B

SERVICE-LEARNING RESOURCES

A good place to start learning about service-learning is the Web. Several extensive Web sites are dedicated to service-learning, and all provide excellent introductions to the topic—and much more too. Here are two of the best sites.

> Campus Compact is a coalition of more than a thousand universities and colleges dedicated to community service and service-learning. www.compact.org

> National Service-Learning Clearinghouse is operated by the Corporation for National and Community Service, an independent federal agency. www.servicelearning.org

For those who would rather pick up a good book for an introduction to service-learning, here are a few excellent first choices:

> Jacoby, B., & Associates. (1996). *Service-learning in higher education: Concepts and practices.* San Francisco: Jossey-Bass.

> Kaye, C. B. (2004). *The complete guide to service learning: Proven, practical ways to engage students in civic responsibility, academic curriculum, and social action.* Minneapolis, MN: Free Spirit Publishing.

> Speck, B. W., & Hoppe, S. L. (2004). *Service-learning: History, theory, and issues.* Westport, CT: Praeger.

All of these provide extensive materials on the theory and practice of service-learning, including the importance of reflection and connections between course work and service work.

Designing and Implementing Service-Learning Courses

There is a wide array of Web sites and books that will help you prepare and teach a service-learning course. The Campus Compact and National Service-Learning Clearinghouse Web sites cited above are good resources, as are the following books.

> Eyler, J., & Giles, D. E., Jr. (1999). *Where's the learning in service-learning?* San Francisco: Jossey-Bass.

> Campus Compact. (2003). *Introduction to service-learning toolkit* (2nd ed.). Providence, RI: Author.

> Berman, S. (2006). *Service learning: A guide to planning, implementing, and assessing student projects* (2nd ed.). Thousand Oaks, CA: Corwin Press.

Service-Learning with Government Partners

Service-learning resources exist for several academic disciplines, from biology to English. However, when it comes to resources specifically emphasizing service-learning with government partners, there is very little. Part of the reason for this is that it is possible to team with government partners to offer service-learning classes in almost any discipline. Thus, many of the examples of service-learning projects with government partners are sprinkled across the many books that focus on specific disciplines. We encourage readers to look through the books that focus on service-learning in their disciplines for examples of courses with government partners and for ideas that might lead to courses with government partners.

A good place to start looking for a book in your discipline is the excellent twenty-one-volume series on service-learning edited by Edward Zlotkowski, *Service-Learning in the Disciplines,* available through Stylus Publishing. The academic areas covered are accounting; architecture; biology; communication studies;

composition; engineering; environmental studies; history; hospitality; management; medical education; nursing; peace studies; philosophy; political science; psychology; religious studies; sociology; Spanish; teacher education; and women's studies.

THE IMPACT OF SERVICE-LEARNING

The question of assessing the impact of service-learning has received a great deal of focus, and the scholarship of teaching and learning, which includes in it much about service-learning, is a burgeoning field. A substantial body of research exists demonstrating the measurable positive impacts of service-learning on students. Some of this work has already been cited, and several of the other important studies are listed next:

Gray, M. J., Ondaatje, E. H., & Zakaras, L. (1999). *Combining service and learning in higher education: Summary report.* Santa Monica, CA: RAND.

Astin, A. W., Vogelgesang, L. J., Ikeda, E. K., & Yee, J. A. (2000). *How service learning affects students.* Los Angeles: University of California, Higher Education Research Institute.

Elyer, J., & Giles, D. E., Jr. (Eds.). (2001). *At a glance: What we know about the effects of service-learning on college students, faculty, institutions, and communities, 1993–2000* (3rd ed.). Washington, DC: Corporation for National Service.

SO MUCH MORE

The materials cited here barely scratch the surface of the enormous service-learning literature. For those who want more, any of the references can serve as a portal to additional material. Readers will also find dozens of service-learning references in the chapters of this book. And in Appendix A, Charlotte Ridge provides short descriptions of more than a dozen service-learning projects at institutions across the country. Certainly everyone who practices service-learning must find their own comfort level with projects, partners, and students, yet there is much to be gained from seeing what others have done. We hope that the chapters in this book serve this purpose as well.

INDEX

Note to index: An *e* following a page number denotes an exhibit on that page; an *f* following a page number denotes a figure on that page; a *t* following a page number denotes a table on that page.